P9-APP-963

THE EMOTIVE IMAGE

The

EMOTIVE IMAGE

Jesuit Poetics in the English Renaissance

By Anthony Raspa

Texas Christian University Press
Fort Worth, Texas
76129

Library of Congress Cataloging in Publication Data

Raspa, Anthony.
  The emotive image.

  Includes index.
  1. English poetry—Early modern, 1500–1700—
History and criticism. 2. Jesuits—England—History. 3. Ignatius, of Loyola, Saint, 1491–1556. *Exer-
citia Spiritualia*. 4. Spiritual exercises in literature.
5. Counter-Reformation. I. Title. II. Title: Jesuit Poetics in the English Renaissance.
PR535.J47R37 1983   821'.4'099222   83–502
ISBN 0-912646-65-9

Contents

Foreword   *ix*

1.   Image, Affections and Love   *1*

2.   The Baroque World View   *11*

3.   Meditation and Psychology   *37*

4.   Poetry of the Will   *61*

5.   Imitation: The World   *83*

6.   The Epigrammatic Style   *117*

7.   Metaphor and Paradox   *143*

Index   *165*

Pour Clara Ethier Raspa

Foreword

A number of people and organizations helped with the following work. These include my departmental colleagues and the administrators of the Université du Québec à Chicoutimi, who granted me a sabbatical leave which the former Canada Council generously supported; the office of the Dean of Graduate Studies and the Département des Arts et Lettres at U.Q.A.C. who awarded publication grants; the Deutscher Akademischer Austauschdienst who sponsored a study session in West German Libraries, and the Social Sciences and Humanities Research Council of Canada.

I am indebted to Allan Bevan, Malcolm Ross, Hubert Morgan, and Nicholas Poburko of Dalhousie University in Halifax, N.S.; to Anthony Camps, the Master, and Ian Jack, Fellow in English, of Pembroke College in Cambridge; and to Edward Synan and Hugh MacCallum of the University of Toronto for their academic help.

A number of libraries cooperated with the use of their facilities over long periods, particularly the Cambridge University Library (Rare Books Room), the English Faculty and the Pembroke College Libraries in Cambridge, the British Library (Museum), the Theology Library at Katholiek Universitiet Leuven (Louvain, Belgium), and the McGill University Library in Montreal. The appearance of Barbara Lewalski's *Protestant Poetics and the Seventeenth-Century Religious Lyric* after the completion of my manuscript changes none of my conclusions.

The following major primary texts were used: Richard Crashaw, *Poems, English, Latin and Greek*, ed. L. C. Martin, Oxford, 1957; John Donne, *The Poetical Works*, II Vols., ed. H. J. C. Grierson, Oxford, 1912; William Alabaster, *Sonnets*, ed. G. M. Story and Helen Gardner, Oxford, 1959; Jasper Heywood, *The Paradise of Dainty Devices* (1576, 78, 80, 85), Scolar Press Facsimile, Menston, Yorkshire, 1972; Robert Persons' *A True Report of the death and martyrdome of M. Edmund Campion*, 1581 (British Library Shelf Mark G11658), from which I draw Henry Walpole s.j.'s poem on Campion's death; Robert Southwell, *The Poems*, ed. J. H. McDonald and N. P. Brown, Oxford, 1967; Ignatius Loyola, *Spiritual Exercises*, ed. Henry Keane s.j., London, 1952; and Eldred Revett, *Selected Poems*, ed. Donald Friedman, Liverpool, 1966, except for the

ix

rest of his verse in the British Library copy of his *Poemes,* London, 1657, (Shelf Mark C. 71a.14).

In my text I refer to these works as Crashaw, *Poems;* Donne, *Works;* Alabaster, *Sonnets;* Heywood, *Paradise;* Walpole, *Report;* Southwell, *Poems;* Ignatius, *Exercises;* Revett, *Selected Poems;* and Revett, *Poemes.* I write of Donne's "La Corona" and "Holy Sonnets" collectively as his religious sonnets to avoid their confusing general title of "Holy Sonnets" in the first edition of 1633.

I wish to thank my editors Dr. James Newcomer and Dr. Marjorie Lewis of Texas Christian University Press for their care.

Université du Québec à Chicoutimi

24 December 1980

THE EMOTIVE IMAGE

CHAPTER ONE

Image, Affections and Love

This work is an examination of the sacred verse of Richard Crashaw and five other English poets in the light of Renaissance Jesuit poetics. Thus, the study is concerned more with aesthetics than philosophy or history, although it necessarily delves into the history of ideas in the sixteenth and seventeenth centuries, both in England and on the Continent, in order to examine the foundations of poetry and meditation. Necessarily, the scope of the work extends to a number of major Renaissance questions like the nature of imitation, epigram, Jesuit meditation, and the morality of verse. I hope to show that such elements converged distinctively in the sacred verse of Crashaw, Jasper Heywood, Robert Southwell, John Donne, William Alabaster, and Eldred Revett and to explain how these English poets were influenced by Jesuit aesthetic verse meditation that was the counterpart of the ascetic *Spiritual Exercises* of the founder of the Jesuits, the Spaniard Ignatius Loyola. The study argues that Jesuit poetics were constituted of three main elements — "image," "affections," and "love" — and that they influenced English poets for diverse historical and literary reasons.

The issues brought up by this study are at once wide and particular. What is meant by "image," "affections," and "love"? How are they meditative? How were they poetic? To answer these questions adequately a new world view succeeding to the Elizabethan world picture in the Counter Reformation mind must be described in the second chapter. Such a step is inevitably contentious. It uses a description of the world to show what poetry is. If we do not accept the world picture described in Chapter II as indeed a contemporary description of the world, then we must also question the feasibility of discussing the verse of Crashaw and his fellow Englishmen in terms of Jesuit aesthetics.

In the light of this possible question, the work concentrates on English verse and on the prose writings of many forgotten or obscure Renaissance men, British and continental, to fill in its intellectual background. Although I use both terms liberally, I attempt to free myself from existing interpretations of the Metaphysical and the baroque which do not allow the exploration of Jesuit aesthetics on their own grounds. As a suitable working principle I adopt Warnke's description of a literary period as a collection of writers more or less possessing a number of

1

common traits.[1] This view of a literary period is useful when critics
disagree over whether the seventeenth century in English literature
forms a separate literary period or constitutes the last stage of the
Renaissance.

The belief that a distinct Jesuit poetic existed is also contentious.
Southwell's biographer-critic, Janelle, argues inconclusively that such a
poetic did exist, and recently, Scallon argued inconclusively that it did
not. Taking a medial position, Grundy hinted at the existence of a poetic
based on Jesuit training.[2]

The current interest in Ignatian meditation as poetry springs from the
acknowledgement that critics of English Renaissance devotional poetry
have given to Martz' *Poetry of Meditation* in the last two decades.
Particularly, Martz' study of the structures of the Ignatian *Exercises* in
the verse of Southwell, Donne, Crashaw, and other English poets
generated a major part of this interest.[3] Gardner, Bald, Lewalski,
Halewood, and Mueller have either minimized the structural influence or
denied it. On the other side, Van Laan, Webber, Mitchell, Ramsay,
Brown, Roberts, and others have supported the position that has become
identified with Martz' name.[4] Indeed, certain kinds of evidence
supporting Martz' position cannot be wished away: the Ignatian
application of the five senses in Crashaw's "Ode Praefixed to a little
Prayer-book given to a young Gentle-Woman" (11. 65-95); the three-part
"Prelude" of *Exercises* both in the same poem and in the verse letter to
the Countess of Denbigh; the presence of the five-part Jesuit meditative
structure in Donne's "First Anniversary" poem to the daughter of his
patron; the structure of Ignatius' penitential meditation in Southwell's
"Saint Peters Complaint," and Crashaw's sixteen adaptations of poems
by Jesuits.[5] The latter adaptations include "Musick's Duell," the
expansion of this poem based on part of Hawkins' *Partheneia Sacra,* an
epigram from Scribanus, and Remond's Alexias elegies, "The Teare"
and "The Weeper,"[6] and Crashaw's contribution of a prefatory poem to
the Jesuit Lessius' *Hygiasticon.*[7]

The lives of Crashaw (1613-1649) and of the other English poets
touched by the debate over the presence of Ignatian structures in English
verse span the rise, flowering, and disappearance in England of the
Counter Reformation Jesuit poetic movement. Donne's maternal uncle,
Jasper Heywood (b. London, 1535; d. Naples, 1598) was the Jesuit order's
leader in the English mission field briefly in 1581 until his arrest and
condemnation to death for treason, a sentence that was not carried out.
He contributed to the first edition of the Elizabethan miscellany
Paradise of Dainty Devices (1576), and more of his poems appeared in its
later editions (1578, 1585), even after his exile. William Alabaster (b.
Hadleigh, Suffolk, 1567; d. St-Dunstan's-in-the-West, 1640) was a Jesuit
novice for a time and was supervised in Ignatius' *Exercises* in London by
the leading recusant Jesuit John Gerard. He was a secret Catholic
emissary on the Continent, was arrested and later returned to the fold of

the Established Church. Although his meditative sonnets were the first in English, they circulated among his contemporaries only in manuscript copy. They remained largely unpublished until the twentieth century.[8] The Jesuit Robert Southwell (b. Horsham St-Faith's, 1561: d. Tyburn, 1595) became the most reputable English poet of his order in the late sixteenth and early seventeenth centuries with the publication of the first collection of his *Saint Peters Complaint, With other Poemes* in London, only two months after his execution for treason. The collection ran rapidly through two other editions. John Donne (b. London, 1572; d. London, 1631) became the greatest poet of those touched by Ignatian meditation partly by reason of his spiritual struggles which were known even to his contemporaries. With the exception of the "Anniversary" poems, his poetry also remained unpublished until 1633, two years after his death. Eldred Revett (b. Beldeston, c. 1635;[d.n.d., n.p.]) who is the least known of the six poets, has left us little biography besides the fact of his origins in the East Anglian gentry. The first edition of *Poemes*, published in London in 1657, reveals Revett's receptivity both to meditative and Cavalier traditions of verse.

The conditions for survival of the English Counter Reformation Church were a considerable force behind meditative poetry. The Church was an underground recusant organization with its headquarters shifting with the changing locations of the English seminary colleges, mainly Jesuit, between St. Omer, Rome, Rheims, Douai, and Antwerp. Its leaders were Englishmen like Donne's Jesuit uncles, Jasper and Elias Heywood, great-nephews of the executed Chancellor Thomas More, recruited from among the young men of the still Catholic great families of Britain. The Church's writings were surreptitiously published at home and openly abroad with a heavy concentration on polemics, though giving significant place to poetics.[9] Ignatian aesthetics in England assumed disproportionate dimensions because the Church of Rome, its English hierarchy now swept away, survived principally in the hands of the Jesuit mission priests. The late Elizabethan, Jacobean, and Caroline struggle against Rome on English territory was practically exclusively anti-Jesuit.[10] The "seminarist" priests, the other contemporary manifestation of Catholic clergy in Britain with whom the Jesuits differed doctrinally,[11] were as numerous as the members of Ignatius' order. However, they were headed by Rome-appointed arch-priests few of whom had native roots in England, and they proffered no literary movement. For all practical purposes, the Counter Reformation baroque movement in English poetry was preponderantly Jesuit.[12] Significantly, it declined rapidly with the civil strife and the Restoration, between 1640 and 1660, when political issues like the accession of a Catholic English monarch became dissociated from the Jesuits.

In the mainstream of this movement, Crashaw's development as a poet was more noteworthy than that of his English predecessors. He was not the greatest writer to be caught in its stream as Donne surpasses him, and he is not the foremost example of the Metaphysical school to which his verse belongs. The movement nevertheless casts light on certain aspects of his art more pervasively than Donne's, where the influence seems to be limited to "La Corona" and "Holy Sonnets".

Crashaw's verse represents the flowering of the Ignatian tradition, and he treated the imagistic text of a poem with significant difference from Heywood, Southwell, and Alabaster. His poems are often marked by an epigrammatic shift from text as symbol to text as poetry. His treatment of a poem as an emotive image, however, follows his predecessors. In "Lauda Sion," the ode to the young gentlewoman, "Adoro te," the second poem to St. Theresa, and "To the Name" Crashaw began discussing verse paradoxically by talking about another text. His emotive text nevertheless always surfaces as its significant concern. For example in "Lauda Sion," the bread of the Eucharist which is "this day's Triumphant Text" is supplanted by the "song" of divine love describing his poem a few lines later (11. 7-8, 13). The same movement from text as symbol to text as emotive poem occurs in the ode to the gentlewoman. Crashaw prefigured his prayer book as "a little volume, but great Book." The "Art" of reading it is soon revealed to be his practice of verse and produces poetic "Words . . . not heard with Eares" (11. 1, 36-38, 65). Again, in the "Apologie for the Fore-going Hymne," Teresa's written works are at first Crashaw's subject and later the spiritual meaning of the "song" that represents his verse (11. 2-4). Finally, in "Adoro te," Crashaw initially preferred faith's "powerful words" to reason ("Discourses dy") in order to adore the Host. Yet, such words, even though they prefigure a superior force of faith, are, like reason, soon inadequate for his task. They are replaced by the "witnesse" of poetry that in questions of belief in the transubstantiation speaks "as lowd as" the assertions of doubting Thomas when he finally accepted the possibility of a risen physical Christ (11. 5, 14, 31-32).

Among other manifestations of Ignatian influence on English verse, the references to the affections and to the primacy of love were more frequent than allusions to the emotive image. They also recurred more frequently from the very beginning of the meditative tradition. For example, although Heywood's "Complaint of a sorrowful Soule" is noteworthy for its adaptation of the Ignatian meditation on personal weakness to the Elizabethan verse plaint, its thematic development of the affections of "greefs" is more important from an aesthetic point of view (11. 14, 19, 24). The traditional lyricism of the plaint which still dominates the poem's style recurs in "Saint Peters Complaint." There again, however, the emphasis is on affection rather than on narrative or plan which elsewhere were at the heart of Renaissance explorations of Aristotle's meaning for fable in questions of genre.[13] Southwell's "greeves," like Heywood's, are the theme of his poem; the Biblical account of Peter's denial of Christ in the courtyard on Holy Thursday is the mere illustration of such affection. Similarly, in the first of his sonnets "Divine Meditations" Alabaster writes of "my love" filling "this book" to create "thoughts inflamed with such heavenly muse" that "the coldest fear of ice may not refuse" (11. 11, 13-14). Though Alabaster remains a sonneteer, the Petrarchan love tradition is no longer the emotive force of his verse. The new force, which he described in his cabalistic work *Apparatus,* has become universal feeling.[14]

The strain between genres and the new aesthetics of meditation in Heywood, Southwell, and Alabaster is absent in Crashaw's verse. Here, the affections found freer expression. This is illustrated in the discussion of the epigrammatic style in Chapter VI which indicates how Crashaw's adaptation of "Sospetto d'Herode" from Marino's *La Stage de Gl' Innocenti,* for example, followed Southwell's precedent in "Saint Peters Complaint." It altered Marino's plan to develop a narrative and dealt rather with the affections. The opening lines announce Crashaw's "theame" of hate, and only secondly is the story of Herod of importance (11. 1-4). Marino's original mannerist poem declared its intention of dealing with a misguided cruel king, and did not prescribe an affection (*cantiam lo sdegno / Del crudo, Rè / che mille Infanti afflitti*).[15]

Elsewhere in Crashaw's poetry, the preeminence of the affections and the primacy of love are equally compelling. The primacy of love for him even bespoke the role of other affections. His "loftyer Song" at the beginning of "Holy Nativity," for example, is inspired by the Christ-vision of the love symbol "Noon." While the vision paradoxically keeps the world dark, more enigmatically it compels other worthy affections like "joy" to look merely "well-stoln" (11. 2-5). Again, in "Lauda Sion" Crashaw called early "Come, love!" to assist him to "work a song / Lowd & pleasant" in order to prefigure the "solemn joyes" of the Eucharist in poetic language (11. 13-14, 16). In "Adoro te," Crashaw elaborated on the primacy of love as well as on its universal presence. He called on the affection because it alone could "Plead" like a lawyer for artistic "powres" for him to turn verse into love (11. 19, 36). Yet elsewhere, in "To the Name Above Every Name," the "Heirs Elect of Love" in the opening lines, which were suggested to Crashaw's religiously eclectic mind by the Puritan Register of the Elect, are the "everlasting life of Song" (1. 10). Every saved soul in the poem has a fourfold function of which the greatest, the last, is poetic. The soul contributes its earthly name first to the Puritan Register, second to the symbol of the unmentionable name of the Old Testament Yahweh, third to Christ's "unbounded Name," and fourth to the poem's symbolic language. From the love represented by Christ, Crashaw took leave to "awaken" himself and to "sing" his lines (11. 9, 12-13, 15).

In the opening lines of Crashaw's Teresian trilogy, as in "Sospetto d'Herode," the affection and the primacy of love replace the role of a narrative story. Crashaw's Teresian trilogy is really a series of poems connected by their treatment of something absolute called love rather than the saint. Teresa was only chosen after a careful process of selection to illustrate the overwhelming superiority of a personal, cosmic, and unending force:

> Loue, thou art Absolute sole lord
> Of Life & Death. To proue the word
> Wee'l now appeal to none of all
> Those thy old Souldiers, Great & tall,
> Ripe Men of Martyrdom, that could reach down
> With strong armes, their triumphant crown;
> Such as could with lusty breath
> Speak lowd into the face of death
> Their Great Lord's glorious name, to none
> Of those whose spatious Bosomes spread a throne
> For Love at larg to fill: spare blood & sweat;
> And see him take a priuate seat,
> Making his mansion in the mild
> And milky soul of a soft child.
>
> (11. 1-14. p. 93)

By Revett's time, the exploration of the self and the universe by means of the emotionally oriented verse that flowered in Crashaw had largely vanished. Of Jesuit aesthetics as a wide cultural phenomenon in Revett's work, only two qualities remained, first the epigrammatic style discernable in poems like "The Teare," "Jesus Wept," and "The Water Made Wine," and second the long thematic paradoxes of other poems like "The Sepulchre" and "Our Saviour cradled in the Manger." The influence of the Jesuits in England that had first made itself felt in Heywood's tentative exploration of new poetic experiences, was evident for the last time in details of style and narrative development. The religiously intense years covered by the world view of the affections, responding to the dismemberment of the soul of Christendom with the Reformation and to the scattering of its parts with the so-called new sciences, had already begun to subside. The new world view appears to history as a momentary response to the division of the conceptually indivisible spirit of Christ and to the extreme danger this begot for English Catholics. As soon as the first shock of that division was past, the experiences which the world view bespoke were no longer entertained. The obscurity of Revett's life brings into relief the quiet disappearance of the poetic sensibility that the world view had fostered.

The Ignatian meditation appears as the one coherent explanation of a Catholic poetic sensibility in England among the numerous experiments in religious verse that accompanied the spread of the Counter Reformation. Its attraction lay in the modernity of its approach. It ignored the traditional formalities of its origins and bespoke the intensity of the present, particularly in an historical situation where the Jesuits incarnated almost single-handedly the residual efforts of English Catholicism to stay alive. The growth of a vital Ignatian poetic in

England is understandable only as the aesthetics of a disaffected religion, as the poetry of the priest's hiding "hole" in the country's usually surreptitiously Catholic houses. Its intensity and relentless piety, often resulting in a lack of poetic discipline, grew naturally out of the political pressure on its writers.

Notes

[1]Frank Warnke, *Versions of the Baroque* (New Haven, 1972), pp. 1-4.
[2]Pierre Janelle, *Robert Southwell The Writer, A Study in Religious Inspiration* (Mamaroneck, N.Y., 1971), pp. 119-123; Joseph D. Scallon, s.j., *The Poetry of Robert Southwell, s.j., Elizabethan and Renaissance Studies* 11, *Salzburg Studies in English Literature* (Salzburg, 1975), p. vii; Joan Grundy, "Introduction," *The Poems of Henry Constable* (Liverpool, 1960), p. 79.
[3]Louis Martz, *The Poetry of Meditation* (New Haven, Conn., 1962), pp. 39-40, 43-46, 116-117.
[4]Helen Gardner, *"The Poetry of Meditation, by Louis Martz," Review of English Studies* (1957) n.s. 8: 197; and "Introduction," Donne's *Divine Poems* (Oxford, 1964), p. liv; R. C. Bald, *John Donne, A Life* (Oxford, 1970), pp. 39-40; B. K. Lewalski, (review) "Donne, *Devotions Upon Emergent Occasions*, ed. A. Raspa," *Renaissance Quarterly*, XXX, 2, Summer 1977, p. 263; and *Donne's Anniversaries and The Poetry of Praise* (Princeton, 1973), pp. 76-77, 82-83; William Halewood, *The Poetry of Grace* (New Haven, 1970), p. 74; J. M. Mueller, "The Exegesis of Experience, Dean Donne's *Devotions*," *Journal of English and Germanic Philology* (1968), 67:12, pp. 5-7; Thomas Van Laan, "John Donne's *Devotions* and the Jesuit *Spiritual Exercises*," *Studies in Philology* (1963), 60:197, pp. 194-195; Joan Webber, *Contrary Music* (Madison, Wisc., 1963), p. 184; W. F. Mitchell, *English Pulpit Oratory* (London, 1932), p. 183; M. P. Ramsay, *Les Doctrines Médiévales Chez Donne* (London, 1924), pp. 35-36; N. Pollard Brown, "The Structure of Southwell's 'Saint Peters Complaint,'" *The Modern Language Review* (1966), Vol. 61, p. 6; John R. Roberts, "The Influence of the *Spiritual Exercises* of St. Ignatius on the Nativity Poems of Robert Southwell," *Journal of English and Germanic Philology* (1960), LIX, p. 451.
[5]Martz, *The Poetry of Meditation*, pp. 222-226; Brown, "The Structure of Southwell's 'Saint Peters Complaint,'" *MLR* (1966), Vol. 61, p. 6. In his "Commentary" in *Poems*, Martin lists sixteen Jesuit sources for Crashaw's verse, seven for Marino, and five for medieval hymns, with references to *Thesaurus Hymnologicus* (London, 1855), 2 vols., Vol. 1, pp. 447-448, and *passim*. More general Jesuit and continental influences on the verse of Crashaw and other English poets are discussed by

Austin Warren, *Richard Crashaw, A Study in Baroque Sensibility* (London, 1957), pp. 69, 71, 78, 80 and 89, who names the Jesuits Bettinus, Biderman, Remond, Bauhusius, Hugo, Hawkins and Pona in Crashaw's ancestry; by Mario Praz, *Secentismo e Marinismo in Inghilterra* (Florence, 1925), *passim*; and by Douglas Bush, *English Literature in the Earlier Seventeenth Century*, Vol. V. *Oxford History of English Literature* (Oxford, 1962), p. 147, while Marc Bertonasco, *Crashaw and the Baroque* (University of Alabama, 1971), pp. 4–5, and Martin, "Biography," *Poems*, p. xxii, call them into question.

[6]In *Poems*, pp. 438-439, Martin includes Strada's original poem for "Musicks Duell" and points out Crashaw's expansion of it (11. 36-49) in his own lines 57 to 156; this addition to Strada's poem appears to the present writer to originate in the description of the flight of the nightingale in Henry Hawkins' *Partheneia Sacra* (Rouen, 1633), pp. 141-143; in "Commentary," *Poems*, p. 435, Martin points out the origin of Crashaw's epigram "Dives asking a drop" in the Belgian Charles Scribanus' celebratory volume *Amphitheatrum Honoris Iesuitici*, Antwerp, 1605. Martin suggests that Crashaw actually imitated the poem's translation by his father William in *Iesuites Gospel* (1610). In *Gospel* (second ed., 1621), p.4, the elder Crashaw also charged Scribanus with idolatry in another poem to Mary, *Amphitheatrum* (second ed., 1606), p. 356. This provoked John Floyd's defence of poetry as meditation in *The Overthrow of the Protestant Pulpit-babels*, St. Omer, 1612. In "Commentary," *Poems*, pp. 432-434, 450, Martin discusses the original poems by Remond for "The Weeper," "The Teare," and the "Alexias" Elegies, as does Ruth Wallerstein in *Richard Crashaw, A Study in Style and Poetic Development* (Madison, Wisc., 1959), pp. 99-100.

[7]Leonard Lessius, *Hygiasticon, Or, The right course of preserving Life and Health unto extreme Old Age* (Cambridge, 1634), which was a translation of *Hygiasticon seu vera ratio valetudinis bonae et vitae*, (Antwerp, 1614).

[8]G. M. Story and Gardner describe the circle of Alabaster's manuscript readers as probably small, and the readership of his printed poems as becoming significant only with Dobell's discovery of a manuscript in 1903 and the subsequent publication of several of his poems ("Introduction," Alabaster, *Sonnets*, p.v.).

[9]John Bossy, *The English Catholic Community, 1570-1850* (London, 1975), pp. 197-202; Augustus Jessopp, *One Generation of a Norfolk House* (London, 1879), p. 97.

[10]Bossy, *Catholic Community*, p. 204; Iain Fletcher, "Introduction," *Partheneia Sacra*, by Henry Hawkins (1633) (Aldington, Kent, 1950), pp. vii, ix; Janelle, *Southwell*, p. 39; Grundy, "Introduction," *Constable*, pp. 38-44; M. D. R. Leys, *Catholics in England* (New York, 1961), pp. 28-32.

[11]The many documentations of the quarrel include: *The Wisbech Stirs*

(1595-1598), ed. P. Renold, *Catholic Record Society,* LI (London, 1958), *passim;* Thomas James, D.D., *The Iesuits Downefall, Threatned Against Them by the Secular Priests for their wicked lives, accursed manners. Together with the life of Father Parsons An English Iesuite* (Oxford, 1612); Grundy, "Introduction," *Constable,* pp. 37-38; Christopher Bagshaw, *A True Relation of the faction begun at Wisbich, by Fa. Edmonds, alias Weston, a Iesuite, 1595, and continued since by Fa. Walley, alias Garnet, the Provinciall of the Iesuits in England, and by Fa. Parsons in Rome, with their adherents: Against us the Secular Priests their brethren and fellow Prisoners* (London, 1601); for the numbers of priests in England, Janelle, *Southwell,* pp. 44-45; Bossy, *Catholic Community,* pp. 217-228.

[12]Fletcher, "Introduction," *Partheneia,* pp. vii-viii; Rosemary Freeman, *English Emblem Books* (New York, 1966), pp. 180-181.

[13]Plato, *Republic,* XXXV (x, 595), trans. F. M. Cornford (Oxford, 1941), pp. 317–318; Aristotle, *Poetics,* II, xxii, ed. T. A. Moxon (London, 1947), pp. 3, 7, and I, iii, p. 37. J. E. Spingarn, in *History of Literary Criticism in the Renaissance* (New York, 1924), p. 11, discusses fable and imitation in the Renaissance as a question related to medieval allegory.

[14]*Apparatus in Revelationem Iesu Christi, Nova & admirabilis ratio investigandi Prophetiarum mysteria ex scriptura seipsam interpretante* (Antwerp, 1607), p. 171.

[15]Marino, Giambattista, and Crashaw, Richard, *Sospetto d'Herode,* with commentary by Claes Schaar (Lund, 1971), p. 32.

CHAPTER TWO

The Baroque World Veiw

1

Several definite ideas accrue to the term baroque world view in this work. The moral assumptions of the baroque here are, first, that the universe was pleasurably meaningful; second, that its forces could best be represented by mythological figures; third, that these mythic forces were emotive; and fourth, that man's faculties controlled his contact with the universe. The baroque is taken to suggest these attitudes to the self and the universe in the Counter Reformation mind in the period roughly bounded by the last quarter of the sixteenth century and the middle of the seventeenth. The term refers to the sensibility created by the gradual collapse of the set hierarchies of the Great Chain of Being, and by the rise and decline of the emotive world view that succeeded it in the Counter Reformation mind. No attempt is made to define the baroque as a term universally applicable to art, culture, or history beyond the limits of time imposed on it here. Nor, as Warnke has shown, is there much to be gained by considering it in a survey of other definitions of the baroque in the last hundred years.[1]

In the English literature of the period in question the baroque is best represented by the poets who were absorbed by its moral assumptions. But it does not exclude the participation of other writers who stood on the periphery of its underlying historical currents. A number of these men, particularly scientists trained in late sixteenth-century astronomy, astrology, medicine, and alchemy, are referred to in succeeding paragraphs.

The baroque here is therefore a working principle and not a philosophical or historical absolute. Its relevance to a study of Jesuit poetics in the English Renaissance is that it fills in their indispensable background. The Ignatian meditation sprang from the fourth moral assumption of the baroque about the human facultative control of the universe. While this chapter deals with the baroque world view, the next chapter examines the sort of man who possessed that view, the kind of meditation which he considered to be its great experience, and the influence of this experience on English verse.

The baroque world view was understood and expressed in terms of its moral assumptions, as are concepts of the universe generally. A world view is meant to answer to our moral expectations of the universe and to our presuppositions about its metaphysics. The baroque channeled these general human needs into a specific form. It shaped the Counter Reformation mind's estimate of the galaxy, the earth, its creatures, and human life. Such an estimate, a world view always demands and imposes on us. It touches on the matter and spirit, image and idea, body and soul of everything, including ourselves. We may form opinions concerning man, the earth, and the galaxy separately. However, as though some form of logic inevitably linked them, these opinions produce a coherent vision transcending their disparity. The baroque world view was no different. By way of contrast, we may consider illustratively, though briefly, how in modern philosophies like existentialism and Marxism the universe corresponds to the moral expectations of existentialists and Marxists.

The existentialist determines his moral philosophy of work and its necessary absurdity by experience.[2] He decides what moral behavior is after concluding that the universe is not so much nihilistic and hostile as empty and indifferent, in spite of its stars. So too for the existentialist all human behavior is indifferent in response to universal emptiness. The universe is not really forbidding; it is quite simply hollow. In the great "something" there is "nothing" and the existentialist responds to the magnitude of something that is void. One must be the equal personally both to the magnitude and to the void.

For the Marxist, by contrast, the universe is occupied by earth-bound human masses in whose hands alone lie the causes and effects of history.[3] Among the stars of the concave universe and beyond it, there are no influences pressing upon man to compel him down this or that historical course. History and the universe are synonymous, and the first of these is delimited by men's actions. History reaches its great moments according to how, when, and to what purpose men relinquish their individual sensibilities to collective goals. Morality — that is, what one should do — relies on how much one contributes to the overall good. This overall good is clearly defined in terms of certain material acquisitions. The good is as wide as what is collectively desirable in an immediate present for living men. The universe of the Marxist has no past, present, or future, and no mythological significance except in terms of the continually evolving overall material good. For the Marxist the exercise of power is necessary as long as there are non-Marxists who threaten to re-invade his collectivity with the individual sensibility. Morality is determined by the need to protect the collectivity so far achieved with politics and wars until the masses are everywhere in one Marxist accord.

The baroque world view, unlike the two more modern views just discussed, assumed the inherent pleasurableness of the universe. As we are all today in some measure existentialist and Marxist because of our constant exposure to both, we may forget that in other world views the inferences of the universe could be both pleasant and urgent at once. The baroque world view was one of these.

If men in the baroque age as defined here had used the term "human condition," there would not have accrued to it the negative sense of human abasement it immediately suggests to us. To be human did not automatically suggest a degrading situation to be solved. It might have suggested that life was problematical but not inherently crushing. The influences of the baroque world view were continually forcing themselves on man to his benefit rather than to his confusion. Even when they were undesirable, like Satan, Donne's "old subtle foe" in "Holy Sonnet" 1 "Thou hast made me" (1.11), like the absent lover-saint Alexis in Crashaw's triology, and like Revett's Herodial figure in "Innocents Day," they were not so much confusing as related to universal hate and sorrow. Baroque man was continually conscious of these universal influences and appreciated them even when they were undesirable as he gained strength from his knowledge of them. When these influences were divine, they were morally good, and when they were satanic, they were recognizably so and were morally bad. There was no confusing the eternal love of Southwell's "Lifes death loves life" with the eternal hate of his "Loves Garden grief." In the first poem love gave significance to life, and in the second poem hate gave significance to its loss. Man was in continual discourse with such universal forces just as the existentialist is in increasing contact with the awesome magnitude of nothing and the Marxist with the forever shifting movements of the masses to their destiny. The first moral assumption of the Counter Reformation baroque world view consequently was that man was always conscious of a meaningful universe and that he was bound to recognize its significance.

The second moral assumption touched on the immediate relevance of the universe to a coherent mythology. Behind each force in the universe there was a mythological god, devil, angel, or the spiritual soul of a once living human being. The visible universe of planets, stars, clouds, trees, men, animals, and rocks was inhabited morally and metaphysically by pure spirits of a mythological significance ranging from the absolute Christian God to mortal humanity. For Heywood and Southwell respectively in "Alluding his State to the prodigall child" (1. 2) and "The prodigall childs soule wracke" (1. 1), the wayward New Testament Son was not a mere arbitrary representation of the affection of "grief." He was its fixed, "eternall," "fatal" incarnation. Sorrow and grief were immanent universal forces that the Prodigal Son in both poems represented as though by divine historical decree.

The "mythological" here does not mean that the Christian God, Christ, and Satan were the metaphoric projections of humanly perceived universal truths. Such projections were Zeus, Apollo, and Aphrodite to the Greek world. The claims of Christianity were and are clear. God like his angels and the souls of men is real. In Christian faith he and his retinue are, first, truths revealed by the Bible and, second, historical truths. The "mythological" here is not concerned with such facts of revelation or historicity, but with a more general matter. It refers to the population of the material universe by creatures who give it significance. What is more important, these mythological creatures because they inhabit the universe give it order. They give it order even when, like God and Satan or the Archangel Michael and Lucifer, they fight. The mythological here means simply that the universe is filled with recognizable material forces and that these material forces are identifiable with known spiritual creatures. In such a conception of the mythological, the figures are absolute in that their roles conform perfectly to their respective significations. This perfection is such that imaginatively, where figure and signification conjoin in myth, they pose no problem of acceptance.

In baroque thinking, the roles of mythological figures were consequently strongly colored by their significations. These significations were constant, and they persisted somehow, somewhere in the universe and there were always mythic figures in existence as persistently to bear them. Within certain limitations, one of these significations could be carried by the various figures of the mythology. Although God could not represent hate and Satan could not represent love, several figures could alternately signify the same meaningful universal affection. The universe was unquestionably held to be filled with joy. Mary the Virgin usually reflected this emotion, but not exclusively. Crashaw wrote a poem "Glorious Assumption" depicting her preeminent significance of joy (1. 63) and he also attached the same meaning to Alexis in his second elegy to the fifth century saint (1. 1). Similarly, in the second poem in "The Sequence on the Virgin Mary and Christ," Southwell declared Mary the "Joy" of the Orient and of peace (11. 1, 3), and in "Davids Peccavi" he also declared that affection the lot of the Biblical David (1. 17). Revett found the origin of grief in the slaughtered children of "Innocents Day" (1. 1), and he attributed that affection paradoxically among an equally disparate number of prospective killers in "The Jews attempting to stone our saviour."

The third moral assumption of the baroque was that the connection between the material universe and its spiritual forces was emotive. God created the world because he loved himself; the Devil inhabited his satanic kingdom because he hated God; good angels and evil spirits and figures like the Virgin Mary unleashed or harnessed the forces of the universe such as death, storms, and harvests by emotions like fear, joy, magnanimity, and sorrow. In the narrative of Crashaw's "Sospetto d'Herode," Satan is the purveyor of hate and becomes indistinguishable from his willing victim Herod. In Heywood's "Alluding his state to the prodigall child," a similar identification involving the poet and the Prodigal Son and the disordered universe and personal sorrow occurs. In such an affective world, the historical figures of baroque Christianity were immediately recognizable as influences exerting power over man. The entire universe was the theatre of the concourse, the exercise, and the war of the affections.

Other poets like Joseph Beaumont and George Herbert sharing in lesser degrees in baroque mythology entitled their poems "Joy," "Love," "Affliction" and so forth according to the names of the affections. In so far as baroque mythology was a wide cultural expression, its influence touched many persons not involved with the Counter Reformation. The mythology was not restricted to those who largely developed its world view. In the poetry of Beaumont and Herbert, nevertheless, the emotive role of the figures of the mythology differed from their role in Crashaw's work. For Beaumont and Herbert this role was pictorial rather than experiential. No mechanism of experience existed in Herbert's and Beaumont's approach between such figures and the beholder. In Herbert's "Affliction," the experience of emotion was volitional and moral rather than universally emotive. One participated in the same emotions as the mythological figures but not as a *sine qua non* of the universe. To perceive was not necessarily to feel. It was to experience in a human, temporal way the emotions that the figures of the mythology underwent separately in the infinite manner of the eternal.

The emotive approach underlying the baroque world view marked a new stage in the influence of the classical affections on Western thinking. It altered radically Aquinas' conception of the affections from which it sprang directly and even more radically its further source in Aristotle. The emotiveness of the world view made mythological, eternal, and universal the affections that in Aristotle's *Rhetoric* II, 1, were only human and temporal.[4] In *Rhetoric,* the affections were the emotions of men awakened, aroused, and directed to the moral end of the oration by the orator. In Aquinas, they had in addition become immortal but nevertheless not universally figurative.[5]

In medieval thinking generally, they were fixed in the historical figures of Christianity separately from man.

In their final transformation in the baroque, the affections became the substance of a spirit world giving meaning immanently to humanity in a temporal world. A similar change took place in the importance accorded to their gradations.

Aristotle had arranged the affections with love and hate sharing a primary place at the top of a ladder of descending antithetical emotions like joy and sorrow. The affections, down to the least feeling, were desirable on one side and undesirable on the other. This ladder is reflected in the *Ars Poetica* of Alexander Donatus (b. Siena, 1584; d. Rome, 1640), a poetical theorist and professor of rhetoric at the Roman College whose work possesses great representative value for baroque Jesuit aesthetics.[6] This ladder is also described by the English mission Jesuit Thomas Everard (b. Linstead, 1560; d. London, 1633), one of the principal translators of recusant continental books, in his version of the Jesuit Balsamo's adaptation of *Exercises* as *Instruction How to Pray and Meditate Well.*[7] The ladder appears in detail, too, in the poet-priest Southwell's *Short Rule of Good Life* which he wrote for laymen, and which was published secretly in England a year after his execution.[8] In such works, however, the affections did not only reflect a gradation of human feeling. They also became the immediate hierarchical significance of the world itself, of matter, space, and time.

For God, the angels, man, the sun, the stars, the animals, and rocks, in the writings of Donatus, Everard, and Southwell, the forces of the universe were a common source of hierarchically graded emotive energy. The writer who attributed eternal love to the Christian God also attributed it to the primary desirable forces of the universe. He was unable to believe in the eternal love of God without enjoying the belief of its immanence in primary graded forms of creation. The world could not be meaningless and yet divine love exist. The gradation of the affections was of necessity matched by a gradation of things. To the baroque man, the sense of abandonment of the faithful Christian in the Anglo-Saxon "Dream of the Rood" and the Medieval "Pearl" was denied. Christ's Agony in the Garden was not for this time a popular or intelligible theme. Southwell in "Life is but Losse," Crashaw in "Bleeding Crucifix," and Donne in "Holy Sonnet" 10 "Death be not proud," celebrated the imminence of death with a daunting equanimity and longing that would have confused the authors of "Rood" and "Pearl."

Finally, the fourth moral assumption of the baroque world view was that man's faculties controlled his contact with the universe's emotive forces. He did not float aimlessly in the universe but steered himself through it from birth to death. He had an inner panel of instruments, his memory, understanding, will, and imagination, and an outer panel, the five senses. With these he controlled his experiences of eternity and time and everything in them.[9] Thus Heywood saw a "greedie" and an "unruly will" as the misguided instrument of a disillusioned man in "Beyng troubled in mynde, he writeth as followeth" (1. 7) and in "Alluding his state to the prodigall child" (1. 7), and Crashaw put the five senses into the service of his meditation in his poem to the Eucharist "Adoro te." Elsewhere, Southwell struggled to put the Apostle Peter's memory under the control of the correct religious affection ("Complaint," 1. 2) and Crashaw hastened the Countess of Denbigh's will to love ("To the Countess," 11. 11-20). The Counter Reformation man's instrument panels guided his emotions through their temporary sensory expression as well as through their profoundest experiences of the eternal. To feel emotion of any sort meant to participate in a metaphysical state of love, hate, sorrow, joy and so forth in eternity and time. To each of these dimensions, each of man's panels of faculties corresponded. The memory, the understanding, and the will answered to the eternal and the five senses to the temporal. The imagination was the watershed between the two where time became eternal and eternity took on the historical images of time.

This view of human nature gave to baroque man's experience a unique quality. He alone among both rational and irrational creatures, spirited beings like angels as well as spiritless beings like dumb animals, was able to experience the emotive energies of time and eternity in a single whole continuum. Nothing else, not even the Creator, shared in one nature man's two sets of faculties. Each of these enabled man to taste separately and yet simultaneously temporal emotions and their eternal counterparts, and nobody but he possessed this powerful privilege. In "Holy Sonnet" 19 "Oh, to vex me," Donne spoke of man's exclusive character in terms of the "contraryes" of mythic emotive force and personal experience meeting "in one" and not of body and soul (11. 1-3). In "Sonnet"15 "My soul a world is by contraction," Alabaster described his soul as "a world," as a microcosm "by contraction," not of a visual universe but of macrocosmic emotive forces (1. 1). Possessing a dual emotive nature unshared by God, Satan, angels, animals, and stones, man was an amphibious creature not between matter and spirit but between sensation and eternal emotion. Even God and Satan, the major contenders for his attention, lacked his time-bound emotion.

The importance of man's emotive duality touched his very existence. Such a characteristic in him was not merely accidental. It was metaphysical in the classical sense of metaphysics as the study of being, nature, and essence as the age understood it. Emotion was the principle of his life as a human being, and his body was the receptacle of the emotion. Man was subject to the constant alterations and coming and going of emotions that characterized rather than detracted from his identity. The baroque human condition is difficult to comprehend without the recognition of its emotional dualism with its fluxes and stable points.

As the Renaissance manifested itself in the Counter Reformation, the faculties of the body and soul, each of which possessed distinct feeling powers, came to define man closely as they characterized no other beings. Though affections like eternal love and immortal hate were present in time elsewhere than in man, they were there unwilled. They had no originally willed roots in time except in man. God's love existed elsewhere on earth, but in his non-human creatures merely as images of himself. Similarly, Satan's hate existed in a willed state on earth only by his seduction of consenting individuals, seduction with hard work as in "Holy Sonnet" 1 "Thou hast made me" (1. 11) or with little effort as in Crashaw's "Sospetto d'Herode" (Stanza 59, 1. 5). In Satan's other manifestations such as the occupation of serpents, hate existed unwilled. The development of Ignatius' *Exercises* and of Jesuit poetry must be understood as having made use of that singular emotive privilege of man. The formal meditation and the poetry it inspired were attractive to the baroque mind because they answered to a hitherto unentertained concept of Christian experience enlisting all the assumptions of a world view. The influence of the baroque world view on the *Exercises* did not lead Ignatius to stop believing in a world of pure spirits which he in fact mentions several times. It did, however, strongly color his approach to these spirits' existence.

2

The Jesuit Bellarmine's little volume on life in heaven, *Of the Eternal Felicity of the Saints,* translated into English (c. 1620) from the original Latin (1616) by Thomas Everard, gives us an insight into the moral assumptions of the baroque world picture.[10] This work by a Roman noble (b. Montepulciano, 1542; d. Rome, 1621), who became a cardinal, a leading Renaissance Biblical scholar, and a controversialist, is a perfect example of the world view popular in England and on the Continent. Although *Felicity* fits into the group of contemporary literature like Southwell's *Short Rule of Good Life* meant for pious reading, the work is noteworthy well beyond piety. For, *Felicity* adapted astronomical concepts and their underlying propositions to an emotive world. It infused into these concepts a series of anagogic meanings on which Counter Reformation thinkers put increasing weight in their gradual retreat from the classical medieval notions of matter and form.

Bellarmine depicted a weirdly cogent world. Its human beings, God, and the angels possessed full freedom of an emotive personal kind. Unlike the Great Chain of Being, his world picture was not a seat of objective activity. Its inhabitants were not involved in detached metaphysical speculation. They were caught in the forever flowing personal crosscurrents of his world's emotive motions and perturbations. Here, humanity could not contemplate its world view except in the light of its immediate experience.

Bellarmine treated the saints of his title from an angel's point of view while adapting them to the subject of his volume. Saints, being dead, in heaven and canonized by Rome, were become angels, saved bodiless souls, nearest to God's heart and his closest image. They lived in the "Supercelestial Heaven," the first of God's six provinces, at the beginning and on the outer ridge of Bellarmine's universe. Everything beneath God in eternity and time was settled in one of this universe's six "provinces" as Everard's translation speaks of them.

The six provinces were arranged conceptually in a series of hierarchical layers unified securely by their emotive, mythological, and anagogic significations. Otherwise, they were scattered fairly loosely through the firmament — mansions, zodiac, degrees, measures, and so forth — of the sixteenth and seventeenth century astronomical universe.

Bellarmine's discussion of his provincial world was intended as a literal description, however anagogic, of the astronomical universe. His universe's provinces followed one another like the layers of an onion, held together by their cogent typological meaning; whatever anagogic qualities his language possesses, it acquired from the universe rather

than from an attempt on Bellarmine's part at poetry. After the
"Supercelestial Heaven," immediately beneath God, the five provinces
were the "Eternall," inhabited by the stars"; the "Aire," home of the
wind, clouds, rain, hail, thunder and lightning; the "water,"
comprehending all earthly aquatic bodies; the "earth" itself, inhabited
by animals; and finally the "subterranean" place, the seat of hell,
inhabited by wicked spirits.[11] These provinces were related to current
astronomical traditions as well as to the associated sciences of astrology,
medicine, and alchemy in which Bellarmine's purely scientific
vocabulary originated. The air of his third province is the astronomical
layer immediately above the atmosphere of the earth in the writings of
Fulke[12] and Recorde.[13] The "eternal" place of his second province
suggests the layer of mysterious atmosphere immediately preceding the
Primum Mobile in, once more, Fulke, and in Burton.[14] His
"Supercelestial Heaven" possesses the pre-lapsarian qualities of the
divine associated with the Primum Mobile in the astronomical writings
of Blundeville and Rastell.[15] The sixth or "subterranean" province is
more difficult to identify and locate than the other five provinces
although it is drawn vividly in the mind of the Herod-Satan figure in
Crashaw's "Sospetto d'Herode." The realm clearly is one of darkness and
evil spirits but its obvious location in the bowels of the earth seems no
longer clear in Bellarmine's day. For example, in Burton's *Anatomy of
Melancholy* the bowels of the earth had already become a mineral source
generally free of spirits.[16]

On the whole, Bellarmine's picture of the provinces was outside the
range of the earlier and even of many of the contemporary meanings of
astronomical terminology. His picture was at most in the range of such
terminology figuratively or allegorically in the anagogic tradition in
which Bellarmine understood it. The significance of his provinces was
anagogic and not astronomical as in the world view of the Great Chain of
Being. The anagogic significance particularly colored his use of current
concepts from both the dying Ptolemaic and the rising Copernican
astronomical systems. The appearance of the vocabulary of astronomy
and astrology infused with anagogic meanings might be viewed as the
last of its possible manifestations as the language of the pseudo-sciences.
This terminology now bespoke a spent science and appears in Bellarmine
to have passed into the philosophic imagination. The difference between
Bellarmine's description of the world and that in contemporary non-
baroque pseudo-scientific works was the product of two varying sciences.
It sprang from two contrasting forms of knowledge. In the pseudo-
scientific works the vocabulary is shaded with lingering scientific
pretensions, but in Bellarmine's *Felicity* the vocabulary served the
philosophic and visionary. Moreover, the different meanings given to the
vocabulary were not the result merely of national, "continental," or
"English" causes.

Bellarmine's figurative use of "provinces" betrays his political origins.

However, although the word has Roman imperial connotations, the imagery of his speech is significant beyond such national considerations. Bellarmine used figurative language to discuss the topics of classical metaphysics, being, essence, and nature which in the baroque mind had become understood as figurative, as well as to illustrate an astronomical world. Figurative language stops being such when used as Bellarmine employed it in response to an equally figurative reality. It becomes a realistic form of speech describing a configurative world. Such figurative language in its day is literal and not poetic. For Bellarmine, to write metaphorically of a world with many levels of meaning was to write realistically.

Everard's translation of Bellarmine's figurative use of language gave this work the same impact in English that it possessed in the Latin original. The cultural concerns that it represented were Western European rather than narrowly national. As an underground mission priest, Everard did not translate *Felicity* as an act of piety, scholarship, history, or partisan Jesuit politics. He projected it as a work of burning philosophical relevance to contemporary Englishmen. The zeal of the Counter Reformation evident in him was still great in the second quarter of the seventeenth century. By that time, the Catholic offensive in England had become the growing target of Puritan attack and now shared the defensive position of the Established Church. By then a Jesuit active in the mission field for about twenty years, Everard was a fast aging man. He translated *Felicity* in order to make easily accessible to Englishmen its contemporary and international world view.

The inspiration for the translation was the cogency of the work's thought in terms of typology and anagogy. If typology is the study of the levels of meanings in things and if anagogy as a system of typology describes the number of these levels as four, anagogy united the elements of Bellarmine's personal vision with the Counter Reformation's emotive approach to experience. In baroque writings generally, anagogy was a term applied both to the whole of the four-level way of thinking and to the fourth of its levels of meaning. This use of the term is retained here as the less confusing of the alternatives to describe anagogy's history in the late English Renaissance. For its part, typology in seventeenth century Britain was generally considered as a two-level way of thinking characteristic of Protestant writings. These uses of the terms contrasted with their original manifestations in ancient Rome, the scholastics, and Dante. There, the typological had usually referred to all four levels and the anagogic only to the fourth.[17] Now, in the baroque, with its four levels of meaning, the literal (historical), allegorical (figurative), tropological (moral), and anagogic (mystical), what was understood as the anagogic method responded to current needs for a suitable manner of considering a dismembered world in flux. And, although the anagogic shared in the impetus in Protestant thinking to consider reality in terms of two levels of meaning, literal and mystical, it profoundly differed from this typology.

The habit of enlisting the anagogic method evident in Bellarmine was a manifestation of the turning that Catholic thinking had taken by the late sixteenth century. Though Bellarmine dealt with anagogy passingly in *Felicity*, he explained it at length in his contested analysis of the Psalms, *Explanatio in Psalmos*, in 1611. Also, in the following year, the Jesuit mission priest and Cantabrigian John Floyd used anagogy at length in what from the point of view of the history of poetic theory was the most important of his controversies. Known more as a controversialist than as a commentator on devotional literature, Floyd (b. 1572; d. St. Omer, 1649) nevertheless took time in his tract *The Overthrow of the Protestant Pulpit-babels* to defend verse as Ignatian meditation and to attack William Crashaw, the Catholic poet's Puritan father, for his abuse of anagogic principles (pp. 67-68). Crashaw, he wrote, could not "discerne the right hand from the left in a mystical sense" (p. 42). Other writers prominent in the same stream of thought were the Jesuit controversialist Anthony Possevine, a common Renaissance authority, who listed in *Apparatum Sacrum* (1608) all the writings of the Church Fathers, the Greeks, the scholastics, church historians, and sacred poets as subjects suitable for anagogic investigation. Yet others like the Jesuit exegete Balsius Viegas in *Commentarii Exegetici* (1601) applied the anagogic method extensively to the last apocalyptic book of the Bible. The Spaniard Luis de Granada, famous to his English contemporaries in Meres' and Hopkins' translations, used the anagogic method to explain both his meditations and the nature of the world.[18] Finally, the French Jesuit Louis Richeome discussed anagogy in detail and adapted it to emblems in his popular book *Tableaux Sacrés*, translated into English as *Holy Pictures* in 1619.

To such thinkers, the universe — pure spirits, the sun, moon, stars, earth, men, animals, and trees — were intelligible from an anagogic point of view. Their differences of opinion with fundamentalist Protestant thinkers did not arise from their use of metaphor to explore metaphysical issues but from the fourfold nature of that metaphoric exploration. Protestant literalist thinking such as Dayrell's in defence of the "matter and form" of the church insisted on only two levels of meaning in the world.[19] Baroque thinkers were otherwise inspired by the decline of medieval logic as an instrument of metaphysical pursuit as well as by the need to replace it as were Protestant thinkers also. The classical and medieval use of logic to tell correct thinking from bad thinking is strikingly absent from baroque writings. The values of anagogy infiltrated all aspects of the baroque vision. In his preface to *Holy Pictures*, Richeome suggests, typically for his age, the breadth of their application:

We have also made many excursions in recommendation of Vertue, and in detestation of Vice, for the institution of manners; and often encited the Reader to the contemplation and love of the celestiall countrey; touching by this meanes the foure Cardinall Senses, which commonly are found in the treasures of the holy Scripture; the Literall or Historicall, which goeth the first; the Allegorical or Figurative, which is the spirit of the Literall; the Tropologicall or Morall, which formes the manners, and the Anagogicall, which shewes the triumphant Church.[20]

Anagogic values made themselves felt in many branches of knowledge in the late sixteenth and seventeenth centuries. But in the baroque they became specifically noteworthy for their general use in the fields of logic and metaphysics by which the earlier Renaissance and the Middle Ages had understood their own visions. In this application of four-level thinking to logic and metaphysics, Richeome's commentary, though originally typical, represents a break with the past. Richeome was ostensibly arguing in behalf of anagogy for emblem literature. His argument for the anagogic method, however, was in essence a defence of its use in the study of being, essence, and nature. He supported the application of the method to the law of Moses in Genesis but not before he first argued for its use in the examination of the "figures" in the "law of Nature" (p. 2). The anagogic that in the scholastics and Dante had been an instrument for the examination of moral values in specific events now surpassed those limits. It became empirical and inductive rather than deductive for the examination of immediate sense impressions.

The "naturall figure" to which Richeome applied anagogy was no mere figure of speech. It was "the outward forme, the lineaments and the proportion of the parts of a Plant, of a Beast, or a Man" (p. 2). Thus assuming some of the characteristics of its material subjects, the four-level way of thinking assured Richeome of a certain empirical approach to the world. Richeome's subjection of his emblems to a four-fold examination was moreover not merely a literary technique. It was also a test of how his emblems corresponded to the inherent realities of the universe. The success of his emblems, he thought, depended on whether they stood up to the rigours of their comparison with creation.

Both need and tradition dictated the adherence of baroque thinkers to the anagogic method. The attractiveness of the method was for them a natural philosophical development. Springing from the same classical and medieval inheritance as the faculties, senses, and affections, the anagogic method filled a void created by the evolution of intellectual history. The late Renaissance inherited in the anagogic method a suitable instrument for examining the eternal emotions to replace a system of logic that had become outdated. The method had been refined first by Aquinas and by Dante immediately after him in terms of the typology found in art, creation, and revelation in the Bible.[21] The capacity of anagogy to deal with these subjects all at once not only permitted it to survive the retreat of logic beyond the close of the Middle Ages and the first stage of the Renaissance, but it also assured it unprecedented importance later in the baroque. With the emotive values of classical rhetoric, the anagogic method became part of the material of human understanding. It thus reached a preeminence it had not enjoyed in a thousand years of medieval thought.

Much Renaissance thinking was a recreation of classical and medieval ideas in a series of new emphases that produced an original effect. The replacement of logic by anagogy as an instrument of metaphysics by baroque thinkers was another such permutation of ancient ideas. As the emotive values of rhetoric subsumed those of classical metaphysics, the anagogic method replaced logic as the instrument for understanding them. In the late sixteenth and early seventeenth centuries in Britain, a syllogistic method to assure correct thinking retained a prominent place in the *curricula* and in the disputations of the schools and universities.[22] Its interests, however, lay in the direction of discourse rather than in the field of metaphysics.[23] Logic was absent from the heart of current philosophical interests. The philosopher Ramus' answer to the contemporary disuse of classical logic was to invent a new logic based on grammatical "invention" and on the concept of wisdom as knowledge.[24] The thrust of his new logic into invention led him further into the art of discourse,[25] and this art was without issue for the development of a new metaphysical tool. Logic was fundamentally expected to serve thought and not art or language. Ramus' attempt to replace the syllogism of the old logic never found roots in the baroque as described here. His new logic lacked the capacity of the anagogic method to respond to the exploration of the new baroque metaphysics.

Old as it was though not as ancient as logic, the anagogic method met the problem of redefining the nature of nature frontally. The use of the anagogic method represented more than an attempt at the readjustment of the old instrument of logic. This employment meant that anagogy itself was being adjusted to the new purpose of filling logic's role in the pursuit of knowledge. Classical logic rested on the use of the syllogism as the chief instrument in the quest of philosophical, scientific, and, later, Christian truth; formed of three premises, the syllogism rested on Aristotle's ten categories, and the ten categories rested on the scholastic dualism of matter and form. Such logic was little adapted to the new metaphysics, which was becoming progressively identified with the emotive values of rhetoric and less and less with Aristotelian values of the categories. The anagogic method was a more suitable instrument than logic for the task of grasping the emotive significance of the baroque world. In the writings of Southwell, Crashaw, Heywood, Alabaster, Donne, and Revett, the evidence for the omnipresence of God was not logic but emotion and usually love. Affections rather than syllogistic sentences were the premises of faith. Where the "sences faile" as evidence of God's existence for Southwell, the truth of God's presence

was "love" ("Of the Blessed Sacrament of the Aulter," 11. 16, 19); for
Donne, the mystical significance of Elizabeth Drury's typological being
was eternal "Heaven joyes" ("The Second Anniversary," 11.
470, 487);
for Crashaw, the typological movement of history from the Old to the
New Testament, from "Types" to "Truthes," yields "love's dawn"
("Lauda Sion," IV, 11. 5, 4).

Similarly in other writings, including the massive body of Jesuit
compositions, and in countless emblem books like the Dutch Benedictine
van Haeften's *Schola Cordis* (1629), the emphasis on anagogy was hardly
unconscious. The removal of emphasis from logic was hardly unwilled
even if its consequences were practically never entertained as such. The
replacement of the syllogism by anagogy for the pursuit of the truth of an
emotive world was not mechanical but was nevertheless steady. In the
section on "The Logick of the Heart" in The *Scoole of the Heart* (1647),
the English translation of *Schola Cordis* by Christopher Harvey, "the
heart / And not the head" becomes the "fountain of this Art" of logic, [26] a
proposition with which classical thinkers and the scholastics would have
strongly disagreed. The poem on "The Logick of the Heart" with three
other poems forms the epilogue of Harvey's translation, and this epilogue
does not appear in van Haeften's original work, but it is a reworking of
his ideas in the first of the four books of *Schola Cordis*. The anagogic
analysis of the poem, "All my invention" and "Method" (11. 13. 19),
would have left classical and scholastic thinkers no less confused. It was
founded on "types" present in the heart rather than on syllogistic
premises (p. 193). The four levels of meaning in the poem's new "logic of
the heart" were an infallible truth-seeking instrument: first the literal
level, "what terms / My Lord and I stand in" (11. 13-14); second, the
allegorical or figurative, "how he confirms / His promises to me" (11. 14-
15); third, the tropological or moral, "how I inherit / What he hath
purchased for me by his merit" (11. 15-16); and finally, the mystical or
anagogic, "My judgment is submission to his will, / And when he once
hath spoken to be still" (11. 17-18).

In Jesuit writings like the second, revised edition of Ribadeneira's
Catalogus Scriptorum (1613), the predominance of typology, anagogy,
and rhetoric over logic and metaphysics is even more striking than in
Schola Cordis. [27] Such evidence is less precise but is more far-reaching.
The bibliography by Ribadeneira, who was one of the most renowned
Jesuit scholars of his day and a pioneer in modern bibliographical work,
pretends to list the order's writings *in toto*. The work spans the first
sixty-three years of the Jesuits' existence, years that covered the rise and
dominion of much Counter Reformation literature. The first and most
prominent section of the bibliography is dedicated to anagogic
interpretations and commentaries, mainly of the Scriptures, and lists
seventy-six entries (p. 256). Later, its section on rhetoric lists forty-three
entries (p. 307). By contrast, the section on *Logica* has only five entries,
and that on *Metaphysica* has only two (pp. 305-306). Even if we group

the eight entries under *Physica* (p. 306) with the two under *Metaphysica* on the grounds that they both pretend to the study of being, essence, and nature, the preponderance towards typology and rhetoric remains overwhelming.

Ribadeneira's bibliography indicates that in the Jesuit movement which spearheaded the Counter Reformation, typology had become the instrument of investigation for an essentially emotive world. The evidence in Jesuit writings demonstrates profound reorientations of scholastic thought. The ancient authorities were the same as in the works of the medieval writers, but the emphases put on them had radically altered. Once circumscribed by figurative literature and morality, anagogy had effectively become the vehicle for understanding a rhetorically-conceived universe.

With their emphasis on mystical meanings and historicity in their considerations of time, Protestant thinkers demonstrated a movement similar to that of baroque writers toward a levelled way of thinking. The development of their thought is therefore interesting in the history of the baroque. For Protestant thinking, too, classical logic had become an inept instrument to examine the truth of contemporary history. As such history in seventeenth century Britain usually appeared in the guise of the Book of Creatures, it was eminently understandable in the light of Biblical prototypes. In *Essays,* although Donne resorted to scholastic terminology to describe the material nature of things, he employed typology to deepen his appreciation of its ultimate worth.[28] Similarly, in so-called secular poems like "A nocturnall upon S. Lucies day" and "The Second Anniversary" poem to Elizabeth Drury, typology determined the nature of his general vision of things. In the first poem the universe is intelligible in the scholastic terminology of privations and absences (11. 16, 26) but its nature is fundamentally metaphoric and visionary. In the second poem Elizabeth Drury is compared to a piece of scroll written on both sides; on one side is the record of her material historical existence, and on the other is her mystical significance in the Protestant Register of the Elect (1. 504).

Thus, although Catholic anagogy served a different cause than Protestant typology, it originated in a similar disillusionment with the older metaphysics. The anagogic method allowed the searcher after truth to look for four levels of meanings in things rather than two and was in that sense more liberal than Protestant typology. In addition, it projected the contemporary imagination onto a universe of eternal affections instead of confining it to correspondences between current history and its Biblical prototypes. The anagogic method was, however, the fruit of the same metaphysical need as Protestant typology. It coexisted with it, not always with contradiction in the general currents of thought in spite of the opposing political ends for church and state to which each was applied. Protestant typology was only less generous and more restrictive on the speculation allowed to the questing human mind than the anagogic method. Imaginatively speaking, as examples of truth, the prototypes of the Bible were less profuse, and their mythological figures tended to be less personal than those in Catholic anagogy. Their inspiration nevertheless sprang from the same philosophical root. The problems of existence that Protestant typology tried to answer were also as profound and, though this typology predominated in Britain even among members of the Established Church like Donne, it did not rule out its adaptation to the Counter Reformation baroque. That adaptation is visible in Donne and Alabaster.

Donne took time to resolve the contradictions created by the presence of both tendencies of typology and anagogy in his work. In his satiric attack on Jesuit meditation in *Ignatius His Conclave* and in his use of the five-part structure of the same meditation in the "First Anniversary" poem to Elizabeth Drury in 1611, he seemed to be arguing in two different directions at once. Later, his "Holy Sonnets" and *Devotions* (1624) also followed respectively the differing Counter Reformation and Protestant typologies. In the more important of Alabaster's two cabalistic works, *Apparatus,* there is less evidence of a conflict, but the fusion of contradictory tendencies is apparent in his interests at least in two different ways. First, he admitted of both as methods of investigation (pp. 14, 261). Second, in Biblical typology he preferred the pursuit of mystical meanings (*sensuus mysticus,* pp. 112, 223) according to the values of two-level typology as in his exploration of Corinthians (pp. 14-15), but one of his most detailed Biblical interpretations is a four-level anagogic interpretation of Daniel (pp. 260-1).[29] Protestant typology and the anagogic method existed simultaneously in Britain. There were always Roman Catholics in that country who developed in their recusant corners the baroque world view together with their fellows on the Continent in reaction to the same positive philosophical impulse which had nothing to do with the political motives for their recusancy.

3

Because language is so closely related to thought, it too was affected by anagogy. Style is not in question here so much as language as a reflection of what it expresses. The nature of language came to reflect the need of old words to conceptualize certain new things. Earlier in this chapter we discussed briefly the literal character of figurative language that described a configurative world. We concluded that the literalness of language is determined by what a given age considers to be historical and literal. This principle was pressingly true in the baroque mentality. The spiritual beings who dominated its mythology existed in time by what we consider to be analogy, they populated it by what to us is metaphor, and their qualities of metaphor and analogy touched language. They gave a metaphoric character to creation which passed into current uses of language. The world which was once considered pseudo-scientifically came to be looked upon as metaphoric and realistic in the terms of pseudo-science itself. The vocabulary of science passed out of the realm of matter into the metaphysics of a metaphoric universe. The concepts of the earlier sciences lost their pretensions to pseudo-science as they passed into philosophy.

From a modern point of view, the emerging world picture had the effect of creating two general kinds of metaphor. First, metaphor was the obvious inventive kind of analogy which we loosely call poetic. That is, it was figuratively decorative. Second, metaphor literally described the world. Of the first kind such are the homely images of ships, seas, storms and stars in *Devotions,* which had been translated by Meres, by the Spanish mendicant prior Luis de Granada. Granada's reputation, already extensive on the Continent, spread to Britain in English versions of his work. Granada's mild and sweet, disarmingly obvious, poetic figures masked the more profound second kind of metaphor that reflected the world as though literally in his writings.

The importance for the modern reader to distinguish between two kinds of imagery in *Devotions* is paramount. Without doing so, the line between metaphysical reality and the writing of poetry becomes obscure. In baroque works, poetic metaphor was an extension into fiction of the already existing metaphor of history. For this reason, Granada's prose shared with Bellarmine's, many long passages in which images are literal descriptions of a metaphoric world. The phenomenon was new in the baroque because it marked a development over the earlier Renaissance. It is nowhere more apparent in baroque writings than when the authors discuss human experience heavily couched in contemporary astronomical and medical language. The demise of the purity of classical metaphysics had itself provoked the new metaphoric character of scientific language. The question at stake is not one of having to identify the vocabulary of a physical science that erred scientifically. It is, rather, to understand the language of a poetic vision of the universe that had absorbed old scientific words.

Classical metaphysics, though now inadequate, had possessed the virtue of keeping clear the images and meanings of words from each other. Although it is true that words are always imagistic in that they are at all times syllabic collections representing an idea, the earlier Renaissance man possessed by education a capacity to keep the qualities of word and idea distinct. Conscious through the training of classical metaphysics of the separate character of matter and form even of words, he could not confuse symbol and meaning. Sociolinguistics as the science of words reflecting unwilled social forces was inconceivable to him. Word as image and word as idea were not, could not, be mistaken for each other. Yet, as things themselves became combinations of image and idea in Counter Reformation thought not through sociolinguistic forces but by a pressing metaphoric vision of creation, it was the very dualistic character of language that was obscured. Words describing creation came to assume metaphoric proportions that seemed literal and historical. Language appeared to acquire a metaphoric character from the world it described rather than to possess it in its own right. When someone like Granada employed the terms motion, perturbation, influence, heart, affection, vapours, and senses, the linguistic clarity of an earlier age, because it had become unnecessary, was eliminated by the new relationship of language to matter. Such a clarity between image and meaning we ourselves find lacking in baroque writings, but it was not essential and had become impossible to its time. The universe had assumed as historical the imagistic values of earlier ages. The problem for the modern reader of seventeenth century prose, particularly that of the Counter Reformation, has its origin in this movement of older values of imagery into the place of empirical realities.

When Meres' translation of Granada's *Devotions* described the heart, blood, mind, and the rest of the body and soul in "devotion," the underlying metaphoric assumptions therefore must always be respected. When Granada spoke of man like the painter having to "mundifie, polish and square the two tables of his soule, which are his Understanding and his Will, this of affections, the other of cogitations," he was consciously drawing a simile. Keeping one's inner life spiritually honed was like being a dedicated artist. With such an obvious simile, it is only too easy to group mistakenly another kind of "realistic" metaphor. This second metaphoric language described the baroque emotive world literally and is more complicated than mere poetry. For Granada spoke realistically, though figuratively, to us, when he added:

> Neither is the heart onely and solely to be kept pure and cleane from noysome & hurtfull cogitations, but also from inordinate affections: for there is not any thing more forcible to disturbe & disquiet it, then naturall passions: as are love, hate, mirth, heaviness, feare, hope, desire, wrath, & other like unto these.[30]

Blood created by the heart was the known carrier of emotions as, for example, Crooke and Bright, the early scientists, agreed.[31] These so-called scientific descriptions were the work of the imagination. However, they came to be used by a baroque imagination fashioned by typology, and they were thought of as producing an empirical picture of human experience.

Again, Granada was knowingly metaphoric when he wrote that there are "winds" that "tosse and turmoile," "cloudes" that "obscure," and "weights" that "depresse" our spirit. However, his subsequent explanation "that passions with their cogitations doe disturbe the heart, with their appetites doe dissever and distract it, with their affections doe captivate it, with their perturbations & inordinate motions doe darken and blinde it," is to be taken literally despite its numerous expressions like "passions with their cogitations," "dissever," and "captivate" that to us are figurative.[32] Conditioned by typological considerations, the baroque philosophical imagination discussed its metaphysical questions metaphorically.

The vocabulary of baroque thinkers like Granada illustrates their metaphoric world better when applied to personal experience than to other things. The reasons for this originate in that world itself. As the emotive forces of the baroque world fused perfectly alone in man, the scientific words related to his experiences describe his anagogic universe consistently with force. Man was the *summum* of the new metaphoric universe so that the language of the self was the referral point of the language of creation. Such language was hopelessly misleading scientifically. Not only was it inherited from a pseudo-scientific past fraught with its inexact deductive guesses of what was supposedly exact inductive knowledge, but it was also submitted to the scientific indignity of metaphor. The vocabulary of personal experience springing from imaginative explanations of the human body was as old as Galen, who was yet the greatest contemporary medical authority, and brought with it concepts eminently adaptable to the baroque anagogic vision. The baroque thinkers absorbed the imaginative appreciations of personal experience floating in the general muddle of the spent pseudo-sciences into their view of the world.

In this development of thought and language the scientific allusions of baroque writers were denied their original denotations. Though the conclusions of the old sciences were imaginative, the original intention behind them relating to man had purported to be scientific explanations of the body. In its new setting, their vocabulary pretended not even to that. Fused into the stream of contemporary anagogy, it became an instrument for the discovery of the mystical significances of the self. The meanings of the words became mystically related to allegory and tropology rather than to the old sciences. On other than baroque grounds, diverse works like Banister's *The Historie of Man* (1578) and Crooke's *Description of the Body of Man* (1615) had already come to suggest that human experience was a kind of "copy" or image of its underlying mystical "type" or significance. Such a characteristic of the pseudo-scientific works of the closing stages of the Renaissance distinguished them from the speculative language of the medieval sciences. The baroque writings of the same period as the later pseudo-scientific works took this tendency to its logical limits imposed by anagogy. For example, which of the three organs, the brain, spleen, or heart, predominated in the body was a current argument though as old as Aristotle.[33] In both *Devotions*[34] and "The Funerall" Donne opted for the brain, as did Banister and Crooke in their work.[35] But he laid stress on the brain's intuitive and mystical aspects according to his views on "Conscience" and the heart in *Pseudo-Martyr* rather than on early scientific conceptions about the brain itself.[36]

The vocabulary of the old sciences influenced by anagogy was unrelated to the image-making of poetry as we understand it. This vocabulary described the role of the self in an anagogic universe and not art. Without distinguishing between our conception of metaphor as verse and its baroque conception as history, particularly in the case of words like heart, affections, blood, passions, cogitations, and spleen, much Counter Reformation vocabulary of medicine, chemistry, and psychology is no more than the servant of our ideas of poetry, of what must appear to have been a simple passion for ornament. In actual fact, it was the slave of an increasingly metaphoric vision of the universe. If the failure of the old scientific vocabulary had been an incipient use of deduction, its new failure in the Counter Reformation was now become a pervasive habit of metaphor. This habit, moreover, was not restricted to Counter Reformation writings. Because of the extensive influence of typology, a number of descriptive affinities prevailed among books of devotion and of astronomy, alchemy, and astrology, both Catholic and non-Catholic, like Donne's *Devotions,* Granada's *Devotions,* Ignatius' *Exercises,* Walter Montagu's *Miscellania Spiritualia,* Bright's *Treatise of Melancholy,* Banister's *The Historie of Man,* Crooke's *Description of the Body of Man,* and Elyot's *Castle of Helth.*[37] This new tradition of language, if such it may be called, came to be adapted to the Jesuit practice of poetry and to the visions of Ignatius' *Exercises.*

The affinities of vocabulary among the above works grew as the sixteenth century wore on, as the seventeenth century developed, and as the baroque literature of the Counter Reformation spread its roots. As time passed, such vocabulary became more cogent and vital to its users. The language of affections, motions, powers, and senses common to Ignatius and Elyot, lacking vitality in *Exercises* and *Castle,* had become uniformly figurative and in that sense alive by the time of Crooke's *Description* and of imitations of *Exercises* like Hawkins' *Partheneia Sacra.*

In those works that branch off into meditation, the vocabulary became part of a new rich expression saying in a consistently visionary manner something about a seemingly metaphoric universe for which it had long been preparing.

The baroque writings like *Partheneia,* harnessing the values of anagogy to an emotive universe, were obviously distinct from the works of scientific thinkers like Bacon and Harvey. However, they represented a force equally new. Their vocabulary was not only an escape from inexpression. It also bespoke a break with the past, from currents of thought about the self and the world that predominated seemingly unchallenged until the early sixteenth century. Even the cloistered, like the Benedictine Abbot of Monteuil Walter Montagu (c. 1603-1677), though a minor figure, could write representatively about this figurative world. In *Miscellanea Spiritualia,* the new vocabulary enabled him to speak about the then present:

> Certain it is, that contemplation may be said to be the best Optick glass for the heavens. For as by the help of such instruments, we discover somewhat more of the magnitude, stations, and motions of the celestial bodies, then we can do

without that supplement to the shortness of our sight, (though they afford us not just measures of any of those so remote objects;) so the same use we may make of our meditation and discourse upon *Divine Providence*; for we may thereby discover somewhat more of Gods method in government, then the weakness of our first and natural apprehension offers us.

Hence it is that while our reason acts but the part of Natural Astronomie, it may make pretty safe calculations; but if it venture into Judiciarie Astrologie, 'tis like to divine very temerariously; that is, while our discourse presses no further than the consideration of that general order of Providence, whereon depends the stations, promotions, and retrogradations of all states and conditions in this world; it may find some reasonable motives to quiet us, in those adverse changes and revolutions which perplex our selves or others. But if we strain our imaginations to reach the precise and special causes of the varying and mutation of private fortunes, we are in danger to make very unsound conclusions. For as we have certain general rules to guide us in the positions and motions of the stars; but none to declare their influences and operations upon our particular free actions: so have we some general notion of Gods order in the common mutation of transitorie matters; but no marks whereby to discern his special design in the changes and variation of particular subjects.[38]

In such a passage, the baroque mind has retreated bravely from the formal hierarchies of the Elizabethan world picture. The Great Chain of Being on which this picture of hierarchical order had loosely hung, had enabled the masses of men to digest the complexities of scholasticism about the Aristotelian categories and about the gradations of matter and form.[39] As the medieval and early Renaissance appreciation of matter retreated, matter itself may be said to have relinquished form and shape. To retain a firm philosophical grasp on it, baroque man turned to the emotive values that scholastic tradition had confirmed for it. Emotion appeared to grow into the form of things. It seemed to become the underlying principle of their existence in the sense that the scholastics had understood such form to be the principle of life. In the baroque, with this stress on emotion, the closed form of art yielded to what Daniells has suggested is baroque open form.[40] When the Jesuit Hugo entitled his emblem book *Emblematis, Elegiis, & Affectibus,* that is, emblems, elegies, and affections, the latter affections were as concrete to him as the traditional elegiac poetic genre and the new literary emblematic genre with which he coupled them.[41] In the same vein Jacob Biderman's "sacred delights" in the prefatory *"Lectores Benevolis"* of his emblem book *Deliciae Sacrae* were "affective," giving his work its substance and content.[42]

In such declarations as Hugo's and Biderman's, whether in the original

Latin editions of their works or in their English translations, the baroque world view succeeded to the Elizabethan world picture as the universe's major support. Although it did not make the Chain disappear from the popular imagination, it replaced it nevertheless. It was no longer important to what extent things participated or did not participate in the Renaissance ideal of pure spirit as reason but how they fitted into conceptions of pure spirit as feeling in so far as reason could comprehend sensation. The nature of reason in the Ignatian tradition of formal and poetic meditation showed the truth of this. Things were no longer graded on either side of a pivotal point called reason in an ascending order of spirituality through the categories of men, angels, and God and in a descending order from men through the categories of animals, vegetables, and finally inanimate matter.[43] With its places and sub-places for angels, devils, popes, kings, cardinals, princes, freedmen, lions, dogs, trees, flowers, stones, and dust, the ladder of being gave up its seat to the ladder of the affections on which its categories might or might not hang. As this change took place, Christian civilization, by which is not meant here Christian religion, may be viewed as beginning to decline into its twilight. Christian faith persisted, but the civilization built on the categories of form and matter and the resulting systems of the ancients had begun to set.

The baroque world was not so much a counter-statement to the nascent physical sciences; it was actually the accompanying philosophical statement of that scientific truth. It often used the vocabulary of the old spent sciences, but so did the new sciences themselves and such vocabulary never set them in opposition. With the new interest in typology and anagogy, the baroque was the first world view and the first popular and yet established philosophy to accompany the empirical reexamination of the material world. The baroque answered to the collapse of the upper half of the Great Chain of Being in the face of the Reformation and the Counter Reformation, while the new scientific thinking answered quickly to the unacceptable deductive speculative study of the material world in the lower half of the Chain. The two movements were accompanying reactions to the same declining civilization that had run its course. The Ignatian tradition of meditation, leaning heavily on the emotive values of the new world view, represented an attempt to re-order human experience into the permanent values of tradition from which it seemed to be straying aimlessly. It re-grouped the still valid concepts of the old philosophies of ancient Greece and Rome and of Europe into the appearances of a new discipline. The practice of poetry that this tradition inspired in Britain represented as well a re-ordering of the genres of received verse to the service of its meditative discipline.

In their time, the baroque and the new sciences did not contradict each other. Countless imitations of Ignatius' *Exercises* spread in numerous languages into all the countries of Europe simultaneously through the same intellectual channels as the announcements of the discoveries of the new sciences. Ignatius' *Exercises* did not follow but in fact immediately preceded all the major announcements of scientific discoveries, whether Copernicus' or Galileo's on the central position of the sun, Tycho Brahe's on the inconstant number of the stars, or Harvey's on the circulation of the blood. The imitations of *Exercises* developed contemporaneously with these announcements. Using the same vocabulary of affections, heart, movement, motions, influences, passions, cogitations and so forth, the baroque and the new sciences reorganized the still valid concepts of the universe bequeathed to them by the old philosophies. For a brief moment in history, the affections, the heart, the brain and the vapors were the common material of the poet, meditator, and scientist, having to describe being, nature, and essence according to the general vision of duality, time, and eternity.

Concomitant with the new sciences, the baroque world view was a reply to the exhaustion of the human mind with the philosophical statements of the immediate past. To set the two movements in opposition is to make the wheel of the history of ideas turn faster than it did. Although it is true that the baroque thinker and the new scientist asked different questions with their common terminology, they were provoked by the same impetus of the first "new" learning of the early humanist revival of the ancients. Paradoxically, the new learning of the seventeenth century spelled the death of the revival of learning of the early Renaissance that had given it birth.

If the names of the new scientists are more prominent in the modern imagination, they were not so to their times. Ignatius may appear less important than Galileo because of the subsequent development of the history of ideas favorably in the direction of science. In addition he is generally classed as a great Catholic saint and the founder of a religious order, which has not helped secular considerations of him as a historical figure. But neither his sainthood nor his religious foundation accounts for his universal attraction to his times, which was as great as any scientist's. In the minds of his contemporaries he was important for the countless imitations in formal meditation and verse that his *Exercises* inspired. A mere saint or founder of a religious order would never have had the effect of someone who successfully redefined the nature of man as a universal feeler. Galileo, Brahe, Harvey, and Bacon must be measured against Ignatius and not against such figures as van Haeften, Hawkins, Montagu, and Everard.

The Counter Reformation baroque may represent the last instance when the ideals of Graeco-Roman civilization filtered through Christian ideals to captivate the imagination of a large segment of western society so that members of that society produced a number of works artistic and scholarly that other epochs may recognize as universal. The extraordinary spread of Jesuit meditation and verse must be viewed in the light of the group and personal pressures produced by the forces of a civilization as described here. *Exercises* represented a retreat from, as well as a final development of, the ideals of the Graeco-Roman world in Christian guise. Beyond the baroque, it may be said, the ideals of Christianity could no longer support the ideals of the ancient world. These ideals, having once died of themselves in Greece and Rome, declined again in the Near-Eastern religion of Christianity. The retreat from Christian ideals came only later, however soon, and for reasons not pertinent here.

Notes

[1]Warnke, *Versions of the Baroque*, pp. 9-10.
[2]Albert Camus, *The Plague*, trans. Stuart Gibbert (Harmondsworth, 1965), pp. 244-245, 251-252.
[3]Arthur Koestler, *Darkness at Noon*, trans. Daphne Hardy (Harmondsworth, 1965), pp. 82-83, 130-131.
[4]Aristotle, *Rhetoric*, II, 1, trans. Lane Cooper (New York, 1960), p. 92: "By these, the emotions, are meant those states which are attended by pain or pleasure, and which, as they change, make a difference in our judgements."
[5]Thomas Aquinas, *Summa Theologica*, I, II, QQ. 22-29, trans. Fathers of the English Dominican Province, Vol. 1 (New York, 1947), pp. 691-717 on the passions, their gradation, and their presence in God *modo analogico*.
[6]Alexander Donatus, *Ars Poetica Sine Institutionum Artis Poeticae Libri Tres*, 1631. The text used here is of the second edition, 1633, p. 178. Carlos Sommervogel, *Bibliothèque de la Compagnie de Jésus* (Brussels, 1890-1909), 10 Vols., III, Cols. 131-133, describes briefly Donatus' career.
[7]Thomas Everard, trans., *An Instruction How to Pray and Meditate Well. . . By the Reverend Father Ignatius Balsamo Priest of the Societie of Jesus* (St. Omer, 1622), p. 271.
[8]Robert Southwell, *Two letters and Short Rule of Good Life* (including "Epistle Unto His Father"), ed. Nancy Pollard Brown (Charlottesville, 1973), pp. 28-32.
[9]For example, Luis de Granada, *The Sinners Guyde*, trans. Frances Meres (London, 1598), pp. 201-202.
[10]Robert Bellarmine, *Of the Eternall Felicity of the Saints. Five Bookes. Written in Latin by the most Illustrious Cardinall Bellarmine, of the Society of Jesus. And translated into English by* A. E. [Thomas Everard], n.p., 1638. The Latin original, *De Aeterna Felicitate Sanctorum libri quinque* (Rome, 1616) was translated into Italian and French in 1616, Dutch in 1617, and Spanish in 1650.
[11]*Eternall Felicity*, pp. 17-18.
[12]William Fulke, *A Most pleasant Prospect Into the Garden of Naturall*

Contemplation, to behold the naturall causes of all kinde of Meteors, first ed. 1563 (London, 1634), Sigs. 2a, 5b.

[13]Robert Recorde, *The Castle of Knowledge, containing the Explication of the Sphere* (London, 1556), pp. 7-8.

[14]Fulke, *Naturall Contemplation,* Sigs. 5a, 6a; Robert Burton, *The Anatomy of Melancholy,* 2, 2, 3, ed. F. Dell and P. Jordan-Smith (New York, 1955), p. 421.

[15]Thomas Blundeville, *M. Blundevil His Exercises . . . Cosmographie, Astronomie, and Geographie,* first ed. 1594 (London, 1636), p. 493; John Rastell, *Book of Purgatory,* II, xx (London, 1530), Sig, e2b.

[16]Burton, *Anatomy,* 2, 2, 3, p. 421, although in the preceding century in Robert Recorde's *Castle of Knowledge,* p. 7, chaos reigned in the bowels of the earth.

[17]Aquinas, *Summa* I, Q. 1, Art. 10, Vol. I, p. 7.

[18]Robert Bellarmine, *Explanatio in Psalmos . . . Lugduni* (1611), pp. 6-8; *Apparatum Sacrum Anton. Possevini . . . Ad Scriptores Veteris & novi Testamenti. Eorum interpretes Synodos & Patres Latinos ac Grecos. Horum Versiones. Theologos Scholasticos quique contra hereticos egerunt Chronographos & Historiographos Ecclesiasticos. Eos qui casus conscientia explicarunt. Alios qui Canonicum Ius sunt interpretati Poetas Sacros. Libros pios quocunque idiomate conscriptos* (Cologne, 1608), p. 40; Blasius Viegas, *Commentarii Exegetici In Apocalypsim Ioannis Apostoli . . . Eborae,* 1601; and Luis de Granada, *Granados Devotion,* trans. Frances Meres (London, 1598), pp. 20-21, 67.

[19]John Dayrell, *A Treatise of the Church* (London 1617), pp. 161-162.

[20]Louis Richeome, *Holy Pictures of the mysticall Figures of the most holy Sacrifice and Sacrament of the Eucharist: Set forth in French by Lewis Richeome, Provinciall of the Societie of Jesus; and translated into English for the benefit of those of that Nation, aswell Protestants as Catholickes. By C. A.* (1619), p. 4. The original edition published in Paris in 1601 was entitled *Tableaux Sacrez des figures mystiques du très-auguste sacrifice et sacrement de l'Eucharistie. Dédiez à la très chrestienne Royne de France et de Navarre Marie de Medicis.*

[21]Dante Alighieri, *Convivio,* II, i, 9-30, trans. W. W. Jackson (Oxford, 1909), pp. 73-74.

[22]Wilbur S. Howell, *Logic and Rhetoric in England 1500-1700* (New York, 1961), pp. 250-251, 285.

[23]Wilbur S. Howell, *Poetics, Rhetoric, and Logic* (Ithaca, 1975), pp. 78-79, 81-83.

[24]Peter Ramus, *The Logicke* (1574), Scolar Press Facsimile (Menston, 1970); Howell, *Logic and Rhetoric,* pp. 148-150.

[25]For the contemporary rejection of Ramist logic: Ruth Wallerstein, *Studies in Seventeenth Century Poetic* (Madison, Wisc., 1950), p. 131; and for its influence on poetic imagery; Rosemund Tuve, *Elizabethan and Metaphysical Imagery* (Chicago, 1947), pp. 281-283.

[26]Benedictus van Haeften, "The Logicke of the Heart," *The Scoole of*

the Heart, or, The Heart of it self gone away from God [.] *Brought back again to him, and Instructed by him*. In *47 Emblemes,* translated by Christopher Harvey (London, 1647), third edition (London, 1675), 11. 5-6, p. 195. The original edition, *Schola Cordis,* appeared in Antwerp in 1629 in four books, the last three only with emblem pictures. Harvey's translation begins with the second book and the four poems of its epilogue rework the ideas of the missing first book (particularly on pp. 17, 20-22, 41-42, 57-59, of the Antwerp Latin edition of 1635).

[27]Pedro Ribadeneira, *Catalogus Scriptorum Religionis societatis Iesu . . . Secunda Editio, plurimorum Scriptorum accesione locupletior* (Antwerp, 1613), p. 232. The first edition appeared in 1602 with the title, *Illustrium Scriptorum religionis Societatis Iesu.*

[28]John Donne, *Essays in Divinity,* ed. E. Simpson (Oxford, 1967), pp. 16, 23.

[29]John Donne, *Ignatius His Conclave,* ed. T. Healy (Oxford, 1969), p. 7; Martz, *Poetry of Meditation,* pp. 222-223; Alabaster's second cabalistic work is *Ecce Sponsus Venit,* London, 1633.

[30]Granada, *Devotions,* pp. 47, 48-50.

[31]Helkiah Crooke, *A Description of the Body of Man . . . Collected and Translated Out of all the Best Authors of Anatomy,* III, 11, first ed. 1615 (London, 1631), pp. 126-127; and Timothy Bright, *A Treatise of Melancholy* (London, 1586), pp. 89-91.

[32]Granada, *Devotions,* p. 49.

[33]Aristotle, *De Partibus Animalium* III. 4, 666a. 10, 20-23, ed. William Ogle, Vol. V, *The Works of Aristotle Translated into English,* ed. J. A. Smith and W. D. Ross (Oxford, 1908-1952).

[34]John Donne, *Devotions Upon Emergent Occasions,* ed. Anthony Raspa (Montreal, 1975), pp. 63-64.

[35]John Banister, *The Historie of Man* (London, 1578), Fol. 6; Crooke, *Description,* pp. 429-431.

[36]John Donne, *Pseudo-Martyr,* first ed. (London, 1610), p. 84.

[37]Thomas Elyot, *The Castle of Helth* (London, 1534), p. 10a.

[38]Walter Montagu, *Miscellanea Spiritualia: Or, Devout Essayes: The Second Part, Composed By the Honourable Walter Montagu Esq; Abbot of Monteuil,* first ed. 1648 (London, 1654 [i.e. 1653]), Sigs, B3 ᵛ, B4.

[39]A. O. Lovejoy, *The Great Chain of Being* (Cambridge, Mass., 1936), pp. 73-75.

[40]Roy Daniells, "Baroque Form in English Literature," *University of Toronto Quarterly,* 14 (1944-45), pp. 396-398.

[41]Herman Hugo, *Pia Desideria Emblematis, Elegiis & Affectibus SS. Patrum illustrata Authore Hermanno Hugone Societatis Iesu* (Antwerp, 1624).

[42]Jacob Biderman, *Iacobi Bidermani è Societate Iesu Deliciae Sacrae* (Antwerp, 1637), pp. 9-10.

[43]E. M. W. Tillyard, *The Elizabethan World Picture* (London, 1960), p. 23.

Meditation and Psychology

1

For about a hundred years after 1548, the meditation in verse and in the adaptations of *Exercises* was a new, creative, and imaginative act of the human spirit. It involved the long received notions of the three powers of the mind — memory, understanding, and will. However, both in Ignatius' *Exercises* (p. 23) and in, for example, two imitations of the manual, the Italian Bruno's *An Abridgement of Meditation* and the Spaniard de la Puente's *Meditations Upon the Mysteries of our Holy Faith,* the meditation seemed wholly without precedent.[1]

Both *Abridgement* and *Meditations* were translated by the English mission priest Richard Gibbons for the recusant field. With Everard and Floyd, Gibbons (b. Wells, 1549; d. Douai, 1632) was one of the principal agents for the dissemination of baroque writings in England. And, although he wrote in *Meditations* that the traditional "supreme faculties" of the "pure spirit" are the instruments of meditation, he shows the three of them to be radically altered from their scholastic origins. Their end was now to provoke the experience of a new world view. Together, the three powers came to be looked upon in the meditation as organizing sensations in the shape of imagery in the imagination. This imaginative arrangement of sensations also involved essentially the reorganization of the elements of the universe. The three faculties thus produced an experience that connected the meditator with the baroque world's forces.

The exercitant's topic and the meditative poem conjoining image and emotion provoked a single human experience that pictured microcosmically an eternity filled with universal affections. Although the poem was on a page and the exercitant's image was in his imagination, their roles were largely similar. Because of their common recourse to the senses, they differed only in the ascetic and aesthetic character of their appeals. Springing from the ancient Aristotelian principle that nothing was in the mind which was not first in the senses, they sought a common meditative effect. Their respective appeals were outwardly psychologically different, but they shared identical sensory and visionary values in the framework of one psychology.

The structure of the ascetic exercise contained basically three parts,

37

Prelude, evacuation of the senses, and application of the senses, and this structure appeared to realize the new experiential role to which Aristotle's principle was being applied. Because of this, the structure accounted largely for the rapid spread of the experience both in formal meditation and in verse. Floyd, for example, invoked the virtues of poetic meditation on the grounds that it presupposed the same sensory channels of knowledge as *Exercises (Overthrow,* p. 43). In the Prelude of the exercise, the meditator drew his topic's image on the inner screen, the *tabula rasa* of his imagination. There in the due course of everyday living, he had first experienced the pictures of the figures that were to make up his meditative image. In the inner personal area where the outer world was constantly becoming familiar to him, he drew an image of his spiritual life or of Christian Mysteries.[2] In the second part of the exercise, *evacuatio sensuum,* the voiding of the senses, he withdrew all five senses successively, sight, smell, touch, hearing, and taste, from their natural response to the physical world. He cut his imagination off from the sense impressions that spontaneous experience was normally flashing on it. In the third stage, with their spontaneity totally curbed, he applied the senses one by one to the image for meditation drawn in his imagination during the Prelude with the intention, as Ignatius wrote, of "running" an "intense affection through all the creatures in my mind" (*Exercises,* pp. 27, 45; Gibbons, *Abridgement,* Sig. ***; Everard, *Instruction,* p. 275; Floyd, *Overthrow,* p. 43). Answering in this way to the emotive exigencies of a relatively unorthodox Christian view of the world, the ascetic experience satisfied its own moral requirements and facilitated its later aesthetic emergence in verse.

The meditation was identified only with the third part rather than with all three sections of the exercise. The reason was that the time, place, and intensity of the visionary experience were determined by the senses' role at the end (Floyd, *Overthrow,* p. 43). Moreover, the visionary experience of the application of the senses possessed its own structure different from that of the exercise as a whole. The exercise and the meditation were not synonymous, and the three-part structure of the one was not the structure of the other. The meditative structure identified with the *applicatio* was founded on the actions of the soul's three powers — the memory, understanding, and will. By contrast, the exercise was based on an external tripartite structure — prelude, evacuation, and application — in which even another person like a supervisor might participate *(Exercises,* pp. 4-6).[3]

The structure of the *applicatio's* meditation was a point of perfect harmony between the meditator's five senses and his memory, understanding, will, and imagination. To this harmony, the two earlier sections of the exercise contributed without taking part. Both structures of meditation and exercise passed into verse some years later. But the passage of the former was by far the more important and more difficult of the two. The challenge to contemporary poetry was not to absorb the structure of the exercise, which was comparatively simple, but rather the structure of the meditation. The absorption of the meditative structure required the Counter Reformation poet to adjust his view of himself as a Renaissance man. Not only had he to imitate in verse the structure of another one of his disciplines, he had also to adapt the fundamentals of his psychology to create an aesthetic response in his reader equivalent to the ascetic experience of the last stage of *Exercises.*

The meditative poem by Heywood and Southwell became an historical reality with the adjustment of the psychology of *Exercises.* In the historical turning that asceticism took into poetry the reader's senses kept contact with the physical world without frustrating the original exercise's visionary end. Language, words, rhythm, meter, symbols, imagery, and lines channeled the senses to the correct affection. In the experience of poetry, they performed the role that the preludial image originally accomplished in the exercitant's mind. With this similarity of verse to exercise in view, Floyd described Scribanus' poem as "a meditation . . . much used by Iesuites . . . applying . . . the internall senses of the soule" *(Overthrow,* p. 43). As like ends begot like reactions, the psychological requirements were unchanged from the ascetic meditation. Once more the memory yielded up its sensations of things past for depicting a meditative topic. And the understanding contributed its residual ideas. Then, as in the exercise, the will, which provoked the individual sensibility, conjoined sensations and ideas into a new experience of the universal in terms of the finite. As Gibbons wrote, the understanding of the meditator created "spiritual conceipts" which were "fit to move our Will to vertuous affections" *(Abridgement,* Sig. **4^{v}).

> To ravishe eyes here heavenly bewtyes are,
> To winne the eare sweete musicks sweetest sound,
> To lure the tast the Angells heavenly fare,
> To sooth the sent divine perfumes abounde,
> To please the touch he in our hartes doth bedd,
> Whose touch doth cure the dephe, the dumm, the dedd.
>
> Here to delight the witt trewe wisdome is,
> To wooe the will of every good the choise,
> For memory a mirrhor shewing blisse,
> Here all that can both sence and soule rejoyce:
> And if to all all this it do not bringe,
> The fault is in the men, not in the thinge.
>
> (Southwell, *"Of the Blessed Sacrament,"* ll. 31-42)

As it realigned the elements of a received psychology about the pivotal point of the senses, the meditation became commonly known as "affectuous." It seemed to be "carnall" in an acceptable sense of taking on physical dimension (Everard, *Instruction*, pp. 21, 275; Floyd, *Overthrow*, p. 46). Commensurately, sensation came to be depicted as "affectuous" rather than as merely sensory as now it suggested deeply both the spiritual universe of the affections and physical things. The senses themselves appeared to undergo change and to become an inner as well as an outer organism. As such, they were elevated to the rank of the five "internal senses" of the earlier tradition of scholastic psychology. However, this elevation was technically erroneous because the "internal senses" originally referred to cognitive powers only indirectly related to the outer world.[4] Because of the attention that contemporary writers like Floyd and Gibbons gave the senses, this unwarranted attribution was not atypical *(Overthrow*, p. 43; *Abridgement*, Sig. ***[IV]; *Meditations*, I, p. 57). Ignatius himself had depicted the ascetic meditation as sensory *(Exercises*, p. 45). This sensory character accounts for the attractiveness of the ascetic meditation to poetry and for its adaptability to aesthetic standards. Poets merely invoked the same powers as the exercitant to justify calling their verse meditative.

In Sonnet 15 "My soul a world is by contraction," for example, Alabaster described his "will" as enticing a collective "internal sense" into his poem's "devotion." The "sense" in question followed a path drawn by his understanding "wit" (11. 11-12, 3). Again in Sonnet 31 "Upon St. Paul to the Corinthians," Alabaster felt compelled to "amend" sense in order to "apprehend" Christ (11. 9-10). Then in Sonnet 64 "Jesu, the handle of the world's great ball," he described "human sense" as enabling him to bring "superessence / Down to us" in verse (11. 5-7). In one of his cabalistic works, Alabaster even found *applicatio sensus* superior to reason for comprehending Biblical language *(Apparatus*, pp. 111-113). His invocation to his "soul's powers" in Sonnet 53 "A Preface to the Incarnation", was a plea for the use of the senses to write poetry according to the requirements of the meditative psychology. Similar pleas are found in Crashaw's "To the Name" ("Powers of my Soul, be Proud!" 1. 91) and in Southwell's "A Holy Hymne" ("What power affords performe indeede," 1. 4).

The same meditative view of the senses recurred in Revett's "Jacobs Vision at Bethel" at the end of the Jesuit tradition. Revett transformed the Biblical Jacob's revelatory vision of the ladder to heaven into an "affectuous meditation" in the manner of Alabaster's "transelementing" sensation into love, in Sonnets 47 (1.9) and 48 (1.11). The thoughts of the dreaming Jacob, he wrote, "doth his sense unwind" not in his body but in "his beauteous mind." They opened his "intellectual eyes" to the "prospect of his soul" in the lines of his poem (13, 18, 19, 22, 23).

The new experience for which the Jesuit meditation appeared to speak in the above poems grew out of the three acts of the understanding. These acts, which emanated from the still present currents of scholastic philosophy, were the "simple apprehension," the "reason," and the "judgment." They represented the activities possible to the second power of the mind, the understanding, and they are not to be confused with the three powers of the mind themselves.[5] As Floyd indicated, the experience of meditation took its name from the first of these activities but appeared to have become a power in its own right *(Overthrow, p. 44)*. The new experience transcended the acts of the understanding and effectively it was a visionary fourth power of the mind which, coming after the will, might be called a "complex apprehension."

This enlarged apprehension, which had been unthought of by the scholastics and their Greek and Roman antecedents, including Aquinas, Aristotle, and Augustine, was composed of a series of simple apprehensions relevant to meditation. It laid stress on the understanding as a synthetic, creative power in contrast to its predominantly logical, rationalistic role in traditional scholasticism. It also placed a new emphasis on the will as the seat of felt experience in order to make human psychology correspond to the demands of a world view based on emotive rather than formal values.

The complex apprehension distinguished Ignatian meditation from other contemporary forms of devotion. It was a vital, interior, and even difficult act for the modern intelligence conditioned by behavioral psychology to conceive. The complex apprehension was deliberate and conscious rather than instinctive and unconscious. It rested firmly on the belief that the meditator was unaffected by the pressures of the world outside his inner self. The new apprehension of this independent inner self bespoke an experience of the senses and the spirit. It united "knowledge and love together" (Everard, *Instruction,* pp. 21-22). Matter and spirit, idea and emotion were involved. At the same time, the apprehension supposed a quasi-instinctive background knowledge of the provocative emotive universe.

In such a guise, intended as the answer of the inner self to the outer world, the complex apprehension had wide connotations. Though couched in scholastic terminology, it was another name for the third, final, and meditative stage, *applicatio sensuum,* of Ignatius' original ascetic exercise *(Exercises,* p. 45; Gibbons, *Abridgement,* Sig. ***2; Floyd, *Overthrow,* p. 43). The complex apprehension also suggested the simple apprehension of its origin in the acts of the understanding. Yet, though both *applicatio sensuum* and simple apprehension helped to explain it, the new apprehension differed greatly from them. Speaking for an experience rather than for part of an exercital structure, its scope was unlike that of the *applicatio.* Whereas the application of the senses referred primarily to sensation, the new apprehension encompassed the fulfillment of spiritual ends as well. It also differed from the old apprehension of its origin as much as art differs from nature. The new apprehension reorganized the material, sensory, emotive, and spiritual values of a number of simple apprehensions into a complex meditative pattern describing both the *applicatio* and its later imitation in verse. The dualistic nature of the simple apprehension permitted this reorganization.

The simple apprehension described the tiny experience of, for example, seeing a green field. In it, the sensation of the color green and the idea of the weald were for a moment one, undivided and unimaginative in that they were three-dimensional and in the outside physical world. To see the weald represented the fleeting, momentary intelligent sensation of the field. Thus far, the Jesuit concept of the experience was in the general run of scholastic thinking. That is, the simple apprehension spoke for the initial integrated experience of perception and sense. Later, the "reason," the second act of the understanding, broke the simple apprehension down into idea and color in the inevitable due course of human experience and, finally, the "judgment," the third act, took over its sundered parts and consigned the sensation to the memory and the idea to the pure part of the reason itself called "intellect."[6] However, by their emphasis on the simple apprehension as an experience of the self as well as an objective form of knowledge of the outer world as it was originally understood, the Jesuits re-oriented it to the baroque world view.

In the ascetic exercise, the human understanding, through its third act of judgment, chose such simple apprehensions stored in the memory carefully. The simple apprehensions had to fit the topic of meditation. They had always to represent suitably the meditative topic in a complex imaginative emotive experience. Gibbons wrote, "Then we must exercise our understanding upon that which the memory hath proposed, and search out diligently, what may be considered about that present object, inferring one thing from another, framing from thence true; pious and spirituall conceipts" in order to create the "Image of the things wee Intend to meditate" (*Abridgement,* Sig. **4ᵛ; *Meditations* I, p. 41). In poetry, the understanding did essentially the same thing. The poet arranged his selected remembered apprehensions into a series of verbal figures. These made up Floyd's meditative "conceipt" *(Overthrow,* p. 47).

The meditative image described in the Jesuit treatises represented the exercitant's imagined topic pictorially. The image was ikonic and was in effect an extended metaphor. Gibbons, whose meager biography leads us to think of him as quiet and scholarly, nevertheless referred to the exercitant's picture vitally as "image" and "similitude" (*Abridgement,* *12, **3). Everard, his fellow mission priest, more tersely described it as a "beautiful Image" (*Instruction,* pp. 21-22). Floyd, who trained for the priesthood at the Jesuit college in Douai in mid-stream of Counter Reformation controversies, referred to it as a "poeticall conceipt" (*Overthrow,* p. 47). Such an image, he argued, was common to the original ascetic Ignatian exercise and to meditative poetry founded on it.

For Famianus Strada, the Jesuit Roman rhetorician, and Donatus, writing exclusively on poetry, the ikonic character of a poem took on similar metaphoric dimensions. Strada in *Prolusiones Academicae* (1617), described it as *figmentum* and Donatus for his part spoke of it as *imago (Ars Poetica*, p. 4). Strada's *Prolusiones* was one of the major statements of baroque aesthetics and its author was one of the most popular Jesuit poetic theorists in England and elsewhere.[7]

The image described in the above works was deeply connected with the meditator's psychology. Much of its character depended on this psychology's affections. Jesuit poetics were the fruit of a confluence of Aristotelian, Thomistic, and Augustinian ideas filtered into Counter Reformation thought with all the continuity and innovation that this confluence entailed; they were not the product of fashionable classical ideas like the Neo-Platonic circulating in the Renaissance.[8] Their psychology sprang from current scholastic concepts like the affections updated according to the pressures of the new world view. In such a context, the Ignatian image had wide psychological implications beyond, for example, the scope of the allegorical "darke conceit" that Spenser imagined could help his weak reader in his quest for virtue.[9] In "Saint Peters Complaint," Southwell spoke of his poem's "texte" as a protracted "endlesse Alphabet" that he "wrung" emotively to his "thoughts." Elsewhere, in "A Vale of Teares," his emotive text was "the dolefulst note" (1. 63).

To plaining thoughts this vaile a rest may bee,
To which from worldly joyes they may retire.
Where sorrow springs from water, stone and tree,
Where everie thing with mourners doth conspire.

Set here my soule maine streames of teares afloate,
Here all thy sinfull foiles alone recount,
Of solemne tunes make thou the dolefulst note,
That to thy ditties dolor may amount.

(ll. -57-64)

So constructed about a central "image," the baroque fourth power of the mind permitted the meditator in *Exercises* and in verse to bring the universe's elements under his personal control. Ignatian psychology was geared to such control to create a dialogue between the meditator and the figures of his mythology. The complex apprehension was therefore founded on the deliberate realignment of received concepts about man's body and soul. The realignment was such that it made mentally disgestible for Counter Reformation man an emotive universe for which the passing formal notions of matter and spirit were becoming rapidly less relevant.

Inspiring like reactions to the universe, the exercitant's image and the poet's poem involved similar complex mental acts. They represented variant uses of a psychology by like means. The image and the poem provoked the new experience first by way of the senses, "appetites," and "concupiscence." Next, they developed it by way of the mind, *desiderium* and *fuga*, or "good" and "bad" desires, "motions," and "perturbations." Then, they concluded it by way of the pure spirit's vision in which the universal affections came into play (Hawkins, *Partheneia*, Sig. Aii^v; Gibbons, *Abridgment*, Sigs. *6, **6, **11; Donatus, *Ars Poetica*, pp. 179-184).[10]

Such affection was more important than image in meditation, although the references to image in the Jesuit treatises tended to precede it. Strada, for example, wrote that emotion was the "soul" of a poem, that in successful poetry it was "made over into a poetic form," that nothing could be "more divinely read" in a poem, that it was "the principal ornament of the poem itself" and that it was the "leading virtue" of verse that men wished "to call sacred" (*Prolusiones*, pp. 158, 169, 170). The image lacking emotive content simply was not verse. For Donatus, the point of view was the same: a religious poem failed if it was not equally made up of *imago* and affection; but the latter was more important because without it an *imago* had no place in verse (pp. 3-4, 178-179, 207). Similarly, Gibbons wrote that the "affection that we would have" preceded its imaginative similitudes in quality as well as in the chronological order of the exercitant's choice *(Abridgement, *12)*. For Floyd, such affection, described in the young Southwell's letter to his father as universal, absolute and fixed in "nature," was the major ingredient of the poet's and the meditator's "imaginations" (*Short Rule*, p. 34; *Overthrow*, pp. 43-45). Crashaw's argument for his verse was constantly in this vein. Even in an occasional prefatory piece for the Cambridge translation of Lessius' *Hygiasticon*, he focused early on the "Certain hard Words" of the poem becoming identified with the experience of the reader: "Hark hither; and thy self be He" (11. 8, 52). Poetry found its value in universal feeling, and Crashaw appeared committed to this principle as early as in his preface to his first volume of undergraduate poems in 1634.[11]

As the choice of affection for sacred verse also influenced its success, love was the best emotion. Love was the first that had existed. It alone corresponded in length of being with God's existence and so, unlike the others, was eternal. As well as having originated before the beginning of time, it preexisted the other affections like pride and hate that had sprung up among the created beings of the timeless spirit universe, Satan and his fallen angels, before the creation of the world *(Prolusiones*, pp. 169-170; *Overthrow*, pp. 44-46; Donatus, pp. 178-181; *Abridgement*, ***2, ***3). Having once shared existence with the Christian God alone, love had inspired him to create both new spirits and the world of time. The commentators considered it as the instrument of experience conforming to the highest standards of *Exercises'* concluding "Contemplation for Obtaining Love."

2

By the use of the three "supreme" human faculties suggested by Southwell, Alabaster, Crashaw, and Revett, English poetry appeared to fulfill aesthetically Ignatius' original ascetic command to his followers. That command had been for his exercitants "to see" Christian realities through "the eyes of the imagination" as if they "were present" at their original historical occurrences (*Exercises,* pp. 42-43; Floyd, *Overthrow,* p. 46). The implications of this command were very great. Without such "affectuous meditation," Gibbons wrote, humanity appeared lost. It was permanently in bondage to its fallen state: "no man can attain any height of Perfection" (*Abridgement,* *7; Everard, *Instruction,* p. 22). Meditation seemed to have become an experience essential to salvation for the post-lapsarian man for whom the universe was fundamentally emotive. With such an approach to meditation, the Jesuit practice of poetry like the original exercise appeared to face the challenge presented to Christians committed to the hopes of the Counter Reformation by the collapse of religious unity and the old world order.

Even before they proliferated in several hundred versions, the forward character of *Exercises'* vision was unmistakable. *Exercises* met the challenge of a recently splintered Christian world with an intense adaptation of current psychological and philosophical principles to contemporary needs. The thoroughness of the adaptation accounted for the work's popularity and its almost immediate influence on verse. To satisfy the needs of his age to remake the world redemptively, Ignatius reconstructed it in the inner self using the reflective capacities of the human reason. The meditative act of looking inward was creative in terms of the world simultaneously with the mind's retreat from it. Consequently, the meditation rested on neither strictly mystical nor logical grounds but on a partial rejection of the world which it hopefully purified in the imagination. Neither traditional logic nor the mystic's loss of his will was involved. This was both new and powerfully attractive to an era that was beginning to reevaluate matter empirically on its own grounds.

The redemptive tone that the meditative tradition bequeathed to Donne appeared to spring from Ignatius' use of the residue of medieval psychology, of memory, understanding, and will in the sixteenth century. Ignatius reinvigorated this psychology by altering the relationships of the three powers in their original hierarchical order and thereby directing them to new effects. He maintained the medieval gradation of the powers with the memory at the bottom, the understanding in the middle, and the will at the top, to which he was deeply attached. But he transformed their activity, meant originally to be outside in the world of nature as well as inside the mind of man, into a wholly inner world.[12] Springing from the decline of the credibility of the Great Chain of Being and from the rising sensory values of the new universal view, the inner world of Ignatius reflected contemporary disillusionment with the consideration of the world in terms of matter and form. He asserted the validity of both man and the universe as divine images in the face of a painfully twice-fallen world without having to get entangled in the fluctuations of fortune to which the earlier psychology, like the old universe, was inevitably tied.

In contrast to Thomas More, Thomas Elyot, and Machiavelli, whose works amply demonstrate the Renaissance interest in statecraft and the proper qualities for courtier and philosopher king, Ignatius showed marked indifference to the public man and the world of polity. The contrast is not only perfunctory. It brings Ignatius' individuality into relief and suggests that another stage in the general current of Renaissance ideas had begun. The peculiar retreat from the world into the self represented by *Exercises* excluded the Renaissance ideal of the civil man as someone versed in public polity. By ignoring the philosophical and ideal character of the political state, *Exercises* appears as the fruit of the older continental Renaissance that had already moved away from the idealism of the civil man with Machiavelli's *Prince*. As such, *Exercises* may be viewed as a counter-statement to More's *Utopia*. It subverted the thinking of the earlier purely humanistic stage of the younger Renaissance in England. *Exercises* typified more the first half of the seventeenth century than the middle of the sixteenth century in Britain when it appeared.

Exercises was a powerful, apolitical yet popular visionary tract, qualities alone permitting it to surpass the ideals it replaced. The work emerged from the same scholastic need as English humanism to explain the nature of man comprehensively, but was post-humanistic in that it precluded the state from his activities. It referred all human activity directly to an emotive eternity and nothing, not even everyday justice, or for that matter not even poetry, to time. In this way, Ignatius founded in psychology a new world outside the context of public polity in which as a Spanish noble he paradoxically had been born to rule.

The ideal Renaissance man in *Exercises* thus became a meditator on the self. He still met the standards of the age as the only creature who participated in the body of animals and in the spirit of the angels below and above him respectively in the old Chain of Being. However, he predominated for his capacities for meditation such as nature gave him and not for his place as an actor in a worldly ladder of being. This concept of Renaissance man as meditator passed into verse. All earthly creatures were subject to man in Donne's "Holy Sonnet" 12, "Why are wee by all creatures waited on?", not because he ruled, but because he meditated. Ignatius thus freed his contemporaries from the consequences of the contemporary fall of the Great Chain of Being to which humanistic notions of the state were attached, at the same time leaving intact the still workable psychology of infinite human reason and faculties which Renaissance works like *Hamlet* continued to reflect.[13] In this way, a whole body of Renaissance religious verse came to be freed from the concerns of the artistically-versed governing courtier that the age so much admired.

As a redemptive document, Ignatius' work sought to inspire its readers to practice the three powers of the mind in a Promethean fashion in the name of being common and everyday. Calling on man to approximate the divine, it encouraged him to imitate in his imagination God's creation of the universe by love. *Exercises* avoided the pitfall of diminishing man by setting out merely to save him from the world, the flesh, and the devil. Ignatius reacted instantaneously to the cultural rather than merely political or strictly religious changes befalling western Europe. Because of this, *Exercises* augured the profound positive adjustments rather than the negative ones that were to redirect Christian sensibility in the next century and that the later political involvements of Ignatius' followers obscured.

Supporting the new role of religious vision in *Exercises* was the apparent necessity of "affectuous meditation" for salvation. The redemptive character of the form of experience advocated by Loyola distinguished *Exercises* from contemporary forms of immersive mystical experiences like those of Teresa of Avila, John of the Cross, and Francis of Sales, from the earlier medieval forms of revelatory religious experience in Julian of Norwich and Richard Rolle, and from the divinely interventional Biblical forms of the prophets Enoch and Elias. A rapid comparison of Jesuit poetry with the lyric mystical verse of John of the Cross bears out its individuality. In *Exercises,* the world appeared to have fallen twice, first in Eden and now secondly in the sundering of the spirit of Christianity. Ignatius' work attempted to redeem the meditator from that impossible twice-fallen state. In that sense, *Exercises* was redemptive rather than penitential and more given to poetic adaptation than to penance. With the regression of the spirit of the medieval and early Renaissance universe, Ignatius did not envisage the withdrawal of the Christian God's presence from creation. However, he conceded the twilight of the hierarchical world in which the position of God was clear, fixed and unambiguous to the beholder. His *Exercises* withdrew human attention from the outer world to an inner world to clarify God's influence on earth once more.

Inspired by contemporary events as well as by their author's personal conversion to the holy life, the very first pages of *Exercises* spoke of man's fallen state as of a vigor immediate to the fall of the whole universe. They were not exclusively concerned with the condition of the individual man (pp. 1-3, 21). The theme of the universal fall was repeated by the imitations of Ignatius' work (Gibbons, *Abridgement,* *7). It created a tone in Jesuit writings suggesting that the splintering of Christianity which was their major historical background event copied archetypally the old story of the fall. Quite apart from the fact that it was also quickly to govern the attitudes of meditative poets towards their verse, such a tone made *Exercises* less partisan in the religious struggles of the Reformation and the Counter Reformation than it might have otherwise been.

Ignatius' conversion was responsible for *Exercises'* tone of universal redemption. This conversion was not extraordinary because Ignatius turned away from personal sin.[14] It was remarkable because by meditation it issued in the exercital four-week long chronological review of the history of Christianity. Only secondly did Ignatius' conversion involve the examination of personal life, and nothing in his biography suggests that he was particularly sinful. His meditations at his original retreat place in Manresa in Spain, his documentation of these meditations in *Exercises* for his followers, and later the poetry it inspired reflected this conversion. The manual that Ignatius bequeathed to the Jesuits rested on a month of exercises on topics ranging, in respect to time, from the creation of the angels to the act of personal love for God as the prelude of one's eternity. The "First Week" was a meditation on the Fall in Heaven and the Fall on Earth, the "Second" on the Incarnation and the Life of Christ, the "Third" on the Passion and Crucifixion, and finally the "Fourth" on the Resurrection and on the concluding "Contemplation for Obtaining Love" (pp. 22, 40, 67, 78). These exercises terminated predominantly not in the alleviation of the exercitant's personal sinful state but in the readjustment of his whole emotive being to the state of fallen man as a way of overcoming the long-ago collapse in Eden.

Ignatius' principal meditations of sins, for example, are on the "Triple Sin" which did not directly spring from the exercitant. The "Triple Sin" was first the Fall of the Angels, second the Fall of Man, and third the hypothetical contemporary perpetuation of evil in the universe. Only later did *Exercises* pass on to the contemplation of personal failings and hell (pp. 22-26). In "The Contemplation for obtaining Love," by *Exercises* Ignatius had not intended to save only man but to save the world for God by man's meditation:

The Second point is to consider how God dwells in creatures, in the elements giving them being, in the plants giving them growth, in animals giving them feeling, and in men giving them understanding, and so in me giving me being, life, feeling, and causing me to understand; making likewise of me a temple, since I am created to the likeness and image of His Divine Majesty (p. 83).

In its quest for a redemptive world, Ignatius' work withdrew the creative human imagination, which the scholastics had considered a mere reflector of outer worldly sense images, back into the self. There, the meditator found time and eternity coexistent once more. *Exercises* and its poetic tradition reactivated the old scholastic imagination to baroque effect. Though still fundamentally passive, the imagination became the meditator's Brave New World in his inner escape from the collapse of the old universal order. Like the sun or earth surrounded by its planets, as though encircled by the five senses, the memory, understanding, and will, the imagination became the center of an unassailable galaxy, a new temporal city in the world and yet outside it.

We find this image variously prefigured in Ignatius, *Exercises,* pp. 23-24; Alabaster, sonnets 15 "My soul a world is by contraction," 11. 1-6, and 73 "O wretched man, the knot of contraties," 11. 2-8; Hawkins, in his prefatory poem to Maffeus' *Fuga Saeculi*;[15] Southwell, "Saint Peters Complaint," 11. 403-412; and Donne, "Goodfriday 1613. Riding Westward," 11. 1-5. In the imagination, no one could depose the earth, reallocate the sun, cast doubt on the primacy of man's created position, or suggest the dispensability of man's inner self in the pursuit of knowledge. The baroque as represented by *Exercises* may be viewed as the first modern form of visionary experience, however totally anchored in Renaissance psychology, if by modern we mean the human response to the first world view to follow the thousand preceding years that covered the emergence, reign, and decline of the medieval hierarchies.

The historic times did not immediately match the new views of *Exercises* and of its prose and verse adaptations. The world of planetary, angelic, human, and political hierarchies that had preceded Ignatius was to dominate the general public consciousness for another half century. However, for all intents and purposes it had collapsed. That world now pictured its own fall as well as its rise. Ambiguously, Christian values supported the remnants of the old world view rather than the old world view sustaining Christianity. Constructed on the remaining foundations of a fallen universe and of fallen man, the old world view had been arranged coherently on the rungs of the ladder of the Great Chain of Being. It had spoken only for a single collective fall touching the universe from the period of the expulsion from Eden to the present. That universal view no longer held and only its traditional association with Christianity sustained it. Even before Western Europeans ceased to believe in the earth as the still point of a galaxy, the divisions of Christianity rather than later scientific discoveries marked the end of the world view of the Great Chain of Being. *Exercises* and its poetic tradition were a reaction to the crumbling of the spiritual upper half of the Great Chain of Being at a moment even when some of Shakespeare's major characters were still to declare its validity.[16]

In their historical context, *Exercises* aimed therefore at filling a void that accompanied the collapse of the old world order. This order had pictured Christian concepts springing from the classical dualism of matter and form. Ignatius sought to alleviate with a new vision of order the strains caused by the shattering of the conception of order in a Great Chain of Being. The Reformation and the Counter Reformation had challenged the conception before the body of this Great Chain was dismembered finally by the announcements of scientific discoveries like the heliocentric position of the sun. To the common imagination the passing of the spirit of the Great Chain of Being was undoubtedly much less spectacular than the loss of the Ptolemaic system. Suddenly to have to live vicariously with the idea that the ground under one's feet whirled about itself and the sun simultaneously, must have stirred the average imagination far more than the comparatively remote arguments of the Reformers and Counter Reformers about the vanished authority of the Pope and kings. However, it was the passing of the Great Chain's unexciting spirit rather than its colorful outward scale, to which *Exercises* and its poetic tradition initially responded with the hope of an inner vision. As a spiritual and poetic force, the international cultural phenomenon that the Ignatian tradition came to represent preceded the wave of new scientific announcements and, indeed, having ridden the wave, outlasted it. Its passing was due to natural developments in sensibility rather than to forms of scepticism inspired by the new sciences.

3

Early in meditative tradition, the church hymn so popular later with Crashaw might be thought to have been the logical instrument of literary change. Southwell in fact twice attempted to use the hymn to that end in "Of the Blessed Sacrament of the Aulter" and "A Holy Hymne," these subjects originating in Aquinas. Crashaw himself later reworked both these hymns into "Adoro te" and "Lauda Sion."[17] However, in Southwell's time the sonnet was already a more current form of personal expression. With its emphasis on communal worship, the hymn was less immediately adaptable to a personal religious role. Its successful adaptation to meditative psychology in poems like Crashaw's "Adoro te,"[18] "Vexilla Regis," "Sancta Maria Dolorem," and "Dies Irae" followed extremely closely on that of the sonnet rather than preceded it, but followed it nevertheless. It is Alabaster's and Donne's sonnets that appear to show Ignatian aesthetics reaching the prime of their influence in England.

Southwell's meditative hymns were tentative because they were premature in the genre's transformation. Hymns as meditation achieved their aims only in Crashaw with the intervening innovations of Alabaster and Donne in the sonnet's inner probings. The sonnet's adaptation paved the way to that of the church hymn, which in the secret services of Britain's recusant Catholics could only be sung with difficulty. The "meditative hymn" appears less plausible than the meditative sonnet and, strictly speaking, it is a contradiction in terms. One cannot sing a song of praise if it is turned into a contest with oneself or with God. However, the contradiction is no greater than the inherent impossibility of a "meditative sonnet." The same impetus underlay first the adaptation of the sonnet and then that of the hymn, and the contradiction in their terminology is of the same order. As in the case of the meditative sonnet, the adaptation of the hymn, however liturgical, to the new devotional psychology gave an ancient genre a new lease on life.

> I Sing the NAME which None can say
> But touch't with An interiour RAY.
> The Name of our New PEACE; our Good:
> Our Blisse: & Supernaturall Blood:
> The Name of All our Liues & Loues.
> Hearken, And Help, ye holy Doues!
> The high-born Brood of Day; you bright
> Candidates of blissefull Light,
> The HEIRS Elect of Loue; whose Names belong
> Vnto The euerlasting life of Song;
> All ye wise SOLVES, who in the wealthy Brest
> Of this unbounded NAME build your warm Nest.
> Awake, My glory. SOVL, (if such thou be,
> And That fair WORD at all referr to Thee)
> > Awake & sing
> > And be All Wing;
> Bring hither thy whole SELF; & let me see
> What of thy Parent HEAVN yet speakes in thee.
> > (Crashaw, *"To the Name,"* ll. 1-18).

The adaptation of both sonnet and hymn — poems to women and songs to God — to meditative verse testified to the inability of existing secular and religious genres of verse to deal with the Counter Reformation world view. Being fundamentally emotive, this world view did not allow the neat categorization of human feeling into the secular and the religious. Nor did it permit the expression of human feeling in the received genres of poetry without changing them. Because of this, a great deal of verse represented by meditative aesthetics refused to be compartmentalized into the religious and the non-religious. As the practical distinctions of the earlier Renaissance between the secular and the religious were invalid, the question of the sacred and profane in verse rearose in Jesuit discussions of poetry. Along with the inadequacy of received notions of verse, the question of the sacred and profane indicated the pressure that the already existing new verse tradition exerted as it tried to find its proper expression.

The ravages of the meditative mentality on received literary genres did not stop with the hymn and the sonnet. They also touched the general flow of the imitations of Biblical verse. Corresponding deeply to the pressures of a world view, the meditative mentality invaded the conventional strongholds of Biblical song and allegory in the work of Alabaster and Donne, for example. Like the sonnet and the hymn, imitations of Biblical poetry appeared outdated. As Biblical imitation had grown theoretical rather than literal, many Biblical practices in poetry followed the sonnet and the medieval hymn into the meditative stream. The fruit of the creative understanding and of the Renaissance ideal of reason rather than of genre, the new meditative mentality appeared to answer to contemporary needs to recreate the world, the universe, human life, eternity, God, the angels, love and hate in verse.

The psychological character of Ignatian meditation, based on redemption by the sensory imaginative experience of time, distinguished it clearly from other contemporary meditative forms. Even the Ferrar family's system of meditation at the Anglican monastic community of Little Gidding, also based on the affections and the three mental powers, provoked a different experience.[19] Friends of the community, Crashaw and Donne were unmarked by the familial, dramatic, and participatory character of its staged exercital productions.[20] These productions shaped prayer and conduced "to the information of the understanding" with moral doctrine rather than with the aesthetic ends of the Jesuits.[21]. The Ferrar meditation was "affectuous" because of its drama rather than of the inner fashion of *Exercises*. By championing moral imitativeness, it assumed the affections as immediately expended by the understanding rather than by the additional intervention of the will. The Ferrar meditation typified the nascent tradition of Protestant devotional prose by Anglicans, Bishop Joseph Hall, Lewis Bayley, Richard Sibbes, Richard Rogers, Isaac Ambrose, and Robert Boyle and, and in some measure, by Donne in *Devotions Upon Emergent Occasions*.[22]

This tradition was noteworthy for its absence of all common form and for its ideal of communicating moral doctrine by discourse. It was identifiable by its objectives rather than by a perceptible shape. The definition of meditation by Hall,[23] who was the leader of this tradition, is a loose imitation of the current Jesuit definition of meditation by someone like John Sweetnam in *Treatise*. It differs significantly from Sweetnam's in its less imaginative use of the understanding. Yet more interestingly what Hall called meditation was a string of sometimes numbered reflections, and its unifying purpose was to draw moral vision out of traditional rhetorical discourse.[24]

Other types of meditation forming strong contrasts to Jesuit meditation also existed. Some, like Edmund Arwaker's emblem book, were based on original Jesuit works. But they lacked the dependence of these on emotive psychology. A devotional writer like Arwaker had an allegorical end in mind leading him to fear Jesuit poetry's sensory dimensions. His alterations to the Jesuit Hugo's *Pia Desideria* in his translation indicate his didactic rather than aesthetic ends. With the purpose stated in his preface of stirring his reader to virtuous action, Arwaker censored Hugo's text of its "fictitious stories" and sensual classical imagery and replaced them with "apposite example out of the Scriptures."[25] Hugo, he said, was "a little too much a Poet." A similar reorientation of a Jesuit meditative work, *The Exercise of a Christian Life* (1579) by the Italian Gaspard Loarte, towards didactic and allegorical ends occurred in Edmund Bunney's Protestant version of 1584.[26] Jesuit verse lacked the informatory and didactic qualities that non-Catholic England appreciated in the late sixteenth and seventeenth centuries. Its striking characteristic on British soil was, however, not even this lack.

Because of its charismatic interpretation of the new universe, Ignatian meditation was remarkable for its ability to adapt to non-Catholic devotion. The tradition infiltrated literary genres such as the sonnet. There, the tradition converted a possible Protestant concern with grace to its emotional ends. The relationship based on distance and discourse between the graced Christian and his saving God that Halewood calls meditative did not exclude Ignatian aesthetics.[27] Nor did the Puritan view of "Conscience" as the great guardian of truth in the heart of the individual Christian described in Donne's *Essays* (p. 7). Crashaw adapted this view of conscience to the creative understanding in "To the Name" ("interiour Ray," 1. 2), "Lauda Sion" ("inquiring ey," 1. 6), and "Adoro te" ("holy dictate," 1. 32), all originally Catholic hymns, while this idea of conscience had its greatest influence only later in Bunyan's works.

That Jesuit verse meditation could pass through the Puritan and Anglican contexts of a poem like "To the Name" and leave these contexts unimpaired, was a measure of strength and flexibility of its psychology. "To the Name" looks backward in time to the Puritanism of Crashaw's father, laterally into his Laudianism, and forward into his Roman Catholicism. Historically, the poem appears to have been a response on the Laudian side to the Puritan argument against genuflection in the liturgy of the Holy Name. The much-repeated "Arte" of the poem (11. 33, 40, 60) rested on the use of the name of the divine Yahweh. Once proscriptively unmentionable according to Old Testament law (1. 1), and later made eminently speakable by the New Testament law, the name of Yahweh became pronounceable in the yet other form of seventeenth-century verse aesthetics.

In "To the Name" Crashaw appealed to the Puritan tenet of conscience and to the abrogation of the Old Law by the coming of Christ to justify his poetic "Arte." Poetry was eternally love-bound and sense-felt. Crashaw ironically directed this "Arte" against the Puritans for using the Old Testament proscription of Yahweh's name. The Puritans argued that all forms of visible church worship were forbidden by the Old Testament prohibition against the pronouncing of "God." Crashaw replaced Jesus' name in his poem with the imagery of Ignatian aesthetics. In this way he imitated the replacement of Yahweh by Jesus in the abrogation of the Old Law by the New Testament.

Supported by Jesuit aesthetics in a special British context, "To the Name" flew in the face of the long-drawn-out Puritan attack, described by Berry, on the Anglican practice of genuflection.[28] Crashaw's imagery of the "panting Turtle-Dove," "diligent Bees," "Mountains of myrrh" and "purple Doores" (11. 108. 153, 186, 217) defended the Laudian sacramental regulation for visible signs of worship against the Puritan position. The poem developed the Puritan idea of conscience in the terminology of Jesuit aesthetics by the adaptation of a medieval hymn to the defence of contemporary Anglican worship. By an ironic imitation of the Old Testament proscription against "Yahweh," the name of Jesus is not pronounced once in the poem.

The extraordinary convergence of conflicting currents in "To the Name" demonstrated the historical depth of meditative aesthetics. Whether Crashaw appropriated these aesthetics directly from Jesuit sources or whether he was partly responding to similar cultural stimuli as the Jesuits, these aesthetics dated back already half a century in England by the time of his argument with the Puritans over genuflection. In addition to the poetry of Heywood, Southwell, Alabaster, and Donne, the works of aesthetic importance in Crashaw's immediate background included the emblem book *Partheneia Sacra,* a version of *Exercises* by Henry Hawkins. Hawkins composed the work for young men too weak yet to perform the ascetic meditation in their "Sodalitie" organization, which was a kind of Marian youth corps. The works in Crashaw's background also included other Jesuit emblem imitations of *Exercises,* either in English or in Latin, like Hugo's *Pia Desideria,* Stephen Luzvic's *Le Coeur Devot* (1627) possibly translated by Hawkins in the unsigned *The Devout Hart* of 1634,[29] and Jacob Biderman's *Deliciae Sacrae.* On the whole, these works followed by some time the origins of verse meditation, but preceded the bulk of Crashaw's poetry. Jesuit emblematists often justified their use of art as a necessary form of condescension to the weaknesses of the exercitant in the performance of the original exercise *(Partheneia,* Sig. Ai^v; *Cor Deo).*[30] Interestingly, the poets never made such a declaration because verse meditation had become an independent art in their hands.

The psychology of the Ignatian ascetic and poetic meditations in the verse of Heywood, Southwell, Alabaster, Donne, Crashaw, and Revett suggests a common stream of inspiration. It does not prove that Jesuit practices always influenced them directly. However, it suggests that the Jesuits, as they sustained the cultural movement of the Counter Reformation in England, spoke most efficiently for those who came under the spell of its poetry or of its cultural forces. Their meditation incarnated the aspirations of that movement's sensibility. As a direct influence and as a representation of a general movement, the meditation spread because of its deep adaptation of contemporary psychology to the exigencies of a new world view. Ignatian poetics could speak for their times in a number of ways. They were not unique because of a conscious, concerted effort by several minor and major Renaissance men to start a literary movement, but because they worked current ideas into the reality of the emotive image that gives this work its title. As such, Ignatian poetics might act directly on some writers who knowingly fell under their influence, and they could also touch others more indirectly as an artistic representation of the age. Writers like Crashaw and Revett with no formal education in meditative aesthetics could experience only some of the same cultural pressures as Southwell and Donne and arrive at the same conclusions about poetry.

In the light of the development of *Exercises* and of its adaptations, the existence of the meditation in England between 1580 and 1650 is self-explanatory. The meditation's psychology conformed to the descriptions of image, affections, and love in Jesuit poetic theory; the presence of this psychology in English poetry was, therefore, witness to the general attractiveness of Jesuit ideas. Poems that dealt thematically with verse image, affections, and love were also influenced by meditative experience. The creative influences of Jesuit poetry are not a modern critical assumption, but were a contemporary way of appreciating the universe, rapidly obscured, unfortunately, by the development of the history of ideas. The late Renaissance Englishmen who lauded these influences and who practiced their principles in prose and poetry filled a desperately large aesthetic void for their compatriots in the mainstream of the Counter Reformation.

Notes

¹Gibbons' translations are first, *An Abridgment of Meditations of the Life, Passion, Death, & Resurrection of our Lord and Saviour Iesus Christ, Written in Italian by the R. Father Vincentius Bruno of the Society of Iesus, And translated into English by R. G. of the same Society. Whereunto is premised a briefe Methode for Instruction & Practice of Meditation*, 1614, Sig. ***; and second, *Meditations Upon the Mysteries of our Holy Faith with the practise of mental praier touching the same. Composed in Spanish by the R. F. Luys de la Puente of the*

Societie of Iesus . . . And Translated into English by F. Rich. Gibbons of the same Societie, 2 parts (Douai, 1610), I, p. 40.

The sources for the powers in the meditation are Augustine, *Confessions,* X, viii, in *Confessions and Einchiridion,* ed. A. C. Oulter, in *The Library of Christian Classics,* Vol. VII (London, 1955), p. 209 (the memory is a "storehouse" of experience: "And yet the things themselves do not enter it, but only the images of things perceived as there for thought to remember. And who can tell how these images are formed, even if it is evident which of the senses brought which perception in and stored it up") and *The Trinity,* XI, 1 (or xii), in *Later Works, The Library of Christian Classics,* Vol. III (London, 1955), p. 91 ("sense and perception belong to the perceiving subject and are independent of the object. The form printed on the sense-organ is product of the object only, of which this form is a likeness or image, distinct from the object itself"); for the understanding, the collective thomistic power of the intellect, the reason, and the intellectual memory (the first "apprehends" truth, the second "moves" from truth to truth, and the third stores up acquired ideas) in Aquinas, *Treatise on Man,* I. Ques. LXXIX, Eighth Article, and Ques. LXXX, Second Article, trans. J. F. Anderson (Englewood Cliffs, N.J., 1962), pp. 81, 93; Martz, "Preface to Second Edition", *Poetry of Meditation,* p. xviii, discusses their roles and sources.

[2]Aquinas, *On Man,* I, Ques. LXXCIII, Fourth Article, p. 65; Augustine, *Confessions,* X, viii, 14, p. 209.

[3]Keane, "Preface," *Exercises,* p. viii, says Ignatius' text was primarily intended for the director of the retreat rather than for the exercitant.

[4]Aquinas, *On Man,* I. Ques. LXXXVIII, Third and Fourth Articles, pp. 60-66, the five "interior" senses being the "proper" and "common" senses, the imagination or "phantasy," and the "estimative" and "memorative" powers.

[5]For this work Edward Synan of St. Michael's College in the University of Toronto translates the section of Aquinas' commentary on Aristotle, in *In Perihermenias,* I, 1.1, explaining the nature of the three acts of the understanding: "As the Philosopher Aristotle says in his third book *On Soul,* the operation of the intellect is twofold: one, indeed, is termed the understanding of atomic items *(indivisibilium intelligentia),* namely, that operation through which intellect *(intellectus)* apprehends the essence by itself of anything whatever; there is a second operation of the intellect, namely that of composing and dividing. A third operation, however, is added too, namely, that of reasoning, according to which reason advances from known items to an inquisition with respect to those that are unknown . . . Now, since Logic is termed 'rational science,' it is necessary that its consideration bear upon those items that belong to the three aforesaid operations. In the book *Of the categories* Aristotle took up his positions with regard to those items that belong to the first operation of the intellect, that is, with regard to those that are conceptualized by

'simple apprehension.' With regard, however, to those items that belong to the second operation, namely, with regard to enunciation, both affirmative and negative, the Philosopher took up his positions in the book *On interpretation*. With regard, however, to those items that belong to the third operation, he took up his positions in the book of the *Prior analytics* and in those that follow, i.e. the rest of Aristotle's logical corpus, the 'organon' in which there is concern with syllogism as such, and also with diverse types of syllogisms and arguments, thanks to which reason advances from one point to another."

[6]Aquinas, *Treatise On Man*, I, Ques. LXXIX, Seventh Article, p. 79.

[7]Famianus Strada, *Prolusiones Academicae, Historia, Oratoria, Poesis*, Rome, 1617; the work ran through several editions, 1619, 1625, 1626, 1627, 1631, 1644, and 1655, and served as a source for many English Renaissance poets (Martin, "Commentary," *Crashaw, Poems*, pp. 439-440), and for Coleridge in *Biographia Literaria* (London, 1960), p. 32, who described Strada as a leading authority on poetic diction; in 1762 (London), *Prolusiones* was published with a collection of epigrams for the use of scholars at Eton.

[8]Ramsay, *Doctrines Médiévales chez Donne*, "*Troisième Partie*"; Eloise Robinson, *The Minor Poems of Joseph Beaumont* (Boston, 1914), p. xli; and K. R. Wallace, *Francis Bacon on Communication and Rhetoric* (Chapel Hill, N.C., 1943), pp. 31-34, discuss the role of medieval and classical philosophy in Renaissance poetry; and de la Puente, *Meditations* I, translated by Gibbons, pp. 8-9, describes its place in meditation. Donatus' discussion of *icastica* and *phantastica* and Gibbons' distinction between similitude and image *(Ars Poetica*, p. 5; *Abridgement*, **3), are based on Platos discussion of the metaphysical realities of likeness and semblance *(The Sophist* trans. F. M. Cornford, in *The Collected Dialogues of Plato*, ed. Edith Hamilton and Huntingdon Cairns, New York, 1961, No. 265a, p. 1013; and *The Republic*, XXXV, x, 595, p. 317). However, the question is peripheral to their discussions of meditation.

[9]Edmund Spenser, "Letter . . . to . . . Sir Walter Raleigh," *Works*, Vol. 1 (Baltimore, 1932), p. 167.

[10]Augustine describes the apprehension as raising thought to "the supreme and most exalted essence of which the human mind is an image"; later, as culminating in "inward vision" in the trinity of the imagination: "When a remembered perception is called to mind, we can observe a corresponding trinity of imagination, this time entirely within the mind, composed of memory, inward vision, and the will which directs attention upon the object in the memory"; and finally, "Thought or inward vision can form images which may differ from the actual content of memory, though it is always dependent on memory, even when evoked by what is desirable by another person. Memory is to some extent controllable by the will, which can abstract the attention from what is

presented to the senses," *Trinity,* X, 19 (or xii), p. 89; XI, 1 (or xii), p. 91.

¹¹In a letter to Benjamin Lany, the Master of Pembroke, prefaced to his first book of verse *Epigrammatum Sacrorum Liber* in 1634, he spoke of poetry in terms of awakening spiritual affections (*"non tam ex ipsius indole & ingenio quàm ex animi sui affectu,"* Poems, p. 6).

¹²Aquinas describes the gradation of the three powers as "relative" according to the order of their usage, rather than as "absolute": *On Man,* I, Ques. LXXCII, Fourth Article, pp. 47-48; Ques. LXXIX, Seventh Article, pp. 79-80; Ques. LXXXII, Third Article, pp. 103-104.

¹³William Shakespeare, *Hamlet,* II, 2, ll. 315-320, in *The Complete Plays and Poems* (Boston, 1942), p. 1062.

¹⁴James Brodrick, s.j., *Saint Ignatius Loyola, The Pilgrim Years* (London, 1956), p. 117, on the first edition of *Exercises* in 1548, and on their composition, pp. 164, 167.

¹⁵Henry Hawkins, trans. "The Translator to the English Reader," *Fuga Saeculi. Or The Holy Hatred Of the World. Conteyning the Lives of 17. Holy Confessors of Christ, Selected out of sundry authors . . . by R. Fa. John-Peter Maffeus of the Society of Iesus* (St. Omer, 1632), Sig. e, ll. 1-4.

¹⁶Shakespeare, *Richard II,* II, 1, ll. 40-64, p. 608; *Troilus and Cressida* I, 3, 11. 81-134, pp. 319-320, in *Complete Plays and Poems.*

¹⁷Martin, "Commentary," *Crashaw, Poems,* p. 448, and Brown, "Commentary," *Southwell, Poems,* pp. 128-130. Brown suggests that Southwell's poems originate in Aquinas' "Lauda Sion" but *"Of the Blessed Sacrament of the Aulter"* echoes both "Lauda Sion" and Aquinas' "Adoro te" as well.

¹⁸Aquinas' "Adoro te," trans. Don Matthew Britt, O.S.B., *The Hymns of the Breviary and Missal* (New York, 1955), p. 188, lacks the "tightly articulated" use of the three powers of the mind singled out by Martz, *The Paradise Within* (New Haven, 1964), p. 23, in *Exercises* and, it must be added, in Crashaw's version as well:

> Hidden God, devoutly I adore Thee,
> Truly present underneath these veils:
> All my heart subdues itself before Thee,
> Since it all before thee faints and fails.

> Not to sight, or taste, or touch be credit,
> Hearing only do we trust secure;
> I believe, for God the Son hath said it —
> Word of Truth that ever shall endure.

¹⁹Nicholas Ferrar, *The Story Books of Little Gidding,* ed. E. Cruwys Sharland (London, 1899), pp. 21-23.

²⁰Bald, *Life,* p. 436, on Donne's known contact with Ferrar; and Martin, "Biography," *Poems,* pp. xxiii-xxiv, on Crashaw's connection with the Ferrar family and Little Gidding.

[21]Ferrar, *Story Books,* pp. 21-23.

[22]Lewalski, "Donne's *Devotions,*" *Renaissance Quarterly* (Summer, 1977) XXX:2, p. 263; also in her *Protestant Poetics and the Seventeenth-Century Religious Lyric* (Princeton, 1979), pp. 151-153.

[23]Joseph Hall, "The Art of Divine Meditation," *Works,* Vol. 6 (New York, 1969), p. 48.

[24]For example, "The First Century of Meditations and Vows," *Works,* Vol. 7, p. 440 and the "Holy Observations" that follow, p. 523.

[25]Edmund Arwaker, trans. *Pia Desideria,* by Herman Hugo (London, 1686), A5^{rv}.

[26]There appear to have been three English versions of the whole or part of the work by Loarte (b. Medina del Campo, n.d.; d. Valencia, 1578); the first is a translation by Stephen Brinkley (alias John Sancer) in 1579, *The Exercise of a Christian Life. Written in Italian . . . And newly translated into Englishe. by I. S.* (London); and the second is *The first Booke of the Christian exercise, appertayning to resolution* published by Robert Persons' press in Rouen in 1582. The third, Edmund Bunney's *A Book of Christian Exercise . . . shewing how that we should resolve ourselves, to become Christians indeed. Perused and accompagned now with a Treatise tending to Pacification,* London, 1584, is an adaptation of Persons' copy; a fourth version by Persons, *A Christian Directorie guiding men to their salvation. Devided into three bookes. The first whereof . . . is only conteined in this volume . . . with reprofe of the corrupt and falsified edition of the same booke lately published by Edm. Buny,* was a correction of Bunney's alterations to Loarte's text. In the meantime, Brinkley's original translation went into a second edition through Persons' press in Rouen in 1584, which must not be confused with Bunney's edition in the same year or with Persons' own edition of the first book in 1582.

[27]Halewood, *Poetry of Grace,* pp. 79-81.

[28]Boyd M. Berry, *Process of Speech, Puritan Religious Writings and Paradise Lost* (Baltimore, Md., 1976), pp. 37-38, 49-58.

[29]Stephanus Luzvik, s.j., *The Devout Hart* (Rouen, 1634), possibly translated by Hawkins, from the original French *Le Coeur Devot Throsne Royal de Iesus Pacifique Solomon. Par le P. Estienne Luzvic de la Compagnie de Iesus* (Antwerp, 1627).

[30]The Jesuit Carolus Musart adds the declaration about the weakness of young men in the Partheneian Sodality in his Latin translation of Luzvic's *Coeur Devot: Cor Deo Devotum Iesu Pacifici Solomnis Thronus Regius. e Gallico P. Stephani Luzvic . . . Latinati dedit, & ad calcem auxit P. Carolus Musart . . . Societatis Iesu* (Antwerp, 1628), p. 4.

CHAPTER FOUR

Poetry of the Will

1

The references to the will in the poetry of Heywood, Southwell, Crashaw, Donne, Alabaster, and Revett often express the yearnings of the redemptive vision that gave Ignatian tradition its strength. As the ultimate redemptive faculty, the will appeared to be the cornerstone for the success of meditation. Because of this, meditative verse was what can be called "poetry of the will." It sprang from the reason and memory, but concluded triumphantly in respect to time in the last used and yet most important faculty.

At the top of the classical gradation of the three mental powers, the will was the faculty to overcome humanity's fallen state. Its role was founded on a number of presuppositions about its redemptive sensory values. The will was thus remarkable for its emotive capacities rather than for its constraining powers. These emotive capacities led to the psychological examinations of the sort we find in the poetry of Heywood, Southwell, Alabaster, Donne, Crashaw, and Revett. These examinations show the poets grappling with the questions touching on their position in the new universe and their relationship to poetry. Significantly, we do not find them in the work of other Elizabethan or early seventeenth century poets or in the same depth in the contemporary religious verse of Herbert, Barnes, Beaumont, Lok, and Brerely.[1]

The argument of the meditative poets about the will tended to be consistent. As one of their regular preoccupations, the will was the home of heavenly desires in man and enabled him to converse with the figures of his mythology. At the beginning of the meditative tradition in England, Heywood set the tone of the discussion for those who were to follow. He spoke of the unredeemed will as imperfect in the sense of depicting the human condition rather than revealing personal failures. In "Beying troubled in mynde, he writeth as followeth," he described himself as suffering from the need of salvation in terms of a "greedie" will that appeared to mislead him. The will conducted him not into personal failings but away from its ultimate redemptive satisfaction. In his poem's emotional experience he pursued the lesser universal affection of sadness to satisfy the will, but kept on yearning with the redemptive desire common to the race of men (ll. 6, 9).

Heywood also considered satisfaction of the will as the main literary success of verse. The sublimest desires of the will were the highest ends of poetry. Heywood's composition of his poem "Alluding his state to the prodigall child" was an exercise in poetic will training. In the extended analogy between the poet and the figure of Christ's parable, the poet attempted to "tread the trackt" of the "unruly will" of the Prodigal Son and to correct it by writing good verse:

> The wandring youth, whose race so rashlie runne,
> Hath left behinde, to his eternall shame:
> The thriftlesse title of the Prodigall sonne,
> To quench, remembraunce of his other name,
> Mate now devide, the burthen of his blame,
> With me, whom wretchlesse thoughtes entised still:
> To tread the trackt of his unruly will.

(ll. 1-7)

However, in "Alluding," as in "the complaint of a sorrowfull Soule" earlier in *The Paradise of Dainty Devices* (ll. 19-36), poetry was not meant to constrain the will. Rather, it was meant to engage it to the limits of its emotive capacities by providing the reader with an escape from the time-bound desires of "concupiscence" into the limitless horizons of spiritual affection:

> Now to come home with him, and pardon pray,
> My God I say, against the heavens and thee,
> I am not worthy, that my lippes should say:
> Behold thy handie worke, and pitie me,
> Of mercy yet my soule, from faultes set free.
> To serve thee here, till thou appoint the time,
> Through Christ, unto the blessed ioyes to climbe.

(ll. 22-28)

At first typified by Heywood's verse, the countless depressive states of mind in English meditative verse reflected the failure of the poet to attain the universal heights demanded of him by the will. For the poet to exercise his will was an admission that he was born deficient in the sense of not being divine. He resorted to poetry to correct that state. Often, this condition appeared the result of Original Sin. However, Original Sin in the sense of personal responsibility as opposed to the human condition it had long ago provoked in Eden was not a major concern of those touched by Jesuit aesthetics, including Donne. Much of the verse of the English poets was "penitential" in the sense of not achieving the emotive height of the universe rather than of the confession of faults. In this, poets imitated the redemptive tone of *Exercises*.

The meditative poem constantly reasserted the decision of the poet to redeem the human condition by making better use of his will and improving his verse. It was penitential in terms of admitting human inadequacy in the face of constantly beckoning universal affections and their poetic expression. So, for Southwell and Alabaster as for Donne, much sacred poetry represented an artistic attempt at fulfilling inborn desires lodged by birth in the will. Man's destiny being heaven, his will instinctively desired to experience it in verse.

Southwell's "Looke Home" is a striking example of this quest for universal redemption. The need for poetry to redeem man transformed the Sidneyean Neo-Platonic theory of verse, the very note on which the poem opened. The mind, Southwell wrote, was a "creature" full of "fayrest formes" adept in poetry at adding "higher skill" to "natures patterns." However, the "force" of the mere form-creating "wit" lacked the "equall power of will." The poet's own will was to imitate God's example when he created Nature, inspired by nothing but love: "His will was followed with performing word. / Let this suffice, by this conceive the rest" (11. 7, 5, 22-23). To "Looke Home," as the title of Southwell's poem suggested, meant that the poet wrote verse fulfilling the will's universal dictates. Poetry did not, as Sidney suggested, primarily bring forth forms greater than nature produced. The poet peered into heaven by the will's "motions" rather than through the superior forms he created in verse.[2]

Similarly, some years later other decisive factors than a sense of personal sin were at work in the redemptive psychology of Donne's "Holy Sonnets." Donne's apparent confessions of lust in his sonnets were counterbalanced by sexual imagery depicting profound spiritual unions. These unions included basic religious relationships between himself and God (No. 14, "Batter my heart, three person'd God," 11. 13-14) and himself and the Church, Christ's spouse (No. 18, "Show me deare Christ, thy spouse, so bright and clear," 11. 9-10). His sexual imagery may be viewed in the light of its emotive origins in forms of willed experience that led men as much to God as to anything else. Donne's redemptive psychology was governed by the failure of human aspirations in an emotive universe. It was not determined by personal sexual failings that could have no bearing whatsoever on "Holy Sonnets" as valid meditative verse.

Meditative poetry was consistently written from the point of view of an emotively yet unredeemed race because such a race was its central concern. Some of Heywood's, Southwell's, Alabaster's, and Donne's best explicatory lines about the redemptive will, therefore, discuss its failure thematically. Paradoxically, these poems tell us more about happy verse like Crashaw's and Revett's than these poets themselves. The self-confessed failings of a poet like Alabaster before the emotional demands of the created universe led him regularly to use lesser affections like joy and sadness to demonstrate the power of the greater will-inspired affection of love. Because of man's fallen state, the lesser affections found much more frequent expression than the universal world's supreme affection of love in meditative verse. However, these affections provided steps to the highest emotion and were not terminal ends in themselves. In Sonnet 15, Alabaster's "will" was the astronomical "intelligence" moving the yet unrealized force of love about the heavenly constellations of the poet's inner world. This will performed "the acts" that, according to the mission priest and translator John Sweetnam, "do accompanie and follow" the understanding in order to "draw forth affectes," and all these affections, as Alabaster's sonnet shows, were to terminate in love.[3] For Alabaster's verse, the will imposed an argument about "teares" and sorrow on his understanding "wit" in the anticipation of love (ll. 4, 8, 11, 14).

Again in Sonnet 10, "Though all forsake thee, lord, yet I will die," Alabaster portioned out the will's role between the Apostle Peter in the octet and himself in the sestet. In the face of his failure to achieve the will's ends implied by such a division, he wrote his poem according to the lesser affection of sorrow. In the sestet, Alabaster also wrote about "hope," but that affection too was the will's surrogate activity which he learned to "say" in place of the greater affection of love (ll. 13-14).

In his verse debate on hope with Cowley, Crashaw also argued for the surrogate role of hope to love quite happily by contrast with Alabaster. He described hope as "love's legacy" (1. 11), then as a kind of *media res* between the extremes of other affections ("a wise & well-stay'd fire! / Temper twixt chill despair, & torrid ioy!" ll. 41-42) and finally as "Queen/Regent in younge lov's minority" (1. 43). Crashaw's poem, unlike Alabaster's, is not a "penitential" sonnet. However, its use of will ("We are not Where nor What we be, / But What and Where we would be," ll. 37-38) presupposes the presence of its affections among the figures of baroque mythology, and the same redemptive psychology as in Alabaster's lines.

Such aesthetics based on the redemptive will in Donne's "Holy Sonnets" were not diminished by his references to divine grace. To consider the sonnets as poetry of grace might seem a natural outcome of their redemptive tone. But his concern with grace in the closing tercets of some of the poems colored his use of the will without altering its emotive ends. In the sonnets Donne's will made an imperfect upward movement towards God, grace made a perfect downward movement from him, and poetry was the expected meeting point of the two. At the end of the first "Holy Sonnet," "Thou hast made me, and shall thy worke decay?", before the inadequacy of human action alone to achieve personal salvation, divine "Grace may wing" the poet to prevent Satan's art from winning him for hell. The poet's inabilty to win grace except as a gift suggests strong Puritan and Lutheran origins. However, as a gift undeserved by men, grace did not eliminate the will as the link between the poet, the baroque world, and meditative verse.

The proof of this is Donne's verse itself. In "Holy Sonnet" 16, "Father, part of his double interest," he exalted "all-healing grace," but he limited its power by declaring "love" the divine "last Will" to stand (11. 11-14). Elsewhere, in "Holy sonnet" 17, "Since she whom I lov'd hath payd her last debt," commemorating the death of his wife Anne More, grace helped Donne achieve salvation. However, salvation was impossible without love. Divine love, which functioned even in the absence of grace, remained the spiritual bridge between himself and his divinity. Donne depicted his and Anne More's affection as a transitory indispensable state in his emotional life but, despite the transitory character of this love, without it, it was as impossible for him to conceive of time as of eternity. Human love was a gateway not to grace but to a greater love called divine. Grace was a gift while divine love was a form of deliberate cooperation. These and similar statements (for example, Alabaster's) — that God exercised his grace through the will of man — make it difficult to view grace as the abnegation of verse as poetry of the will (Sonnet 75, "A New Year's Gift" of poetry "to my Savior," 1. 10).

Grace conditioned the force of the baroque mythology in Donne's sonnets without replacing it. It was therefore thematic and topical where it occurred rather than structural and formative on "Holy Sonnets" as a whole. It fitted into the body of theological ideas regularly dealt with in contemporary English poetry, of which there are countless examples. Some are the soul's graces and the beauty of God's graces in Southwell's "At home in Heaven" (1. 42), the need of grace for joy in his "Sinners Complaint," the "Fields of Grace" at the end of Crashaw's verse debate on hope (1. 90), and the identification of the Protestant Community of Saints with the Jewish Sion in his "To the Name" (1. 2). These ideas do not describe poetry.

The personal histories of English poets also militate against grace as the mark of a class of verse. Grace cannot be used to distinguish a Puritan or Anglican poet from a Catholic one particularly when each of Alabaster, Crashaw, and Donne, to name only three examples, was at some time in some way Puritan, Anglican, and Catholic.[4] The presence of grace in Donne's lines even if it were proved Protestant did not abjure their Ignatian character or their historical connection with, for instance, the Jesuit Francis Borgia's "coronary" linked prayers. Nor does it serve to dissociate his sonnets from the traditional Jesuit divison of meditative topics between the self and Christian Mystery at a moment in English literary history when it was common for a poet to adhere to the theology of one group and write poetry in the aesthetics of another.

Two things support the meditative and the will-oriented redemptive character of Donne's "La Corona" and "Holy Sonnets" with more depth than grace. Whether their composition took place over a long or short period affects neither. The first is the appearance of the sonnets side by side, with "La Corona" in the forefront, in their earliest manuscripts. The second is their publication in this fashion in the first edition of Donne's *Poems*.[5] In their own day, both series of poems were thought of as fitting together. Such evidence is inconclusive because the manuscripts are not in Donne's hand, the first edition of his poems was posthumous, and the arrangements cannot therefore be proved to be his. However, such historical evidence is supported by the generally uniform aesthetics of the sonnets. Like Heywood's, Southwell's, and Alabaster's verse before him, Donne's religious sonnets represented an attempt to reduce the distance between the Christian and his yet imperfect willed experience of divine love.

2

In spite of the growing competition to "reason" from the "will" represented by *Exercises,* the Counter Reformation baroque movement in the English verse of Heywood, Southwell, Donne, Alabaster, Crashaw, and Revett fitted into Renaissance literature and did not constitute a separate literary period. *Exercises* continued to disseminate the Renaissance ideal of reason. This ideal assumed that reason was a reflective power distinguishing man from the animals and revealing his nature to himself. *Exercises* supported this ideal uninterrupted both in its adaptations and in verse until the growth of neo-classical rationalism in the later part of the seventeenth century spelled its end. Human will by way of sense and emotion rather than reason by way of thought and spirit connected man with an eternal world. Yet reason preserved its ideal Renaissance role now by leading human experience out of sensation into the will and eternity. Under this impetus, *Exercises* and its adaptations spread across the face of Europe in the century following Ignatius' foundation of his order as part of the thought of the Renaissance rather than as a movement against it. *Exercises* was disseminated in several hundred versions impossible to number exactly.[6] Becoming more romantic, diffuse, and poetic, the meditation came to rely more and more on metaphor. And, in spite of the political events that contradicted its assumptions, the meditation became an instrument to maintain that ideal in England as elsewhere.

Exercises was not a part of a Counter Reformation political strategy but a reassertion of the primacy of human "reason" in the context of a fundamentally altering world view. It marked both a retreat from a hierarchical world view and a rejection of the world as a setting for human affairs. But it did not renege on the world as the domain of personal human reason. This accounts for its charismatic fascination over men whether Rome-adherents or not for a hundred years. It explains why Jesuit verse could be imitated and Jesuit poetic theorists quoted so liberally even by their politically sworn enemies. Ignatius had effectively remade the world into an unassailable shape in the inner self for all and not only for some of his contemporaries according, no less, to God's traditionally held original plan to keep the material world at man's rational disposition.

Noteworthy for their creative rather than their analytic use of reason, Jesuit writings relegated the rationalistic activities of reason progressively to the background. This too helped reason's passage into verse. While man became a meditator, he also became a consummate thinking artist. With the proliferation of the versions of *Exercises* and its verse and emblem book imitations, reason grew into an indisputable creator of images against the universal sensory background of a "performing will." Floyd described it as the power in which the poet "stayed" *(Overthrow,* p. 44). Floyd's declarations on the nature of poetry as meditation are fundamentally important because, with Gibbons' explanation of meditation in the terminology of verse, they constitute the English Renaissance's major statements on the adaptation of *Exercises* to poetry *(Abridgement,* *12, **3).

Being the creative poetic shaper, as described by Floyd, the understanding exercised synthetic powers that the will lacked because of its emphasis on sensation. That the meditative tradition called reason the "understanding" rather than reason itself suggests its creative role. Lying midway in the classical gradation of the three powers between the sensual, spontaneous, purely memorative experiences below it and the supernatural experiences represented by the actions of the will above it, the understanding showed the way to visionary experience. All contemporary forms of discourse, logic, rhetoric, and poetic invention were subject to it.

Such meditative verse as the understanding created fitted into the stream of contemporary thought that considered poetry as a branch of logic. Spingarn has identified this latter poetry as "puristic," and it contrasted sharply with Sidney's Neo-Platonic verse.[7] The Jesuit practice of verse nevertheless represents a radical shift in the school of "puristic" poetry. By tradition, the creative role of reason appeared to spring from logic but now its spiritual sources became emotive. As Southwell described it in the letter to his cousin prefixed to the 1595 edition of his poems, the understanding was the "wit" that wove a new religious "webbe" in the old secular "loome" of verse for emotive perceptions of the eternal (p. 1). It was the mother of poetic "Arte" and "Invention" which, Southwell wrote to his cousin in the self-derogatory fashion of the times, he claimed not to possess. However, his emotive aims in poetry remained clear.

In Southwell's description, the understanding was the creative instrument in both ascetic devotion and poetry. It was the pivotal link between the two arts fulfilling in both the Renaissance poetic criterion of "virtue" as "goodness." Southwell's references to the creative understanding according to the criterion of "virtue" were original to him among English poets; the understanding showed, he wrote to his cousin, "how well verse and virtue sute together" (p. 1). However, more importantly, he explained in the following prefatory poem "To the Reader" that "thoughts" in the manner of Ignatian meditation rather

than "Prophane conceits" constituted the substance of verse. These
meditative "thoughts" bestowed virtue on the poet's lines (11. 9, 14, 15).
In his "Man's Civill War," the understanding once more arranged the
poet's "hovering thoughts" into a successful virtuous "meditation" (11.
1-3). The poet's "thoughts" were the very "inward eie" that inspired the
meditation and the understanding was the inner faculty to which the
longing Christian, moved by heavenly desires, resorted for his liberation
from captivity to the senses:

> When inward eie to heavenly sights
>   Doth draw my longing harts desire,
> The world with jesses of delights
>   Would to her pearch my thoughts retire,
>
> Fond fancie traines to pleasures lure,
>   Though reason stiffely do repine.
> Though wisdome wooe me to the saint,
>   Yet sense would win me to the shrine,
>
> Where reason loathes, there fancie loves,
>   And overrules the captive will,
> Foes senses are to vertues lore,
>   They draw the wit their wish to fill.
>
> Neede craves consent of soule to sence,
>   Yet divers bents breed civil fray,
> Hard hap where halves must disagree
>   Or truce of halves the whole betray,
>
> O cruell fight where fighting frend
>   With love doth kil a favoring foe,
> Where peace with sense is warre with God,
>   And selfe delight the seede of woe . . .
> (11. 9-28)

Southwell also described the understanding in judiciary terms. Here
his terminology was related to the discretionary third act of "judging"
that followed the simple "apprehension" among the three acts of the
understanding. Southwell's connections with Ignatian psychology were
extensive even in details. He held the creative understanding responsible
for the judicious choice of good and bad images for verse. Thus he
imposed on it its exercital role of selecting the correct material for
meditation. In "David's *Peccavi*" Southwell described the creative
understanding as possessing the characteristics of an artistic arbiter. The
Biblical David's, Southwell's, or any poet's *alter ego,* in the poem held
"wit" responsible for "the plaining voyce" of bad verse and also for its
correction (11. 15, 28). Having become only a wan "Rebell" in the poet's
creative experience, the understanding produced imagery that was a
"dolefull ecchoe" reflecting his "wayling minde." The poet grew unable

to plead even the "excuse" of a "want of skill" in order to justify his failure (11. 28, 16, 21). He simply had to write another poem, this time a good one that provoked the highest affections.

In Crashaw's and Alabaster's verse, the understanding played a creative role similar to that in Southwell's poems. There, however, its manifestations were more aesthetic. Crashaw's and Alabaster's imagery reflected the work of the understanding more poetically than Southwell's. In Alabaster's sonnets such aesthetics were also more formal from the point of view of genre. Yet, in the case of neither Alabaster nor Crashaw were these aesthetics different in kind from each other or from Southwell's verse. Where its role seemed to diverge in Crashaw's and Alabaster's poems, the creative understanding did not so much suggest dissimilarities in aesthetics as differences in manifestation springing from the poets' individual talents and from the historical development of the influence of the "three supreme faculties" on English poetry.

As is clear in Crashaw's "To the Name," the creative understanding was more concerned with matters aesthetic than with matters dialectic. Literary history served Crashaw more efficiently than his predecessors. "To the Name" shows that the discussions of the understanding grew progressively less evident in the rhetoric of verse as they gave way to its increasing practice. The understanding was a creator of images ("proclaim / New similes to Nature") investigating the world ("Warn each severall kind / And shape of sweetnes") and the poet's inner life ("thou art . . . / full of nothing else but empty Me") to provoke profound experiences ("Unfold they fair Conceptions; And display / The birth of our Bright Ioyes") of an emotive universe ("The' attending World . . . / First turn'd to Eyes; / And . . . Turn'd them to Teares, & spent Them too," 11. 95-96, 37-38, 19-21, 163-4, 135-8). Once an evident part of Alabaster's arguments, such discussions were incorporated deeply into Crashaw's religious themes and imagery. The major question of "invention" related to "ornament," argued out in detail with little rhythm, meter, or metaphor in Alabaster's sonnets 53 "A Preface to the Incarnation" and 62 "Omnia Propter Christum Facta," was later submerged in the tauter imagery of Crashaw's verse. The differences between the two poets suggested the evolution of the Renaissance lyric out of the Elizabethan age into the Caroline era rather than divergences in concepts of the nature of verse.

Conforming to the mid-seventeenth century development of meditative aesthetics, the understanding in Crashaw's verse assumed the guise of a symbol. It was regularly pictured as a creative "soul." The symbolic "soul" brought the artistic character of the understanding into relief by showing it at work as though it were separate from the poet. In the hymns "To the Name," "Dies Irae," "Adoro te," and "Vexilla Regis" the "soul" performed the tasks of choosing, exploring, and synthesizing the objects and emotions of imagery. In this way, the soul depicted the age and the depth of the poetic meditative tradition by that time. The understanding's symbolic treatment contrasted sharply with its initial allegorical appearances in English poetry in the work of Heywood and with its somewhat later lyrical handling by Southwell. In the narrative of "To the name," the understanding was an aesthetic muse and artist "soul" constantly creating "Art" as though in a recurrent act independent of Crashaw. Art was for him the lord of nature and experience:

> Goe, Soul, out of thy Self, & seek for More
>   Goe & request
> Great Nature for the Key of her huge Chest
> Of Heavns, the self involving Sett of Sphears
> (Which dull mortality more Feeles then heares)
>   Then rouse the nest
> Of nimble Art, & traverse round
> The Aiery Shop of soul-appeasing Sound.
>   (11. 27-34)

In "Vexilla Regis," a later poem in *Steps to the Temple* of 1648, the presence of the understanding recurred a little less often than in "To the Name." The understanding's creative activities in "Vexilla," however, were no different than in its companion poem. The understanding brought to light the suitable material for poetry as well as Christian truth (Stanzas IV, I). In "Adoro te" in the same volume, it was the power to "consider" and was prefigured in the paradox of the "soul's" closed and yet "inquiring ey." Crashaw rigidly distinguished the understanding from the mere "discourse" of the contemporary books of logic and rhetoric (11. 27, 6, 5). Though less elaborately present in "Vexilla" and "Adoro te" than in "To the Name," the understanding continued to be a reflective power in a mentality in which reflection meant not to contemplate eternal things but to create emotive imagery.

Symbolized in the soul in the dramatic monologues of many of his poems, the creative understanding was more than a decorative figure. It was also the person whom Crashaw addressed. The symbol allowed Crashaw in his verse monologues to assume the detachment of the exercitant from his inner powers. The soul participated with him as though in the shape of an omnipresent *alter ego* in his writing. Rather than talking to himself only with the divine overhearing, Crashaw spoke to his creative understanding as it accompanied him on his poetic journey much as the soul accompanied the exercitant in *Exercises* (p. 83). With the soul, he appeared to debate the question of suitable subjects for verse and its imagery much as the Jesuit Sweetnam discussed the relationship of the exercitant to his soul. Sweetnam (b. Northampton County, 1581), who died in Loretto in 1622, a generation before Crashaw was to do so, said the "understanding employed" its meditative subjects in order to detayne our selves." Its purpose was to "drawe conceipt" (*Treatise,* p. 5). According to Gibbons, writing at about the same time, the subjects of imaginative "conceipt" were the meditative topics that the understanding "determined" with "our selves" (*Abridgement,* Sig. *11).

The dramatic role of the meditative understanding that Heywood had introduced allegorically to English verse lost its didactic tone in Crashaw's poetry. The sententious style of lines like "My mated mynde, that dredes my sutes in vaine" in Heywood's "Beying troubled in mynde, he writeth as followeth:"1.9), ceded its place to the more purely aesthetic figures of better verse. Published in the twilight of Jesuit poetry a few years after the appearance of Crashaw's last poem "To the Countess of Denbigh" in 1652, even Revett's "Meditation" continued to triumph over the facile prefigurations of allegory into which the exercital inner dialogue in verse could have easily fallen once more.

> Thou callest in the thoughts at large
>   by thine arrest;
> And redeliver'st them to charge,
>   of their own brest.

(11. 9-12)

The understanding of Ignatian tradition in Revett's verse resisted a return to its allegorical English origins. Its creative power remained great even when the emotive world view supporting the tradition's style was already in full decline.

Alabaster and Donne had established firmly the use of the meditative understanding in English verse long before Crashaw. That the aesthetics should have survived as late as Revett's time is therefore not surprising. Faced with the very conventional sonnet form, Alabaster and Donne had developed meditative aesthetics beyond their original allegories. With them, the meditative understanding became a force in English poetry through the redefinition of certain basic sonnet conventions to meet the requirements of strictly interior experiences. The understanding left the sonnet's outward appearance intact but as a literary influence altered its psychology. This historical development of the meditative sonnet united Alabaster and Donne and must have made them appear of the same literary generation to their contemporaries, even though Alabaster's verse circulated in manuscript between ten and twenty years before Donne's. Coming chronologically between Heywood's and Southwell's verse on the one hand and Crashaw's and Revett's on the other, Alabaster's verse held a medial position which prepared the way for Donne's religious sonnets less than a generation later. In Alabaster's and later Donne's hands the new role of the sonnet may be viewed as marking a milestone in the history of Ignatian practices in English verse. The inner probings of the secular sonnet sequence which had been governed by the social conventions of courtly love tradition became regulated in the meditative sonnets by the three powers of the mind.

The new literary forces therefore in Alabaster's sonnets extended well beyond theme and imagery. As Sonnet 53 "A Preface to the Incarnation" shows, the sonnet form as well as figurative language was being adapted to meditative tradition. Alabaster asked "Christ, let many worlds be lent / To enrobe my thoughts with all their ornament." Then, in a conventional invocation to the Renaissance poetic criterion of ornament-producing invention, he summoned the "tongues of men and angels" to "join in one, / To spread the carpets of invention." Like the rest of his figurative language, Alabaster's "tongue" image for the understanding lay "Before the eyes of all the firmament" (11. 4-8). However, a more important matter was involved than the scope of a single image. The first analogy of the sonnet's sestet reveals the argument of the preceding octet to be a clever synthesis of image and idea having more than decorative significance. The analogy also depicts the poet's mental powers functioning in the context of an emotive universe: "The temple where I sing is heaven, the choir / Are my soul's powers, the book's a living story" (11. 9-10). Alabaster's analogy reformed the sonnet's basic conventions as well as its imagery. Though the understanding created figurative language, it also provoked the sonnet's adaptation to verse meditation. The poet struggled with God over questions bearing on the new world picture rather than on the traditional hierarchies to which the conventions of the English sonnet sequences originally catered.[8]

Alabaster shifted the sonneteer's address away from an outer object to an inner one. He did not address the lady of the secular sonnet series but an inner being like himself and God in the mythology of the new world view. The change was not merely thematic but also bespoke an inner field of emotive contact. In his prayer to Christ in "A Divine Sonnet" (19), Alabaster enlisted his "thoughts" to "have free scope . . . God's . . . love to explain" (1. 8). In the following sestet his purpose was not only to demonstrate but to experience that love himself. In Sonnet 38, the poet addressed "eternity" not for the aesthetic enjoyment of its imagery but to become emotionally absorbed in a universe brought into the reaches of his experience by his own verse: "O tie my soul unto this endless clew, / That I may overfathom fate and time / In all my actions which I do pursue" (11. 9, 11).

Alabaster's use of the understanding altered the sonneteer's relationship to his imagery as well as changing the nature of that imagery. In order to make the sonnet meditative, the poet not only imposed new aesthetic values on his images but assumed a new stance towards it. Alabaster redirected poetry away from the imitation of the natural world to the investigation of the self. Martz has described the structural values of the Ignatian colloquy on poetic inner probings which, however, possessed other psychological values drawn from *Exercises* more influential than structure. Alabaster's sonnets depended on the reflective, inward-looking capacities of the understanding. These capacities rather than imagery and structure led to the genre's alteration.

> O take thy Cross and nails and therewith strain
> My heart's desire unto his full extent,
> That thy dear love may not therein be pent,
> But thoughts may have free scope thy love to explain.
> O now my heart more paineth than before,
> Because it can receive and hath no more,
> O fill this emptiness or else I die,
> Now stretch my heart again and now supply,
> Now I want space, now grace. To end this smart,
> Since my heart holds not thee, hold thou my heart.
>
> *("Penitential Sonnet"* 19, ll. 5-14).

When the understanding in Alabaster's verse reappeared in Donne's sonnets, it marked him as a consistently unconventional poet. It signified as much a break with traditional verse forms as Donne's lengthened versions of the secular sonnet like "A Valediction forbidding mourning" that respected no more than the genre's conventional statement of problem and resolution. Motivated by the same emotive forces as in Alabaster, Donne's use of the fourteen-line sonnet was not the momentary return to convention of a middle-aged man converted to religion. It represented a fundamental shift in the Renaissance man's view of himself by redirecting his sights into himself in questions of poetry rather than onto the outer world. This shift affected deeply Donne's concept of imagery as "ornament" by forcing him to redefine poetic invention in terms of the psychology of the inner self rather than of an objective, ordered world. A secular form of verse was called upon for the first time in Donne, as in Alabaster, to perform personal, spiritual religious functions in the light of the emotive world view that for such men was replacing the Great Chain of Being.

Although many traditions of Renaissance rhetorical discourse converged in Donne's religious sonnets, the understanding remained governed by a coherent psychology. As well as arguing effectively in Peacham's, Puttenham's, and their master Aristotle's sense of the art of rhetoric as persuasion,[9] the understanding in Donne's apparently conventional sonnets performed the functions allotted to it in meditative thought. An example is "Holy Sonnet" 5 "I am a little world made cunningly," in which he stated the classical Christian duality of human body and soul according to the current metaphysical categories of physical "Elements" and an "Angelicke spright." Donne marvelled at the union of these contrary forces in himself. The spirit of the poet at work in the poem, however, was one that drew analogies between temporal experiences and eternal emotive realities. It was not the logical faculty described in the *curricula* of Renaissance books of education marvelling at man's place in the Great Chain of Being and drawing descriptive figures of speech.

In Donne's sacred sonnets, the emphasis on human nature shifted away from its traditional medieval and humanist elements of body and soul as matter and form. Psychology and the senses became the predominant human traits. They assumed the emotive characteristics of the baroque spirit world that Donne, like one of the explorers to whom he compared himself later in "Holy Sonnet" 5, set out to investigate. Donne's references to tears and emotions in the poem were undoubtedly hyperbolic and poetic. However, hyperbole and poetry had become scientific terms in meditative verse to describe the movements of the thinking man's understanding in a metaphoric universe.

The references to man, reason, and poetry in Donne's works are stronger indicators of his place in the history of Ignatian aesthetics than his factual connections with Jesuit verse. Historical connections are undoubtedly revealing. For example, "La Corona" sonnets were in the tradition of the "Coronary" or "Crowne" prayers on the "principall Mysteries" of Christ's life found, among other places, at the end of the Jesuit Francis Borgia's *The Practice of Christian Perfection. Practice* was translated into many languages, including English, by Everard, in 1620.[10] For evident numerical reasons Donne's seven "La Corona" sonnets appear to reflect the seven linked prayers of each of Borgia's "coronaries" rather than the numerical unparalleled strings of other prayers and poems that were also called "crowns."[11]

The division of Donne's religious sonnets into a "La Corona" series on Christian Mysteries and into a second set on his personal spiritual life called "Holy Sonnets" also imitated Borgia's distinction between "crownes" on Mysteries and those on "the obteyning of Christian Perfection" *(Practice,* p. 229). This division is found in the work of no other English sonneteer except Alabaster and was the major distinction of meditative topics in the tradition of *Exercises (Abridgement* *9).

However interesting these historical facts may be, the creative understanding in Donne's poetry was more formative. It determined the development of a poem, for example, like the fifth "La Corona" called "Crucifying." The understanding connected Donne more deeply to Jesuit verse tradition than historical fact:

> By miracles exceeding power of man,
> He faith in some, envie in some begat,
> For, what weake spirits admire, ambitious hate;
> In both affections many to him ran,
> But oh! the worst are most, they will and can,
> Alas, and do unto the immaculate,

Whose creature Fate is, now prescribe a Fate,
Measuring selfe-lifes infinity to' a span,
Nay to an inch. Loe, where condemned hee
Beares his owne cross, with paine, yet by and by
When it beares him, he must beare more and die.
Now thou art lifted up, draw mee to thee,
And at thy death giving such liberall dole,
Moist, with one drop of thy blood, my dry soule.

Donne's lines betray their meditative origins by depicting the understanding acting on memory and will. Their syntax suggests things suddenly remembered, and these things appear finally in the images of the poem. Donne recalled "the worst are most" and, by association, "Fate." Immediately, the envious men of the poem then "prescribe" that "Fate" unknowingly to themselves. At the poem's opening, those who possessed "affections" of "envie" and "ambitious hate" clustered beneath the robes of the figure of the "immaculate" Christ to avoid the destiny of time. Such possessors of base affections were only images. They were no more than the handy illustrative thoughts recalled by the poet to exemplify the miracle of human salvation in the crucifixion.

The picture of the crucifixion drawn in terms of the affections of hate and envy was Donne's act of the will. This act made the poem meditative. Images of hate and jealousy paradoxically depicted his noble wish to be "lifted up." He desired to be elevated in order to resemble Christ by an inner experience of love like his in the crucifixion. The creative understanding at work provoked the meditative experience by presenting Donne with a picture of emotion. Sweetnam described that understanding in his preface to Molina's *Treatise of Mental Prayer:*

Meditation is nothing else but a discourse made by the understanding, in which it considereth something or other, & from that draweth other different thoughts, conceits, or considerations, gathering one thing from another: In the same manner as when one is alone, plotting some thing which he is to do, & considering that he must do it in this, or that manner, for this reason or for that; and that he must procure this thing, and take heed of the other, for such and such reasons; & many other like things which the Understanding frameth, all directed to attayne to the end which he pretends. In this very manner is meditation of spirituall things, that the Understanding considering one of the mysteries of our Faith, maketh discourses upon it, and conceites, of what it behooveth us to love, and what to hate; of what we must seeke to procure, and what to fly and take heed of, and the like. And this is properly meditation. (pp. 1-2)

3

Although the meditative image relied heavily on the will and the understanding, its use of memory, at the bottom of the classical gradation's three mental powers, was equally indispensable. The meditation rested on memory in a different fashion than on the understanding and the will, but responded to similar psychological pressures. In a sense the whole meditation seemed to begin chronologically with the memory. By an initial upward motion from the memory, the poetic experience appeared to move through all possible levels of human knowledge.

The memory served the creative understanding immediately above it. As such, it represented in the Ignatian tradition an alteration of more recent scholastic notions. The memory was sensory according to Augustine's description of it as the storehouse of the sensation of things, rather than pictorial according to Aquinas' depiction of it as the storehouse of their images.[12] The notion of memory as sensation was much more pertinent to the personal experiences of meditation and to an emotive world than were figurative representations. In his sonnets, Alabaster referred several times to the sensory dimensions of memories according to their description by Augustine as "prints of experiences."[13] In Sonnet 50 "To his Sad Friend," he spoke of "passions" as "but the prints that do respect / The form of things" (11. 3-4). In "Penitential Sonnet" 15 he described his "thoughts" as relegating his poetic "conceits" to the past and then resurrecting them in the shape of emotions for present verse (11. 15-16).

In "The Weeper," Crashaw spoke of experiences as memories in the same fashion as Alabaster with identical consequences on his poetry. "Time layes" up his experiences of the Magdalen's sorrow, he wrote, and resurrects them for imagery in the present through his memories. He punned on the word "memory" to denote both his own power to recall and the Magdalen's fame as a religious convert (XXV, 1. 6; XXVI, 1. 4). In his "Description of a Religious House," a remembered experience was a recalled emotion: "The self remembering Soul sweetly recovers / Her kindred with the stars" in poetic experience (11. 36-37).

In Heywood, Southwell, and Revett the references to memories were less obtrusive, but these poets shared the same point of view as Crashaw and Alabaster about their place in verse. The Augustinian attitude towards memory as sense governed the memorative relationship of all three poets with the past. The past seemed to revive memories relevant to alleviating the consequences of the general Fall of Man. For the new redemption, sensation in verse seemed beautifully instrumental. Feelings of the past appeared to be of greater value than its pictures.

In "The complaint of a sorrowful Soule," Heywood described his remembered "secret thoughts" as new experiences. These "thoughts" assumed the proportions of "fiers assaults" that forced him to write good verse (11. 16, 14). Elsewhere, in Revett's "Jacobs Vision at Bethel," thought ended in prayer and sleep. Both prayer and sleep led to the poet prefigured as Jacob; he recalled his thoughts as a dream-like phenomenon which, indeed, did in "his sense unwind" (4. ll. 1-2; 5, ll. 1-3). Unwinding sense in verse was "vision":

> Where richly melting in his thought,
> and soft perfume of Prayer,
> His lids as sweet a slumber caught
> as he had slept on Aire.

> Now with a ravishing too theame
> that doth his sense unwind,
> The joyes of a delicious dream
> run through his beauteous mind.

> A golden seale doth from him rise,
> the prospect of his soul,
> That lifts his intellectual eyes
> to where the Clouds unroul.

> And the fair Gate of Heav'n lies
> with bright expanded leaves,
> Whence he the sacred treasuries
> with extasie receives.

> (Stanzas 4 to 7).

Finally, in Southwell's "Josephs Amazement," the memories of "his former love" became "goulish thoughts". They turned "sence" in poetry into a "wakefull spie" (11. 17-18, 7). In another of his poems, "A Phansie turned to a sinners complaint," in which the same connection between memory and sense held sway, "sence" once more became "passions spie." Recalled "thoughts" appeared like "ruines olde" in Southwell's experience as they failed to produce the desired poetic vision of his other verse (11. 37-38).

The notion of memory as primarily sensation was pivotal whether Ignatius consciously planned it or not. The notion corresponded to his meditation's sensory requirements. The fact that memory as sensation in the meditation replaced the Aquinian view of memory as pictorial image served to alter scholastic psychology itself. Nothing was in mind which was not first in the senses, but what came into the mind now in the baroque world was stored there according to the sensory standards of personal experience rather than according to the pictorial norms of an outer world. The manner of the consignment of things into the mind and their recall also bespoke a different value system for the world. It marked the birth of a sensibility concerned with the details of personal vision as the fundamentals of philosophical truth. The new sensibility suggested the response to a view of reality stressing emotion and metaphor by which personal vision was achieved.[14] It also spelled the decline of the old world view emphasizing matter and form that the concept of memory as pictorial image in the former psychology had served.

The changes wrought on memory by Jesuit writings, which Ignatius had inspired, heightened its original sensory Augustinian character. Having become part of a closely articulated psychology with the understanding and will, the memory appeared to increase the expectations of Jesuit writers of personal sensation. Sensation was called upon to picture an inner world immediately recognizable in the universe's emotive forces. The emotive world was made to appear present to the beholder in his personal past. Once primarily a question of concupiscence and appetite, personal sensory experience became the universe's microcosmic picture. Memory that in Augustine had been the gateway to the exploration of already perceived supernatural truths became the door to the experience of an already-felt world. Although it gained nothing in depth over its Augustinian origins, memory grew considerably in sensory scope. By the exploration of what was known and understood rather than of what was known but not yet comprehended, the Augustinian pursuit of vision through memory was adapted to the Jesuit meditation. Poetry came to appear to pursue unique sensory ends in which sensation immediately suggested spirit.

Once revived in meditation, memories yielded attractive, one might even say loving, patterns of associated ideas. The personal past was not recalled haphazardly but according to definite plans. As memories were connected to sensation and sensation to universal Christian emotions, their related ideas referred to God, Satan, angels, rocks, men, stones, and so forth. From such ideas and their related sensations, the exercitant and the poet chose images suitable for a meditative topic. At the beginning of "Adoro te," Crashaw closed all the "doors" of the senses (11. 5-10) to the outside world (an image originating in Augustine)[15] but not to the experiences recalled for the purposes of imagery. The poet did not summon the affection of love to "alleage & show" the offerings of an outside world. He called on it to describe the new metaphoric writings of faith "writt" in the inner self by the thought of Christ's Resurrection.

Similarly, much of the verse of Heywood, Alabaster, Southwell, and Revett is synthetic in the sense of awakening past experiences to new effects. This is true no matter which of the formal traditions of genre, sonnet, hymn, epistle, or lyric their verse followed. The instrument of this reawakening was the will, the most important of psychology's three powers. However, even before the will was brought into play, their poetry was easily distinguished from that of Vaughan and Traherne, whose aesthetics, though also based on memorative experience, were other.

Vaughan and Traherne pursued a course of visionary experience more reminiscent of Plato and of his Renaissance Neo-Platonic followers than of the writers of the meditative tradition.[16] They explored memory to discover insights explaining the world according to their Christian beliefs. Bennet has pointed out this use of memory in Vaughan's investigation of nature.[17] Traherne and Vaughan did not investigate memory for the sake of experience. Their poetry displayed imagistic modes more relevant to allegory and symbolism than to aesthetic meditation. Unlike the poetry of Traherne and Vaughan, the work of Heywood, Southwell, Alabaster, Crashaw, Revett, and sometimes Donne recalled memories for their material usefulness to verse, to already set patterns of discourse, to clearly defined topics of meditation. Memories did not reveal things as in Vaughan and Traherne, but demonstrated them vicariously. Because of this use of memory, the verse of the meditative poet was quite paradoxically "poetry of the will" rather than of moral discovery.

Notes

[1]Joseph Beaumont, "Psyche," IV, 102, ll. 3-5, *The Complete Poems of Joseph Beaumont*, ed. A. B. Grosart (Edinburgh, 1880), p. 68, and "Loves Monarchie," ll. 3-6, *The Minor Poems*, p. 94. Also, Henry Lok, *Ecclesiastes . . . English Poesie, According to the Analogie of Scripture* (London, 1597); John Brerely, *Virginalia, or Spirituall Sonnets in prayse of the most Glorious Virgin Marie, upon everie severall Title of her Litanies of Loreto* (London, 1632); Barnabe Barnes, *A Divine Century of spirituall sonnets* (London, 1595); Malcolm Ross in *Poetry and Dogma* (New Brunswick, N.J., 1954), p. 228, describes the verse of the latter poets as "abstract."

[2]Sir Philip Sidney, *A Defence of Poetry*, ed. J. A. Van Dorsten (Oxford, 1966), p. 23.

[3]John Sweetnam, trans. *A Treatise of Mental Prayer in Which Is briefly declared the manner how to exercise the inward Actes of Vertues. By Fr. Ant. de Molina Carthusian. Whereunto Is adioyned a very profitable Treatise of Exhortation to Spirituall Profit. Written by F. Arias of the Society of Iesus . . . translated out of Spanish into English by a Father of the Society of Iesus* (St. Omer , 1617), p. 3.

[4]William Halewood, *The Poetry of Grace*, pp. 74-75; also C. S. Lewis, *English Literature in the Sixteenth Century, The Oxford History of English Literature* (Oxford, 1968), pp. 17-18, 42-44, on the Calvinist nature of the Elizabethan Church; Martin, "Biography," *Poems*, pp. xix, xxiii, xxxiii, on William Crashaw's Puritanism, his son Richard's ordination to Anglican orders and his conversion to Catholicism. Barbara Lewalski treats of some crosscurrents of Christian theology and literary

traditions in *Protestant Poetics and the Seventeenth-Century Religious Lyric,* pp. 14, 202.

[5]Gardner, "Introduction," Donne, *Divine Poems,* p. xxxviii, n. 4, describes the manuscripts; several major opinions for the ordering and dating of the composition of Donne's "La Corona" and "Holy Sonnets" exist, including: Grierson, *Poems,* II, pp. cxlii-clii; Gardner, "Introduction," Donne, *Divine Poems,* pp. xxxvii-xlvii; and Martz, *Poetry of Meditation,* pp. xi, 53-56.

[6]A. C. Southern, *Elizabethan Recusant Prose, 1559-1582* (Glasgow, 1950), pp. 30-43; Martz, *Poetry of Meditation,* pp. 5-9; A. F. Allison and D. M. Rogers, *A Catalogue of English Books Printed Abroad or Secretly in England,* 2 vols. (Bognor Regis, 1956), I, pp. 12-13, 30-31, 71-72, and II, pp. 100, 114-121, 131-132, but *passim;* Helen C. White, *English Devotional Literature Prose, 1600-1640* (Madison, Wisc., 1931), pp. 138-139.

[7]Spingarn, *Literary Criticism,* p. 11.

[8]Story, "Introduction," *Alabaster,* p. xxxi; J. W. Lever, *The Elizabethan Love Sonnet* (London, 1966), pp. 146, 160-161.

[9]Aristotle, *Rhetoric,* I, 1, p. 7; Henry Peacham, *The Garden of Eloquence,* intro. William G. Crane, *Scholars' Facsimiles and Reprints* (Gainesville, Fla., 1954), A B iij; George Puttenham, *The Arte of English Poesie* (1586), ed. G. D. Willcock and Alice Walker (Cambridge, 1936), p. 23.

[10]Thomas Everard, trans. *The Practise of Christian Workes. Written in Spanish by the R. Father Francis Borgia, sometymes Duke of Gandia, and the third Generall of the Society of Iesus. Togeather with a short Rule; How to live well. Englished by a Father of the same Society,* 1620, p. 202.

[11]Gardner, "Introduction," Donne, *Divine Poems,* p. li, n. 2, discusses other groupings of seven prayers apparently not called "crowns;" Martz, *Poetry of Meditation,* pp. 107-108, discusses "coronaries" in both poetry and formal prayer.

[12]Aquinas, *On Man,* I, Ques. LXXIX, Seventh Article, p. 79.

[13]Augustine, *The Trinity,* XI, 1 (or xii), pp. 91-92; the idea of the memory as the "print" of experience recurs in the English translation of the Belgian Jesuit Leonard Lessius' *Hygiasticon,* p. 166, for which Crashaw wrote a prefatory poem.

[14]Augustine, *Confessions X,* viii, 14, p. 209: "Out of the same storehouse, with these past impressions, I can construct now this, now that, image of things that I either have experienced or have believed on the basis of experience — and from these I can further construct future actions, events, and hopes; and I can meditate on all these things as if they were present."

[15]Augustine, *Confessions,* X, 13, pp. 208-209.

[16]For example, Spenser in "A Hymn of Heavenly Love," 11. 1-4, *Works, The Minor Poems,* Vol. 1, p. 213.

[17]Joan Bennet, *Five Metaphysical Poets* (Cambridge, 1964), p. 75.

CHAPTER FIVE

Imitation: The World

1

English meditative poets pictured their subjects according to the general Renaissance criterion of "imitation." This criterion required the poet to recreate his subject according to various standards of form, beauty, and function.[1] However, in so far as verse fulfilled the ends of Jesuit meditation as well as those in the mainstream of Renaissance poetics, it posited two imitations in a single poem. One was an imitation of "things" and the other was an imitation by "words" *(Donatus,* p. 70). The first imitation involved the representation of meditative topics, strongly influenced by the rules governing knowledge. For its part, the second imitation touched on figurative language as a picture of active, sentient human life. Donatus distinguished between them by comparing them with the art of painting. The imitation of things resembled the shape of an object in a painting, and the imitation by words resembled its sensory details in the colors of various paints (pp. 5-8, 75). This chapter deals with the first imitation, that is, with the objective world pictured in meditative poetry. The next two chapters will deal more exclusively with the patterns of human feeling and figurative language suggested by the second imitation.

The Jesuit imitation of things focused not on structures in verse but on outer reality. The imitation reorganized the objects of the material world according to their sensory qualities in the lines of verse. However, the imitation of things was not simply concerned with patterns of unified emotional experience that such qualities might be made to suggest. It was concerned rather with their capacity to give the objective world life in poetry. For Donatus, such poetry was not only *imitatio* as it was generally discussed by poetic theorists. It was *imitatio rerum,* the imitation of things, his preferred term (p. 70).

The lack of concern in the imitation of things with a unified picture of emotional experience is its principal characteristic. The imitation rested not upon emotive concepts of sensory uniformity but on how the knowledge of objective things acquired a quality of distance in being transmitted to the self. We must remember that meditative psychology was based on the Aristotelian and scholastic principle that nothing was in the mind which was not first in the senses. This principle now stressed the detachment of the self from things as a characteristic of the acquired knowledge of the world.

Such detachment of the self characterized deeply the Jesuit approach to imitation. The detachment gave a distinct flavor to the long classical heritage of poetic imitation. Springing from Plato's *Republic* and Aristotle's *Poetics,* the question of imitation took a turning away from the aesthetics of verse concerned with purely formal considerations. It now reflected concerns with knowledge as well as with poetic mode.

Imitation, which had once enabled writers to break away from the medieval concept of verse as allegory,[2] now allowed meditative poets illuminated by Jesuit poetics the additional liberty of depicting knowledge as the microscomic picture of the universe reflected in the human understanding. These poets moved away not only from medieval allegory but from verse as well and to the poet himself.

Heywood, Southwell, Alabaster, Donne, Revett, and Crashaw can be said to have expected such human fulfillment of verse in those of their poems that may be regarded as meditative. There is the example of Southwell's "Decease Release" in which the style of verse is described as leading to the poet's emancipation:

> My life my griefe, my death hath wrought my joye,
> My frendes my foyle, my foes my weale procur'd,
> My speedy death hath shortned longe annoye,
> And losse of life an endles life assur'd.

> Rue not my death, rejoyce at my repose,
> It was no death to me but to my woe,
> The budd was opened to lett out the Rose,
> The cheynes unloo'sd to lett the captive goe.

> A prince by birth, a prisoner by mishappe,
> From Crowne to crosse, from throne to thrall I fell,
> My right my ruthe, my titles wrought my trapp,
> My weale my woe, my worldly heaven my hell.

> By death from prisoner to a prince enhaunc'd,
> From Crosse to Crowne, from thrall to throne againe,
> My ruth my right, my trapp my stile advaunc'd,
> From woe to weale, from hell to heavenly raigne.

> (Stanzas 5, 7-9)

As the imitation of things in lines like the above put increasing emphasis on the poet, it also came to suppose that he perceived the outer world in a series of separate sense impressions. An "impression" was not a suggestion of an ideal nature to the mind but a kind of knowledge. It was a print in the self of the mould of things outside. The imitation of things was a collection of such prints according to meditative psychology into the shape of a poem. The imitation depended on the rules that governed things but according to the conditions by which things were thought to become objective knowledge. The Ignatian imitation of things contrasted strongly with a number of other contemporary approaches, for example, Aristotle's newly revived prerequisite "plan" for a good poem, Milton's "elegantly drest" representation of truth, and Sidney's "speaking picture" of a yet better world than this one. Nor did it resemble Puttenham's "counterfeit" image bringing out the life of nature, nor Jonson's "feigned" device subserving nature's forces.[3]

The implications of the Jesuit imitation of things for poetic practices and meditative psychology were enormous. It is true that no matter what theory underlies it, poetic imagery is always a picture of things. Nevertheless, in the meditative poem, the poet never "imitated" anything in the way we commonly think of him as reacting aesthetically to the world. His meditative temper and his poem's aesthetics sprang from his view of knowledge. As the everyday knowledge of the outer world seemed to be conditioned by the quality of distance adhering to sense experience, his meditative temper involved deliberately widening that distance in the lines of verse.

Created by exaggerating the already existing distance between the poet and the world, the meditative temper governed the poet's approach to all questions of imitation. With such a temper, the poet developed a suitable contemplative inner state, a proper attitude towards the world that his imitation recreated for his reader. As the poet retired into a prerequisite meditative inner state as part of his act of creation, his distance from the world became a *sine qua non* of recreating it in imagery.

Many English meditative poems begin with the poet's describing that emotional seclusion and its attendant contemplative inner state. Its examples are countless. Southwell's "prodigall child" of the poem of that title is "Disankerd from a blisful shore" in line one and is "lancht into the maine of cares" in line two. In "Saint Peters Complaint," the poet's main character launches "Foorth my Soul into a maine of teares" and, in the second line, "Full fraught with grief" is "The traffick of the mind."

In Heywood's poems, the making of distance appears more interior than in Southwell's verse because it is more ascetic. Yet, this distance-making serves the purpose of separating the poet from the outer world for poetic imitation. Often, Heywood's separation adopts a litany-like tone. In "Beying troubled in mynde," "bitter sweate" first "straines my gelded harte." Then, "the carelesse count," "the doubtfull hope," and "the pensive path" successively concluded in the same inner "warre" (11. 1-5). Separated from the world, the poet did "drive my daies in troubles and desease" of mind (1. 12). Similarly, in "Alluding his state to the prodigall child," the imitation of the story of the Biblical "wandring youth" was the point of Heywood's personal departure form the world:

"Mate now devide the burthen of his blame, / with me" (11. 5-6). Heywood's personal distance from the world also characterized his other distinctively meditative poems like "Complaint of a sorrowful Soule," "Easter day," and "Who wayteth on this wavering world." It distinguished the openings of these poems particularly from his stricter imitations of "Miscellany" doggerel like "Looke oe'r you leap" and "A witty and pleasant conceit."

2

In the fashion of *Exercises,* the inner distant state depicted by meditative poets referred both to the self and to Christian Mysteries. It not only referred to the personal predispositions suggested by the self but also to sublime Christian events. The inner state was contemplated directly by means of the self and indirectly through the intervention of Mystery. The meaning of Mystery altered from its theological tradition reflected in medieval hymnals and widened to cope with diverse emotions.

> With all the powres my poor Heart hath
> Of humble loue & loyall Faith,
> Thus lowe (my hidden life !) I bow to thee
> Whom too much loue hath bow'd more low for me.
> Down down, proud sense ! Discourses dy.
> Keep close, my soul's inquiring ey !
> Nor touch nor tast must look for more
> But each sitt still in his own Dore.
>
>   Your ports are all superfluous here,
> Saue That which lets in faith, the eare.
> Faith is my skill. Faith can beleiue
> As fast as loue new lawes can giue.
> Faith is my force. Faith strength affords
> To keep pace with those powrfull words.
> And words more sure, more sweet, then they
> Loue could not think, truth could not say.
>
>   (*"Adoro te,"* ll. 1-16)

The inner state touching directly on the self, moreover, dealt not only with personal sinful alienating situations, but also covered the possible relationships between God and the individual person resulting from the fall of man. These relationships included those for which the poet was responsible as well as those for which, because of man's destiny, he was not. Poems like Southwell's "A Phansie turned to a sinners compaint" and "decease Release" evoked general states of human weakness like despair and death more fitting for poetic meditation than personal treatments of weakness such as appear in his other poems like "Sinnes heavie loade." The nature of imitation encouraged the discussion of psychological and moral states as impersonal and general. Its sensory images were constantly impressing their universal character on the poet's imagination. Even the most personally felt state of alienation, like that due to mortality in Donne's "Holy Sonnet" 10 "Death be not proud," ended quickly in the consideration of the universality of the demise of death not in the self but in the world (11. 11-12).

Poetic imitations dealing with Christian Mysteries were marked by the same universally oriented character as those dealing with bare states of the soul. These imitations moved the poet to relate the general states of man to Christian mythological truths. Christian Mysteries came to represent inner states by way of worldly states. Through an inner state, the poet comtemplated a Mystery as a condition of the world. Mystery, like the self, explained that state. Crashaw's "Nativity" and "Epiphanie" were hymns because their genre suggested songs of divine praise, as did Southwell's "A Holy Hymn" and Revett's "Christmas Day." All of them dealt with miraculous historical events. In the four poems, however, contrary to the original idea of a hymn as impersonal, the "I" of the poet surfaced. The figure of the poet, a pivotal point in meditative psychology, was necessary for the imitation of Christian Mystery.

The presence of the poet in meditative verse enlarged upon the medieval tradition of Mystery as Biblical event. Mystery came to include all supernatural events evoking human emotions directly. The poet's presence consequently served to remove stress from the medieval tradition of Mystery based on certain major theological conceptions. This tradition had stressed the sacraments of initiation and their few related events in the lives of Mary and Christ.[4] The tradition of Mystery as divine historical event occurring in the sixteenth and seventeenth centuries as well as in Biblical times was more pertinent by far to a typological conception of the universe. Mystery came to denote practically any miraculous Christian event, Biblical and in the present, that was rationally inexplicable to the human mind. Mysteries subjected to meditation not only necessarily touched on Christ as man and on Mary as the Mother of God, to which in their theological medieval veneration they had referred. Now, they also covered everything that was logically unintelligible because of some interference of a spirit world in the other world of time.

Contemporary interest in Biblical typology evidently accounted for the proliferation of stories about Christ and the Apostles in all devotional verse of the period. Any Biblical event was suggestively poetic as the world to Catholic, Anglican, and Puritan seemed in some measure to be closely constructed on the same typological principles as the Bible. In this general scriptural current, the most suggestively poetic Biblical events to the meditative mind were those that seemed to enlighten it deeply about its own self and creation. The favourite events in all conceivable genres of verse from epigram, to sonnet, to hymn in English meditative poetry touched extensively on strongly personal situations in the early period of Christ's immediate family: the Immaculate Conception of Mary, her betrothal to Joseph, the Annunciation, the Visitation, the birth of Christ, the coming of the Magi, the Circumcision, the Presentation, and the flight of the Holy Family into Egypt. A few examples are Southwell's "Sequence on the Virgin and Christ" and "Josephs Amazement," Crashaw's "Our Lord in his Circumcision" and the "Nativity" and "Epiphanie" hymns, Revett's "Christmas Day" and "Our Saviour circumcis'd," Nos. 2-5 of Donne's "La Corona" sonnets, and Alabaster's "Incarnation" sonnets Nos. 53 to 67 and "A New Year's Gift to my Savior" No. 75.

There were likewise recurrent Biblical events from Christ's ministry evoking strong personal situations similar to those suggested by early incidents in Christ's immediate family. These tended also to touch on the spectacular interference of a spiritual mythology in the world of time and very little on Christ's teachings and on the organization of the Church. Some much used events were Lazarus' resurrection, the miracle of the wine at Cana, and Mary Magdalen's conversion as in Southwell's "Mary Magdalen's Blush," Crashaw's "To our Lord, upon the Cross" and "Water made Wine," and Revett's "The water made wine" and "Lazarus and Dives." Then a large jump in the period of time covered by the New Testament occurred, and the choice of Biblical themes in meditative verse next came to rest on the very late events of Christ's life that also demonstrated spectacularly the relation of the baroque mythology to the present world. The favourite events were Christ's suffering on the Cross and the Resurrection as in "Southwell's "Man to the Wound in Christ's side" and "The virgin Mary to Christ on the Crosse," Crashaw's "Sancta Maria Dolorem," "Vexilla Regis," and "Easter day," Revett's "Christ naked and wounded on the Cross," Heywood's "Easter day," Donne's "La Corona" sonnet "Resurrection," Alabaster's three sonnets entitled "Upon the Crucifix" Nos. 30, 32 and 34 and "Upon Christ's Saying to Mary 'Why Weepest Thou?' " No. 21.

A number of events, like Saint Peter's denial of Christ in three of Southwell's poems and the ascent of Christ's spirit to his Father on Mount Olivet in Alabaster's verse, reflected personal interests. Southwell's sympathy for Peter sprang from his own possible temptations to deny his Church before the political exigencies of the Act of Supremacy. And, in four sonnets (Nos. 3-6) in "The Portrait of Christ's Death," Alabaster found his conversion to a visionary life easily analogous to the ascent of Christ's spirit before his death.[5] The striking aspect of these scriptural themes is that in the Jesuit meditative tradition they all became known as "Christian Mysteries." The contemporary interest in Biblical events originating in a concern with typology became characterized by Mystery.

In *Exercises* Ignatius himself infused the approach to Mystery as Biblical event and as history into meditation. His list of Mysteries for meditation included the theological ones of the Annunciation and the Nativity of Christ, but their overall number had jumped dramatically to fifty-two. Among others, they included the temptation of Christ in the desert and the turning of water into wine at Cana (pp. 91, 92, 96, 97). Meditative Mystery was not the medieval question of devotion inspired by certain favorite theological conceptions about Christ, Mary, and the sacraments, but was a matter of personal historical experience. Theological realities now became related to typology, and the stress on Mystery changed accordingly. The Biblical events that had served as the subjects of the allegories of medieval "miracle" and "mystery" plays had now, by the extension of present history into theology and typology, become "Mystery."

By becoming Mystery, all the inexplicable events in the history of Christian mythology grew pertinent to human feeling. Mystery came to be understood as the personal appreciation of the inexplicable method of the Christian God's historical functioning among the figures of his mythology. It enjoyed the objectivity characteristic of history, yet also a subjective character due to its immediate relevance to personal salvation.

Such personal immediacy made Mystery as attractive a meditative topic as the bare states of the soul, and it led the poet to the same contemplative ends. The inexplicable events of Christian history thus became excellent topics for verse imitation. Donne haphazardly mixed the Mysteries pertaining to Christ and Mary in "La Corona" sonnets guided more by the personal connotations of the new concept of Mystery than by the theological statements of its old concept. The figure of Donne is ever present in the poems relating the worldly mysterious event first to himself and then to universal truth ("I againe risen may / Salute the last, and everlasting day," 11. 13-14, "Resurrection"). The poet's position was a watershed between the new kind of Christian Mystery and its meaning in verse. To write poetry was a personal spiritual uplifting comparable to Christ's Ascension in Donne's "La Corona" sonnet bearing that title:

> Salute the last and everlasting day,
> Joy at the uprising of this Sunne, and Sonne,
> Yee whose just teares, or tribulation
> Have purely washt, or burnt your drossie clay;
> Behold the Highest, parting hence away,
> Lightens the darke clouds, which hee treads upon,
> Nor doth hee by ascending, show alone,

> But first hee, and hee first enters the way.
> O strong Ramme, which hast batter'd heaven for mee,
> Mild Lambe, which with thy blood, hast mark'd the path;
> Bright Torch, which shin'st, that I the way may see,
> Oh, with thy owne blood quench thy owne just wrath,
> And if thy holy Spirit, my Muse did raise,
> *Deigne at my hands this crowne of prayer and praise.*

The meditative poet's creation of distance also affected other important matters, some literary and others not, besides Mystery and the bare states of the soul. Formally speaking, the poet's distance-making altered both the general tradition of Metaphysical poetry and the received genres of verse, particularly the sonnet, that fell within its range. Moreover, the nature of this distance changed as the Ignatian tradition developed.

In Alabaster's and Donne's poems, the making of distance between the poet and the imitated world colored the abrupt openings, such as "For Godsake hold your tongue" in "The Canonization," typical of much Metaphysical poetry. The abrupt colloquial openings of Metaphysical verse tuned the reader in dramatically to the poet's thoughts. In the branch of this poetry illumined by Ignatian psychology, the address to the reader informed him specifically on the meditative topic to be considered. The abrupt address to the reader became coincidental in that the poet spoke out loud to himself in order to retire from the world. The reader was enlightened only accidentally and suffered the abruptness of the poet to himself rather than to him. Such a coloring suggested the growth of the sixteenth-century traditions of genre into those of the seventeenth, marking at the same time the development of a form of Metaphysical poetry.

Creating distance between the poet and the world tempered a genre of Metaphysical poetry like the sonnet in a different and more extensive way than the minor convention of the colloquial opening. The argumentative nature of the sonnet imitation markedly altered in the hands of both Donne and Alabaster. This is true equally of their sonnets dealing with Christian Mysteries and of those treating with aspects of their personal spiritual lives. The octet of the conventional sonnet now became invariably directed to the needs of meditative distance rather than to argument. Alabaster's "Penitential Sonnet" 13, "My soul within the bed of heaven doth grow," which fits into the category of meditations directly on the self, is an example. The point at issue in Alabaster's poem, as in all meditative sonnets, was not the inadequacy of the world to picture the poet's destitution. The poet began his poem already conceptually triumphant over destitution and his "soul" was fixed, as Alabaster writes, "within the bed of heaven" (l. 1). The world, not his soul, nor for that matter not even his poem, failed to correspond to the poet's already achieved expectations of his life. Alabaster painted a white world black, "withered and unsound" (l. 7). But he wrote a sonnet in this fashion to describe his conviction that repentance, by taking one's distance from the world, was a state *per se* of holiness and that poetry was equally *per se* as worthy of its expression.

Donne's "Holy Sonnet" 13 "What if this present were the worlds last night" also fits into the category of meditation directly on the self. Its picture of the world acts to much the same distancing rather than confessional or argumentative purpose as the description of the universe in Alabaster's verse. The world appears imminently menacing in his first line, "What if this present were the worlds last night?" This picture's purpose was to encourage Donne to reject the world while he was in no state of personal guilt because of his association with it ("tell / Whether that countenance can thee affright," ll. 3-4). Poetry like "Holy Sonnet" 13 was written to separate the poet from the world and force him to consider it correctly in terms of the spiritual universe. The sonnet paints the world black to bring into relief the inherent moral realities of the poet's and reader's lives. Donne's black world was a provocative imitation of a desired inner state rather than its fair copy.

The imagery in Alabaster's and Donne's sonnets on Christian Mysteries imitated the world in the same fashion as the sonnets on their spiritual lives. The argumentative tone marking the conventional sonnet opening ceded its place there too to the distance associated with meditation. The octets of Alabaster's and Donne's sonnets on inexplicable historical events argue nothing about Mystery and much about the imitation of verse as Mystery's picture. The opening of Alabaster's first sonnet on the Mystery of the Crucifixion (No. 1) "The night, the starless night of passion" is therefore both personal and objective in putting distance between the poet and the world. In the same breath, the sonnet's opening speaks of "passion" in terms of individual emotion, but it also talks of it as Christ's divine universal suffering. It paints a forbidding picture of a "martial" yet peculiarly abstract world, repugnant equally to the suffering Christ on Calvary and to the feelings of the seventeenth-century English reader. The poet takes his distance from the world at the same time that the dying Christ suffers his passion and, by doing so, he approaches his universality of character. With Christ in verse picturing an inadequate world, he sets out to conquer time (ll. 1-4). The distance between the poet and the world is strikingly, sublimely immediate.

> The night, the starless night of passion,
> From heaven began, on heaven beneath to fall,
> When Christ did sound the onset martial,
> A sacred hymn, upon his foes to run;
> That with the fiery contemplation

Of love and joy, his soul and senses all
Surcharged might not dread the bitter thrall
Of pain and grief and torments all in one.
Then since my holy vows have undertook
To take the portrait of Christ's death in me,
Then let my love with sonnets fill this book,
With hymns to give the onset as did he,
That thoughts inflamed with such heavenly muse,
The coldest ice of fear may not refuse.

Alabaster writes that "passion" in its two senses of personal emotion and of Christ's suffering originated in the "starless night." This night without constellations is a supra-terrestial world before the beginning of time. The passion liberally provoked by that night, rather than the historical fact of Christ's death, was the object of his "fiery contemplation / Of love and joy" (11. 5-6). Seeming to spring from an emotive universal type pre-dating time, Christ's passion though past gave the poet's present experience meaning.

The opening lines of Donne's first "La Corona" sonnet were later to repeat Alabaster's idea that universal passion was the criterion of unworldly distance. The innocent world again suffered its black dismemberment in poetic imagery for the benefit of meditative states of the soul. The first "La Corona" sonnet was in fact devoted to no "Mystery" as commonly accepted even in the new litany of miraculous historial events. Instead, it sprang from the "thirst" of universal passion afflicting the poet (1. 12). History was made up not only of events here but of emotional states infinitely extended. Donne wove a "crown of prayer and praise" but in a mood of "devout melancholie" (1. 2) more applicable to the following six sonnets on Christian Mysteries than to the first which introduced them. Change, the "fraile bayes" of secular verse, and riches were in Donne's lines the properties of a weak world from which he took his necessary distance to achieve the meditative ends of his poems.

In the light of meditative poetry that preceded his, the so-called continental sensuality of Crashaw's verse was consequently not a singular English phenomenon without native roots. The sensory character of his lines was, rather, the last stage of a long historical process. Beyond it in Revett's poetry lay inevitably a decline as is the fate of all literary movements. The meditative sensory character in the religious verse of Crashaw and Revett was more obvious and consistent in its appearance than had been the case in the work of the earlier poets. However, the reasons were related to English literary history rather than to contemporary importations from the Continent. Crashaw's verse is more sensual than that of his predecessors, but this characteristic is the result of the perfection of a habit practised over many generations of the poet creating distance from the world.

Fulsome examples of meditative aesthetics existed not only in Crashaw's and Revett's verse; they are also found earlier in Heywood's "Easter Day" and Southwell's "Burning Babe." The moral assumptions of the old world view of the Great Chain of Being with its respect for the hierarchical values, however, lingered long in the handling of verse topics and imagery. The imitations in Crashaw's and Revett's verse, in terms of creating distance from the world, represented a more consistent liberation from the old view by having benefited from the passage of time.

As in the meditative poetry of Heywood, Southwell, Alabaster, and Donne, the world in the making of distance in Crashaw's verse was regularly indifferent. It was neither bad nor good except as the reflection of the moral condition of the individual soul born into a fallen world and sharing that fall. Crashaw tends to speak of the procedure of creating distance symbolically at the beginning of many of his poems, and such procedure appears more detached than in the work of his predecessors. For example, the opening lines of his "Nativity" hymn are sublime in their indifference to the world. Their imagery depicts the world's indifference rather than its adversity to the new "Noon" of the poem's "loftyer Song" (11. 1-2). Crashaw pictured eternal emotive truths in the figurative expressions of the temporal world, using words such as "night" and "sun" (11. 2, 4) not to suggest darkness and light, ignorance and illumination, but to develop notions of contrast. He thus brought into relief emotive realities to which traditional concepts like material darkness and light were irrelevant.

Similarly, the paradoxes of the opening lines of Crashaw's "Epiphanie" hymn and "Sancta Maria Dolorem" were secondary in importance to his imitations of a distant world. The first poem is celebratory and happy and the second is profoundly dispiriting. However, in spite of this difference of tone, the imitations of both poems reflect concern with meditative distance. Both imitations are founded on meditative notions and not on considerations of paradox. Crashaw's paradoxes were a style of poetry but, unlike imitation, they were not a copy of the world. The cross, Christ's body, and marble in "Sancta Maria Dolorum" (11. 1, 6, 11) were the elements constituting a number of paradoxes, as were the morning, kingship, and the meridian in the "Epiphanie" hymn (11. 2, 7, 17). However, these objects derived their meanings in Crashaw's lines from emotive forces related to meditative distance and imitation outside the normal contrastive attributes of paradox. The later stanzas of "Sancta," for example, bring the emotive realities to the foreground of the poet's concerns:

> O teach those wounds to bleed
> In me; me, so to read
> This book of loves, thus writ
> In lines of death, my life may coppy it

With loyall cares.
O let me, here, claim shares;
Yeild something in thy sad prerogative
(Great Queen of greifes) & give
Me too my teares; who, though all stone,
Think much that thou shouldst mourn alone.
Yea let my life & me
Fix here with thee,
And at the Humble foot
Of this fair Tree take our eternall root.
That so we may
At least be in loves way;
And in these chast warres while the wing'd wounds flee
So fast 'twixt him & thee,
My brest may catch the kisse of some kind dart,
Though as at second hand, from either heart.
(Stanzas VI, VII)

In the opening paradoxes of "Epiphanie" and "Sancta," worldly
objects as in the above lines no longer referred to each other but to the
force of the affections. The images having this effect in Revett's verse are
less consistent than in Crashaw's. But where they occur, as in many
figures of "Christmas-Day," they are striking and attain the meditative
ends of the verse of his master. The world of "Christmas-Day" was an
easily and deeply plundered body for verse imitation. The example of an
extended meditative imitation in Revett is rare because he never settled
his identity as a poet between the conflicting attractions of Crashaw for
verse on Mysteries, Herbert for verse about the self, and Marvell for
secular poems. "Christmas-Day" is all the more to be welcomed as a late
example of a class of meditative poetry on Christian Mystery in the work
of one man. Revett wrote that angels "broak" the day in a universe
covered by a "half asleep" dawn of the mere world, as did Crashaw in the
opening lines of the "Nativity" hymn. But as in Crashaw's poem the day
that Revett's spiritual creatures heralded had no genuine connection
with the sun that was also rising over the natural world (11. 6-7). In
Crashaw's "Nativity" and "Epiphanie" hymns and Revett's
"Christmas-Day," the material world was abandoned in favor of its
poetic reorganization.

Come we shepheards whose blest Sight
Hath mett loue's Noon in Nature's night ;
  Come lift we vp our loftyer Song
And wake the Svn that lyes too long.

To all our world of well-stoln joy
  He slept ; and dream't of no such thing.

While we found out Heaun's fairer ey
And Kis't the Cradle of our KING
Tell him He rises now, too late
To show vs ought worth looking at.
Tell him we now can show Him more
Then He e're show'd to mortall Sight ;
Then he Himselfe e're saw before ;
Which to be seen needes not His light.
                              (*"Nativity,"* ll. 1-14)

The distance between the poet and the world in English meditative verse is open to other explanations. It might be true that practically all seventeenth-century religious verse, because it is both religious and poetic, shows us the poet separating himself from matter. Such distance might also appear meditative because the religious mind always views the world of time contemplatively from afar. The possibility exists as well of identifying such distance of the poet from the world closely with *evacuatio sensuum* of *Exercises*. In effect, this distance answers to the psychological needs of the Ignatian voiding of the senses. That the poets consciously described this distance so often at the beginning of their poems might even induce us to consider it as a structural element imitating the exercital *evacuatio.* An apparent voiding of the senses might have become an opening theme of much meditative verse.

But both the first suggestion of religious detachment and the second suggestion of the *evacuatio* simplify the imitation of verse too much.

The imitation of things in English poetry which we may discuss in terms of Jesuit verse was a determining influence in its own right. It was a vital issue and it forbids the consideration of the poet's distance from the world as a general stance. Because of this, Donatus in *Ars Poetica* described imitation speculatively and at length as though he were a scholastic philosopher contemplating syllogistically an illusive metaphysical point.

Imitation, Donatus said, was the form of things in verse. Claiming Plato as his authority, he wrote that it was "the cause of images" and "the reason why" they existed *(Ars Poetica,* pp. 3-4). However, the poetic imitation existed not according to Plato's idealistic standards but according to the mimetic standards of the new world view.[6] Imitation was not an abstraction or a matter of speculation. It had become an independent subject of study in Jesuit books of poetic theory, free of the mirror-like derogatory qualities attributed to it by Plato. Imitation became a creation as respectable as a philosophical text and Plato, who had written against it, became one of its supporting authorities by the selectivity of Renaissance writers to choose from his works only what they wanted.[7]

As Alabaster demonstrated in Sonnet 70, "A Morning Meditation," in a single text in the special domain of matter called poetry, his verse imitated the world, himself, and the universe of affections all at once. The meaning of his verse imitation was separate from that of the objects it depicted, and the purpose behind his text was the meditation of his title:

> The sun begins upon my heart to shine,
> Now let a cloud of thoughts in order train
> As dewy spangles wont, and entertain
> In many drops of his Passion divine,
> That on them, as a rainbow, may recline
> The white of innocence, the black of pain,
> The blue of stripes, the yellow of disdain,
> And purple which his blood doth well resign;
> And let these thousand thoughts pour on mine eyes
> A thousand tears as glasses to behold him,
> And thousand tears, thousand sweet words devise
> Upon my lips as pictures to unfold him:
> So shall reflect three rainbows from one sun,
> Thoughts, tears, and words, yet acting all in one.

The purpose behind the imitation in lines like Alabaster's was regularly at the heart of discussions of meditative verse. It was impossible to talk about poetry without also discussing the world and its meditative experience. Imitation in verse was governed by the principles of that experience which was founded in turn on the principles of creation and the self. The causality between self, world, and meditation in poetry was inextricable, leaving little room for conjecture or pure aesthetics.

The weaving of all three — self, world, and meditation — into poetic imitation required constant vigilance. The poet was bound to avoid superfluous properties such as a too great personal concern with the self and too many examples from nature. Yet he was consistently required to keep the self in the forefront with nature interposing between him and the universe of the affections. This was as true for poems on or about Christian Mystery like Donne's "La Corona" sonnets and Crashaw's "Nativity" as for direct contemplations on spiritual life. The first of Donne's "La Corona" sonnets which introduces all seven poems is the first link in a "crown" of prayers remarkable for the tension typical of Ignatian verse. There is constant strain in the sonnet's lines between the self (Donne's "white sincerity"), the world ("treasury"), and meditation ("heart and voice be lifted high," 11. 6, 3, 13). The self had always to be kept face to face with emotive universals. Neither was the self nor an emotive universal to be submerged in the other. The poet also pretended that the meditative experience of the reader like his own was yet to be achieved. In reality it had already been realized from the first line.

3

The need of imitation to exist from a poem's first line, even from its first word, distingiushed meditative verse fundamentally from *Exercises*. Imitation was the crucial element making poetry differ from *Exercises* at the same time that the poem copied Loyola's work. Reading *Exercises* and reading a meditative poem by Donne or Crashaw were deliberately different experiences. *Exercises* was a manual on how to have a meditative experience later. Not only was it not needed for the crowning meditative experience of the third part of the exercise, but it was not necessary for the three-part exercital structure, though it could be used for it. In fact, Ignatius said the manual of *Exercises* was handier for the retreat master than for his exercitants (p. 2).

These preliminary exercital steps either directly in the hands of the exercitant or indirectly in those of the retreat master were impossible to poetry. The experience of meditative poetry began with the first of its words and concluded with its last. Poetry must be looked upon as having recreated aesthetically from its first to last syllables, uninterrupted, the triumphant experience of the universal affections of the exercise's concluding third part. The history of Ignatian psychology in English verse from Heywood to Revett is understandable only in terms of such a standard of verse. Otherwise, meditative verse was a mere rhymed and metered version of Ignatius' manual. Whether meditative verse was directly influenced by *Exercises* and its copies, or by Jesuits writing verse or comment on poetry, or by broad cultural forces explained alone by their psychology would also become entirely irrelevant. Without having inspired some form of verse aesthetics, *Exercises* would have been nothing for meditative verse except a topic of conversation, occasionally exerting passing structural influences in conventional poetic genres. That meditative verse was not this is evident in the poets' concepts of experience. Meditative verse resembled *Exercises* because its imitation recreated the exercital experience of the affections. It departed from the manual because that experience was of an aesthetic rather than of an ascetic order.

The repeated appearance of the exercital structure in English poetry in no way detracts from the meditative experience it inspired. The structure in verse in fact brings that experience into relief. The appearance of the Ignatian Prelude, voiding of the senses and application of the senses is to us an important clue of *Exercises'* greater relevance to aesthetics than to structure. Although the discovery of the exercital structure in verse was the key to Martz' pioneer literary criticism, it was the meditative experience that gave sense to the structure's poetic use.

Meditative poetry was not meditative only in those moments when it structurally relied on one or all parts of the original exercise. It was meditative according to its own aesthetic principles springing from the experience of *Exercises*, whose ascetic character in the name of verse it necessarily rejected. A reader's experience of meditative verse began at its start. Within his reading of a successful poem he did not have the opportunity of pausing lengthily to compose a picture of his meditative topic in his imagination. Nor could he go through the procedure of removing his senses from their contact with the outer world. His senses had to maintain their contact with the poem in that world and could not be withdrawn to an inner imaginative self where the poem, unlike the exercital picture, did not exist.

In the imitation of the meditative poem, therefore, the structure of the original exercise was an historically interesting element but was secondary. Its presence suggests the attraction of *Exercises* to a century of Counter Reformation sensibility. The structure does not, however, explain that attraction to poetry. There are many important historically revealing examples of the structure in English verse, but they are aesthetically inconclusive in the long run of understanding meditative poetry. To see this, we may survey these examples.

In Crashaw's "Adoro te," the senses are voided one by one, "Touch," "tast" and so forth at the beginning of the poem (11. 6-10). The ear is left figuratively "open" but the reasons are related to style discussed in the next chapter. The voiding is not present in the medieval hymn which is the source of Crashaw's poem. It is also absent in Southwell's imitation of the same hymn in "Of the Blessed Sacrament of the Aulter," although Southwell emphasized the inactivity of the senses without going so far as to depict the *evacuatio*. He may have nevertheless had *evacuatio* in mind as in the sixth stanza the application of the senses occurs unequivocally.

Many instances of the practice of the three Ignatian Preludes *(Exercises,* p. 40) are also evident in the poetry of the time. The Preludes appear in three rhetorical exclamations at the beginning of Heywood's "The complaint of a sorrowfull Soule" ("So many Judges shall against me sentence give"; "So many pleaders shall confound my carefull case"; "So manie shall that time, against me witnesse beare", 11. 7, 9, 11). In Crashaw's epistle to the "Countess of Denbigh," the Preludes reappear as rhetorical questions ("What Magick-Bolts, what mystic Barrs"; "What Fatall, yet fantastick, Bands"; "Say, lingring Fair, why comes the Birth", 11. 11, 13, 15). They occur again in the three propositions in the early lines of his ode "to a young Gentle-Woman" ("It is, in one choise handfull, heavenn"; "It is love's great Artillery"; "It is an armory of light", 11. 11, 15, 21).

In the same poem to the gentlewoman, a large section describes an application of the senses. First the "Eares," then the "eyes," the nose ("exhalations"), touch ("embraces"), and taste ("sweets", 11. 65, 70, 77, 83, 94)) are successively applied to the topic of divine love. Of such an "application" in verse, Southwell's use of the exercital structure a half-century earlier in "Of the Blessed Sacrament of the Aulter" had been the forerunner. Southwell had applied the senses to the same topic ("ravishe eyes," "winne the eare," "lure the tast," "sooth the sent," "please the touch," 11.31-35). In Crashaw's ode to the gentlewoman, moreover, the exercital structure seems more pervasive than in the poem by Southwell. Following on the three early Preludes (11. 11-26), the application of the senses also occurs and suggests that the ode rests practically on the entire exercital structure. The exercital voiding of the senses between the Preludes and the application is missing. But the emphasis on divine love in the concluding section (11. 96-124) vividly recalls the "Contemplation for Obtaining Love" at the end of *Exercises'* "Fourth Week" (pp. 82-83).

Again, Heywood's and Southwell's poems contain marked examples of Ignatius' three contemplative "points" for the Preludes at the beginning of both his manual's "First" and "Second Weeks." The points were meant to inform the meditator about his topic by considering it repeatedly (p. 2). Early in "A Vale of Teares," Southwell recreated the order of the points for "seeing," "hearing," and "considering" matter for a Prelude in the "Second Week" (pp. 41-42). After the preludial "composition of place" depicted in the vale of the first stanza (1. 1), the three points were arranged in a series of structurally matching subordinate clauses. They covered the second, third, and fourth stanzas:

> A vale there is enwrapt with dreadfull shades,
> Which thicke of mourning pines shrouds from the sunne,
> Where hanging clifts yeld short and dumpish glades,
> And snowie floud with broken streames doth runne,
>
> Where eie-roume is from rockes to cloudie skie,
> From thence to dales with stonie ruines strow'd,
> Then to the crushed waters frothie frie,
> Which tumbleth from the tops where snow is thow'd:
>
> Where eares of other sound can have no choice,
> But various blustring of the stubburne winde
> In trees, in caves, in straits with divers noise,
> Which now doth hisse, now howle, now roare by kinde:
>
> Where waters wrastle with encountring stones,
> That breake their streames, and turne them into foame,
> The hollow clouds full fraught with thundring groans,
> With hideous thumps discharge their pregnant wombe.
>
> Stanzas I-IV

The three contemplative points also appeared in Heywood's "Alluding his state to the prodigall child" immediately after he declared his intention in the first stanza "To tread" the "trackt" of his "unrulie will." In this case, the three points did not recur three times as in Southwell's

"A Vale of Teares" but twice in quick succession as in Ignatius' "Second Week." Yet, Heywood's technique of drawing parallels reminds us of the occurrence of the Preludial points in the meditation on the "Triple Sin" at the beginning of the "First Week" (pp. 24-25) rather than of the catalogue of the "Second." In stanza two, Heywood's three Preludial points as in "Second Week" touched on the son's outward journey ("He tooke his childes part"; "He traveld farre"; "False queanes did him," 11. 8, 10, 12). By contrast, in the fashion of the method in the "Triple Sin," the repetition of the points in the third stanza forming analogies with his own life touched on his final degradation ("they drove him out"; "He was full fayne"; "Through hunger huge", 11. 15, 17, 19).

In Southwell's and in Revett's verse the three Preludial points occurred in different ways. Normally, in Southwell's poems like "The prodigall childs soule wracke" and "Man to the wound in Christs side," they came towards the middle of a poem whereas in another poem like Revett's "The Taper" they tended to fill all of it. In addition, the recurrence of opening key words in Revett's points imitated the exercital practice of mentally savouring the meditative object.

In "The prodigall childs soule," after six stanzas depicting the poet's tempestuous inner state vividly in terms of wild nature, three stanzas show him exploring it. Each stanza covers a preludial point. First, "I plunged in this heavie plight"; second, "I felt my inward bleeding sores"; and, finally, "I cried truce, I craved peace" (11. 25, 29, 33). In "Man to the Wound in Christs side," three stanzas serving as an Ignatian "compositon of place" precede the three points. The points cover the fourth to sixth stanzas, and they investigate the symbolic picture sketched in the poem's earlier stanzas. Southwell wrote: "Heere must I live, heere must I die"; second, "Heere would I view that bloudy sore"; third, "Heere is the spring of trickling teares" (11. 13, 17, 21).

In Revett's "The Taper," four Preludial points, such as are found in the concluding "Contemplation" of *Exercises,* recur. The points perform much the same role of exploring the significance of certain natural scenes suggestively as in Southwell's two poems. The repetitive words in the first four stanzas of the poem are "how" and "now." Stanzas three and four add the exclamatory command of "see," which Revett's editor Friedman describes as suggestive of the Ignatian "composition of place."[8] "The Taper," like Southwell's "Man to the Wound in Christs side," concludes with a brief prayer of recapitulation on the inner state of the poet.

The structure of the ascetic exercise fails to explain the above poems in two different ways. First, the occurrence of the structure is never wholly formative, even though it covers much of Crashaw's ode to the gentlewoman. In none of the poems are all parts of the structure present. The structure appears to account for the disposition of certain images, key words, and stanzas. But in no way does it consistently account for the fabric of whole poems either as poetry or as meditation. Its parts are locally formative rather than determining. In so far as poetry invariably imitates the outer world, the structure accounts for the arrangement of parts of that world but not for its coherence as imitation. The question at stake is not one limited to the gap that always exists between the opinion of a group of writers of what verse is and their actual poetry. This gap results from the fact that language is an inheritance common to all men. It is not easy to prove that the poetry of many writers achieves their expectation of symbolic figures without ever failing, when everyone shares in their language. However, more is in question here than that gap between common language and poetics.

The failure of the exercital structure to explain poetry springs from its original devotional source. The experience of formal Ignatian meditation was unshared. By contrast, a basic premise of formal Ignatian poetry is that it would be read and, therefore, shared. What must be compared between *Exercises* and the verse it inspired are not similar or dissimilar structures but common experiences. Such experience rather than structure was adapted to and eventually infiltrated countless verse genres. The poetic imitation recreated this experience and explains poetry's devotional character.

The devotional poem which Jesuit practices influenced imitated the typology of the baroque universe. Because of this, Ignatian poetry also pretended to imitate the ascetic experiences outlined in *Exercises*. As the meditative poet considered the various orders of religious verse open to him, he was not only generally different from Brerely, Constable, and Barnes because he used the exercital structure; rather, he shared with a number of other poets the belief that poetry, by imitating the typology of the world, also provoked a particular meditative experience. In this experience there lay the lines between "sacred" and "profane" or "obscene" verse. Much of the imitation of things of Jesuit-inspired verse was understood in the terms of these categories of poetry.

4

What made a poem sacred, profane, or obscene? Historically, the question of the morality of verse in Christian Europe sprang from the arguments over the distinction between poetry and allegory in the fourteenth and fifteenth books of Boccacio's *De Genealogia Deorum*.[9] From these arguments, the "puristic" tradition of poetry, to which Jesuit verse was later to belong, developed freed of medieval conceptions of allegory. But, practically speaking, the answer to the question of what induced Jesuit writers to distinguish between sacred, profane, and obscene verse was related to their view of matter and feeling in the typology of the universe.

If the ultimate significance of the baroque world was emotion, meditative poetry brought out its deepest affections. In that sense, poetry was an answer to a world vision. Those who put their faith in the emotive world view also shared a belief in its purpose in poetry. The emotive world's role in verse was not open to debate. This explains the contemporary approach to meditative poetry in terms of the sacred, profane, and obscene instead of as an inclusive class of religious poetry. Because it was also understood among meditative poets that sacred verse gave experiences of universally good affections and that bad verse provoked the feelings of inadequate affections, the categories were likewise generally shared. What was not shared was how the imitation of verse achieved the distinction of being good and bad and how such distinctions were transmitted practically into the categories of written verse. Southwell in the letter to his cousin, Crashaw in the two poems to the "young Gentlewoman," and Donne in the "Anniversary" poems and the first "La Corona" sonnet did not discuss whether, but how, sacred, profane, and obscene poetry existed. Southwell wrote about sacred poetry:

> But the vanity of men, cannot counterpoyse the authority of God, who delivering many partes of Scripture in verse, and by his Apostle willing us to exercise our devotion in Himnes and Spirituall Sonnets, warranteth the Arte to bee good, and the use allowable . . . But the Divell as hee affecteth Deitie, and seeketh to have all the complements of Divine honor applied to his service, so hath he among the rest possessed also most Poets with his idle fansies. For in lieu of solemne and devout matter, to which in duety they owe their abilities, they now busy themselves in expressing such passions, as onely serve for testimonies to how unwoorthy affections they have wedded their wils. And because the best course to let them see the errour of their workes, is to weave a new webbe in their owne loome; I have heere layd a few course threds together, to invite some skillfuller wits to goe forward in the same, or to begin some finer peece, wherein it may be seene, how well verse and vertue sute together.
>
> *(Poems, p. 1)*

The question of the sacred, profane, or obscene character of verse was, therefore, understood in the current, quite often technical, vocabulary by which poetry everywhere was studied, debated, lauded, or condemned. Among theorists like Donatus and Strada, it was discussed in the popular terminology of "versimilitude," the "probable," the "adornments," the "fictions," the "fable," and the "invention" of verse. To such terms, matters concerning the morality of verse were usually referred.

Of these terms, verisimilitude or *verisimile* touching on the likeness of imitation to truth was the most important. Verisimilitude was a pivotal concept in the moral relevance of aesthetics, and it was constantly at the centre of the discussions of verse. In the "puristic" tradition the *verisimile* was defined according to the "ideal representation of life" of the mid-sixteenth-century Italian critics Muzio and Robortellus.[10] Muzio's and Robortellus' approach, being broad, permitted the reintegration of "fictions" into "puristic" verse under the pressure of the new popularity accorded to Aristotle's "fable" with the numerous sixteenth-century translations of *Poetics*. Thus, a vast number of literary terms with classical and medieval as well as Renaissance origins were enlisted to describe meditative verse. Renaissance poetic terminology came to explain verse forms that explored the profoundest emotive levels of the typological universe.

In the Ignatian tradition, the sacred poem was one that awakened the highest emotions of the soul by its subject's historical imitation. The sacred poem achieved its sublime imitative ends by the Renaissance concept of "scheme" as a figure of thought. That is, it pictured its subject "schematically" rather than by the symbolic and imagistic representations of trope. For its part, profane poetry achieved the same emotive heights, but it did so by trope, by the figurative language of image and symbol, rather than by figures of thought. By contrast obscene poetry, which was occasionally also called profane, for example, by Southwell in his "To the Reader," failed to awaken human emotion beyond the typological level of time. If sensation rather than imagination could be considered as illusory, obscene verse of the sort which Donne accused the Jesuits in *Ignatius His Conclave*,[11] created its illusions. Obscene poetry possessed no valid emotional level in terms of the baroque universe.

From the point of view of its sacred, profane, and obscene imitations, meditative verse was consequently written and read in four different ways. First, a poem could be historical and sacred in the sense of being completely executed in Renaissance schemes. Written alone in figures of thought, its imitation was what Donatus, quoting Plato's term for a direct copy of eternal forms, called a "likeness" *(Ars Poetica, p. 21)*. The sacred poem lacked the fictional "fable" that Aristotle had supposedly described as "essential to a poem."[12] Immediately, the Jesuit approach suggested the imitative tradition of Muzio and Robortellus that set apart Aristotle's "fable" for fiction. This tradition described the fable as a cogent fiction, and excluded it from the historical verisimilitude.[13] Donatus also called historical verse a "verisimilitude by words" *(verisimilitudo verborum)*. This verisimilitude was an imitation of reality formed by what he referred to in the mind as *icastica*, and it made up one of his two main branches of verse imitation. Gibbons used the term "proper sense" to describe such an historically-oriented meditative image *(Abridgement, Sig. **5ᵛ)*, while Strada spoke of it as written without the fictions elsewhere allotted to poetry *(Prolusiones, p. 158)*.

Second, another approach by which the Jesuits considered the imitative character of sacred poetry made their position in the mainstream of Muzio's and Robortellus' tradition more specific yet than their stand on the fable. Sacred poetry might also be written as an imitation of reality but not strictly so. Its imitation could be interspersed with odd fictional images and symbols. The imitation of a poem might be basically one of reality, but its figures of thought could be sprinkled with fictional figures of speech. These figures, which Strada called "adornments," were individual tropes, unconnected to the cogent narrative fictions that Aristotle had supposedly referred to as fable *(Prolusiones,* p. 160).

Third, a poem written according to the whole "fiction" supposedly stemming from *Poetics* became usually known as profane verse. Its imitation was a "verisimilitude of things" *(verisimilitudo rerum)* composed strictly of figures of speech. It was thus opposed to the "verisimilitude by words" written wholly in figures of thought. Donatus identified the verisimilitude of things with Plato's "semblance," formed by the imaginative faculty that the Greek master described as *phantastica.* Strada spoke of this verisimilitude as an imitation by fictions, and Gibbons as image's second main branch after the historical *(Ars Poetica,* p. 20; *Prolusiones,* pp. 170-171; *Abridgement,* Sig. ***). This imitation was profane in the sense of setting a fictive screen between the reader and the sacred object of his meditation. Strada found its imaginative coloring sublimely helpful for men to attain the desired emotional reaches of poetry. "What can one do," he wrote. "Those things are felt little that are tasted at a distance . . . extraordinary things are conveyed to us by transmission in fictions ."

The fourth point of view from which poetry was regarded simply considered that it failed as imitation because its emotional range was inadequate. This poetry was neither an historical likeness nor a fictional semblance of the world. Even though it might be intended as one or the other of these, it provided no contact with the profoundest level of meaning of the typological universe. Such poetry was usually called "obscene," for example by Donne.

5

Because of the connection between creation and typology, nature was often a key concept in the discussions of imitation, verisimilitude, fiction, and history. Nature referred to the material world as though it, nature, represented a level of meaning above the lower level of mere uninterpreted historical event, and it came to describe the contents of the meditative poet's imitation of things. Nature appeared to assume the level of meaning in verse that Catholic and Protestant arguments attached to allegory. Allegory did not mean here the didacticism of medieval art like the Mystery or Miracle Play, whose personifications moved the abstract ideas of its message to their predetermined moralistic end. Rather, allegory referred to a typology containing a figurative level of meaning called nature and a literal level called historical fact.

The allegory associated with nature and history in current approaches to typology thus passed into verse imitation without its original medieval moralistic connotations. Allegory gave order to a topic in verse without a moral end, and it was noteworthy for its organization of nature rather than for its laws. As such, it appeared to bestow sense and direction on verse imitation. Having nothing to do with the laws of nature in Bacon or the natural law in Hooker, allegory came to be used repeatedly to discuss meditative verse imitation hand in hand with nature.

Southwell depended regularly on the allegorical use of nature to discuss the contents of his verse. His references to art, sense, and emotion were all directly in nature's scope as the meaning of allegory. Nature, he wrote in "A Vale of teares," was "disordered order," and, he added, in it "nothing seemed wrong yet nothing right" (11. 27, 32). However, its virtues were apparent once it was ordered in verse. There, "All pangs and heavie passions" in man could be explained, revealing "A thousand motives suitly" for all emotions. In nature, "sorrow springs from water, stone and tree, / Where everie thing with mourners doth conspire" (11. 53-54, 59-60). Nature was a constant source of analogies that gave it better ordering in poetry than in the world. This ordering differed fundamentally from Sidney's concept of the ideal "forms" bettering nature produced by verse. For Sidney, such ideal forms were the terminal imitative ends of verse. In the meditative tradition, by contrast, the terminal mimetic ends of poetry were the emotions incarnated by the imitation by words that complemented the imitation of things.

As in "A Vale of Teares," in the pseudo-epic invocation to the muse at the opening of "Saint Peters Complaint," the dark "mud" of the "cleerest brooke" was a natural analogy to describe Southwell's subject. The stream's murkiness was a fitting comparison for the "plaint" of the Apostle Peter at his denial of Christ three times on Good Friday (11. 2-3). The contrast of the "mud" and the "cleerest brooke" reflected the indifferent "disordered order" of nature. Nature received meaning by describing a topic in verse rather than from the normal connotations of darkness and light associated with earth and water.

> Yet natures worke it is of arte untoucht,
> So strait indeed, so vast unto the eie,
> With such disordred order strangely coucht,
> And so with pleasing horror low and hie,
>
> That who it viewes must needs remaine agast,

Much at the worke, more at the makers might,
And muse how Nature such a plot could cast,
Where nothing seemed wrong, yet nothing right:

Here christall springs crept out of secret vaine,
Strait finde some envious hole that hides their grace.
Here seared tufts lament the want of raine,
There thunder wracke gives terror to the place.

All pangs and heavie passions here may find
A thousand motives suitly to their griefes,
To feed the sorrowes of their troubled minde,
And chase away dame pleasures vaine reliefes.

Let former faults be fuell of the fire,
For griefe in Limbecke of thy heart to still
Thy pensive thoughts, and dumps of thy desire,
And vapoure teares up to thy eies at will.

Let teares to tunes, and paines to plaints be prest,
And let this be the burdon of thy song,
Come deepe remorse, possesse my sinfull brest:
Delights adue, I harbourd you too long.

                    (*"Vale of Teares,"* ll. 25-33, 49-56, 69-76)

The sonnets of Alabaster and Donne show the same approach to imitation governing even the nature of the human Christ. By fulfilling the promises of the Old Law of a redeemer, the historical Christ was a theological necessity. But the Christ appearing in the meditative poem was less noteworthy for this traditional theological incarnation than for his allegorical meaning for the material world. In Alabaster's Sonnet 58, "Christus Recapitulatio Omnium," the world was a "storehouse" lying "undigest." Its "inventory" was not yet drawn until summed up in a "brief introductory" nature of Christ's loving heart (11. 2, 4, 8). Again, in Sonnet 68, "A Morning Meditation (1)," the dawn was unlighted and totally insignificant, remaining in this state until the "sense and object" of worldly things were fitted together by the nature of Christ in Alabaster's lines (11. 3, 8). Christ did not seem to incarnate only God but the world as well for the sake of poetry.

Donne added a tone of urgency to the quest for allegorical meanings in nature. But the urgency sprang from the poet's temper rather than from nature's lack of sympathy for verse imitation. In the series of pressing rhetorical questions in the octet of "Holy Sonnet" 12, "Why are wee by all creatures waited on?", as in Southwell's verse nature was neither good nor bad. It gained its real meaning for Donne by making Christ's eternal character comprehensible in verse. The subjection of all things to man's dominion was of a startling indifference, but this paradox was not only designed for witty effect. It also set into relief the divine purpose of the indifferent "Created Nature." By including even Christ, this nature, once imitated in verse, was a picture of the ultimate significance of time. Christ was not "tied" to nature but followed its course to give it meaning elsewhere than in time (ll. 12-13). For Donne, the imitation of things in verse expressed this meaning momentarily.

Later, in Crashaw's "To the Name," the urgency of Donne's quest for ordering nature in verse was altered. Crashaw was motivated by a more consistently immediately felt sense of the emotive realities behind nature and was untouched by Donne's need to draw parallels between Biblical prototypes and their copies in nature. Crashaw's vision of an indifferent yet organizing nature for the imitation of poetry nevertheless remained unchanged from Donne.

Divine poems like Crashaw's "To the Name" and his elegies to Saint Alexis exemplify the adaptability of the Jesuit verse imitation of things to varied existing genres via nature or allegory. The hymn, the verse letter, and the elegy all became subject to the new aesthetics. Their original rules were suffused with the idea, if not with the law, of nature as a term suggesting analogies giving order to a topic in verse. This order appeared to become primordially important in understanding nature. The hymn lost its liturgical character, the verse letter ceased to be addressed to a living person, and the elegy relinquished its dirge-like tone to the presuppositions of ordering the universe for meditation. Obeying the new concepts of imitation, the arguments of Crashaw's two trilogies praised the lives of his characters, Saint Teresa and the wife of the sixth-century Saint Alexis, as sublime examples of nature. In each trilogy, the argument repeated his assertion in "To the Name" that poetic art was the "key" to open the "huge chest" of nature for imagery (ll. 29-30), and here, poetry was meant to re-order the lives of Teresa and Alexis. In the first poem to Teresa, her "rare Workes" or mystical writings recording "Love's noble history" were an integral part of nature. As such, Teresa's writings became part of the substance of Crashaw's lines (ll. 155-158). In "An Apologie" that followed, the poem was the "worthlesse song" into which Crashaw "transfus'd the flame / I took from reading thee." The flame broke "from thence into the wondring reader's brest" (ll. 2-3, 25). In the final poem, "The Flaming Heart," the "larg Books of day" of Teresa's writings became the anticipated success of his humble verse song (ll. 88, 62).

> By all thy dowr of LIGHTS & FIRES;
> By all the eagle in thee, all the doue;
> By all thy liues & deaths of loue;
> By thy larg draughts of intellectuall day,
> And by thy thirsts of loue more large then they;

> By all thy brim-fill'd Bowles of feirce desire
> By thy last Morning's draught of liquid fire;
> By the full kingdome of that finall kisse
> That seiz'd thy parting Soul, & seal'd thee his;
> By all the heau'ns thou hast in him
> (Fair sister of the SERAPHIM!)
> By all of HIM we haue in THEE;
> Leaue nothing of my SELF in me.
> Let me so read thy life, that I
> Vnto all life of mine may dy.
>
> *("Flaming Heart,"* ll. 94-108).

The same unified picture of order, reading, and nature bound the three elegiac complaints to Saint Alexis. The first "Complaint" was an imitation of nature's "blest starres" of which number the wife of Alexis became "a new name" through the medium of verse (1. 24). She and poetry possessed the same emotive meaning. In the "Seconde Elegie," the wife pursued the "Hills & relentlesse rockes" to "Expostulate" her woes (11. 16, 14). The expression of these woes in nature imagery was the poem and, once more, the woman and verse shared one significance. In the third "Elegie," which is really a verse letter, "Nature's virginity" ("seas," "sacred shores," and "mountaines") was broken by being made to represent Alexis' emotion. In the imagery of the poem, nature depicted the wife as the receptacle of this emotion (11. 6-9).

The new shades of meaning in nature were related in large measure to the Jesuit imitation of things. Nature no longer referred only to the physical world yet untouched by the hand of man. It came to signify everything in an outer world, including history, that could be worked into imitation as a suitable representation of truth. "Indeed," wrote Donatus, "do you not perceive that [the poet's choice] stretches beyond the limits [of history] and comprehends universal nature." And he concluded, "We exclude nothing from poetry" *(Ars Poetica,* pp. 15-16).

Donatus' approach to nature seemed to him suitably to replace Aristotle's fictional fable for the imitation necessary for any good poem. Donatus thought that not only a fable but "whatever nature has set in heaven," including apes and fish, could be worked into a verisimilitude. "Except a man write about God and the angels," he continued, "will it not be poetry?" *(Ars Poetica,* pp. 14, 16). Through nature, allegory, and typology, verisimilitude in the imitation of things replaced "fable" as the aesthetic staple of verse. Imitation, which Donatus had declared to be "the cause of the image" of a poem, now came also to be understood as a verisimilitude depicting the whole outer world. Providing that it provoked a suitable experience, Strada wrote, poetry could depict anything *(Prolusiones,* pp. 159, 189).

Several of Crashaw's poems appear to show the imitative view of the Jesuits at work. The sources of his figurative language were invariably broad. Yet, in his poetic imitation of the world, he sought incessantly a series of ordered effects. His choice of images cannot be explained alone by the practice of Metaphysical poetry to yoke discordant things together into sometimes developed figurative language. At stake in his verse were imitative principles involving varieties of images as well as the habit of Metaphysical poets to force comparisons by contrasting widely dissimilar things.

These imitative principles cannot be identified with the strictly pictorial designs of Cavalier lyrics. The lyric grace at which the Cavalier poem aimed, fulfilling its aesthetic purpose, was terminal. It suggests no typological level, no probing into an emotive universe. As some of Revett's poems like "The Nymph" and "Astraea recall'd" in the Cavalier style show, lyric grace did not work to the ordering of the ideas of a poem to meditative experiences. Rather, it sought to glorify these ideas in graceful forms, bettering the appearance of a generally morally deficient world.

A number of Crashaw's poems like the verse letter to the Countess of Denbigh traverse the breadth of imagery suggested by meditative aesthetics several times. Written on the Continent and first published in Paris in 1650, the verse letter encouraged the Countess to follow Crashaw's path into the Church of Rome. We do not know whether Crashaw was successful as we do not have the lady's answer. However, like so much of his verse, the poem is a stunning demonstration of Crashaw's ability to meander in and out of his sources of imagery without ever getting lost because principles of verisimilitude provide the necessary guidance.

The verse letter to the Countess opens with images suggesting the little emblem pictures of the time, which probably had their origin in the medieval romances. The Countess is then described in conventional nature and classical imagery. She is a "heav'n-beseiged Heart" standing "Trembling at the Gate of Blisse," hesitating to cross the threshold into Crashaw's newly adopted Catholic religion (11. 1-2). The woman's will is restrained from assenting to his faith by "Magick-Bolts" and "mystick Barrs" (1. 11). Later, the Countess' spiritual condition resembles the winter: she is like "Poor Waters" of nature that lie "Fetter'd and lock'd up fast" in the hibernal season "In a cold self-captivity" (11. 20-24). Crashaw then compared her indecision to the inability of the waters to move. Classical imagery follows but is soon confused with the poem's central nature paradox: the countess is at once a captive and her own captor. She is compared to the "astonish'd Nymphs" who deplore "their Floud's strange Fate / To find themselves their own severer Shoar" (11. 25-26).

The three kinds of imagery recur a little later in positive terms mixed with yet a fourth — the Christian. These images make the Countess' condition more vivid because they contradict rather than describe it. They represent the decision that she should have taken instead of her indecision. Conventional nature imagery occurs first: "Both Winds and Waters urge their way" unlike her "and murmure if they meet a stay," while she utters no sound over her inactivity (11. 39-40). Second comes classical imagery. The goddess Diana's "Chariot of chast Loves" representing the decision that the Countess should have taken speeds purposefully through the sky of Greek mythology in pursuit of her loved one. The chariot is not drawn by mythological horses but by a drove of non-classical "neat Doves" — the Christian symbol for peace and the Holy Ghost — and these doves constitute a third kind of imagery. Last follows emblem imagery with which the poem began: the figure of magnetic steel and compass ("So lumpish Steel, untaught to move, / Learn'd first his Lightnesse by his Love") describes the Countess as, unlike steel, possessing the power to move herself, but she stays still (11. 51-52). A fifth kind of imagery — the Biblical — in another poem "Vexilla Regis" suggests the eclectic character of Crashaw's choice of figures yet further. His selection of imagery was wider than any one poem reveals. In "Vexilla Regis" Christ's cross on Calvary is imaged by God the Son's throne now transposed by poetry to the Psalm of Solomon (IV 11. 5-6).

6

The diversity of the sources of imagery in the verse of Richard Crashaw clearly revealed its Counter Reformation character. But long before the younger Crashaw was writing his poem, his father William Crashaw, the Protestant divine, had attacked his Counter Reformation treatment of imagery in the *Iesuits Gospell* as had John Donne in *Ignatius His Conclave*.[14] These attacks were more properly an assault on some aspect of a vision of the world rather than on kinds of imagery. Both the elder Crashaw and Donne, echoing Plato's condemnation of poetry as a misleading imitation of a copy of reality,[15] charged that the Catholic practice of sacred imagery obscured the Biblical prototypes which it was the function of poetry to maintain evident to the reader.

Donne explained his position amply in "The First Anniversary." The role of sacred poetry was to fuse Biblical prototypes with their copies in the Book of Creatures (11. 455-474). The poet thus indicated to the contemporary reader the mystical significance of current events in the seventeenth century according to their divinely revealed meaning in the Bible. He also demonstrated who was and who was not inscribed in the metaphoric Register of the Elect. With the Bible, one of Donne's two books of life, the Register of the Elect was the list of saved souls in eternity, forming the mystical level of meaning to the lower typological level of time in the Book of Creatures. The same "Register of heaven" in the Jesuit Henry Walpole's poem on the death of Edmund Campion constituted the superior typological level of meaning of both Campion's life and Walpole's verse. However, significantly, in Walpole's Counter Reformation argument, the inscription of Campion's name in the Register was not the end in itself of sacred verse. Above, or on the same level as the Register, there was the yet other mystical dimension of meaning called "love" (11. 7-12).

A number of Donne's sacred poems show more exclusively than others his approach to sacred verse as a fusion of Biblical prototype and copy in current history. As such, they contrast revealingly with his meditative sonnets. In "The Crosse" Donne found first a series of "material" crosses in nature like the "birds on crossed wings" and "the Meridians crossing parallels." Next, he discovered a series of "spiritual" crosses in himself like "dejections" and "concupiscence of wit." The fusion of prototype and personal history concluded in the identification of human suffering with Christ's (11. 25, 22, 24, 26, 53, 58).

Then, in "A Hymn to Christ, at the Author's last going into Germany," current history imitates not one but two prototypes, one each in the Old and New Testaments. Donne's ship, the North Sea between Britain and the Continent, and the clouds form a copy in the contemporary Book of Creatures. This copy in present time prefigures both the Biblical archetype of Noah's ark, the deluge, and Yahweh's anger, and the fulfillment of the promise hidden in this Old Testament archetype in the New Testament incident of Christ's sacrifice of his body, blood, and suffering on the cross (11. 2, 4, 5).

However, the literalist or fundamentalist position of Donne and the elder Crashaw did not automatically exclude the Counter Reformation world view. Undoubtedly, it consistently denied the validity of the exclusively sensory aesthetic areas of the meditative view of verse. But the Protestant position did not make it necessarily impossible for one system to harmonize with the other. This is particularly true of the areas that separate Donne from the elder Crashaw.

The elder Crashaw's position was thinner than Donne's in that being regularly controversial, all of its elaborations were disputatious. William Crashaw's theological disputations and even his rare translation of a medieval poem like the "Dialogue, Betwixt The Soul and the Body of a damned Man" are devoid of experiments in either genre, theme, or style. The absence of experiment in the elder's Crashaw's work may be the result of temperament as well as his Puritan controversialist position. The same may not be said of Donne. Both because of his Catholic recusant upbringing and of the wider range of his literary output, Donne explored the aesthetic possibilities of his Biblical literalist position into the Counter Reformation world view.

Donne's Catholic recusant upbringing is more purely a matter of biography than of literary criticism. As such, it adds fuel to the controversy over Catholic and Jesuit influences on his verse without the hope of ever settling it. Nevertheless, the religious contents of Donne's verse have been regularly discussed in terms of his life. If we pursue this habit now, we find that the internal evidence of his poetry illuminates the history of the man. In terms of Jesuit aesthetics, as these have been discussed here, the evidence of recusant influence on Donne conforms with little mystery and without misleading us to the known facts of his upbringing.

Donne was born and brought up a Roman Catholic, the great great-nephew of the executed Chancellor Thomas More, the nephew of the Jesuits Jasper and Elias Heywood, the elder brother of Henry Donne, who died in jail in London, albeit of natural causes, for hiding a Catholic priest, and he avoided taking a degree at Oxford or Cambridge because of his inability to swear to the Act of Supremacy. To suggest that such a history could have left him intellectually unmarked is unrealistic. No man's life works that way. In addition, in attempting to determine the strength of Catholic influences on him, to argue that there appear to have been only a few Jesuits in England in the crucial early years of his upbringing in 1581 or that in fact there were very many is secondary in the light of the mass of devotional Jesuit recusant literature known to have circulated in England between 1570 and 1650, forming the backbone of British Catholic sensibility.[16]

The corollary to believing in a strong Jesuit and Catholic influence on the young Donne is not that Donne became an Anglican because he was an ambitious courtier. An ambitious man, unless he is stupid, which Donne was not, does not marry the wrong woman, lose all preferment, and land in jail in a courtier's era that was particularly inclined to consider marriage as an institution of personal advancement for both male and female. Donne's "Holy Sonnet" 17 tells us if we did not already know that he and Anne More loved each other desperately. An ambitious man would have also jumped at James I's offer of religious preferment, which Donne for years steadily resisted.[17] He would not have waited in obscurity in relative financial straits for a suitable secular opening in a court in which secular and religious preferment, quite contrary to what we consider them, were politically closely identified.

To question the great depth of Donne's residual Catholic and Jesuit sensibility obscures his honest motives, having nothing to do with ambition, for becoming an Anglican. His reluctance to take Anglican orders and, by inference, because of the King's encouragement a high post in the Established Church, is itself a clue to his motives. We have only to note the surviving comments about the changes of religion by Alabaster and Southwell's father Richard to suspect what went on in his mind.[18]

Donne would appear constrained from accepting James' offer of preferment by his residual Catholic sensibility and by the possibility of adverse judgements by his fellow courtiers. If it is true that Donne feared to bring his new-found church into disrepute, his motives represented an act of unparalleled scrupulosity uncalled for in a courtier's world for whom jockeying for position was the expected way of making a living. This is a much more logical supposition than that he resisted religious preferment to await an even higher secular post.

Intellectually, Donne's reasons for becoming an Anglican appear fairly certainly to have been twofold, and to have a primordial bearing on his poetry. They were also related to each other in the nature of history. First, he became a member of the Established Church because, as he informs us in *Pseudo-Martyr*, he believed that the Church founded by Christ was capable of not only one expression, as claimed by Rome, but of many historical structural expressions simultaneously.[19] So that as an Anglican, Donne had not left the Church of Rome, which in *Pseudo-Martyr* he described as a valid Church. Rather, he was merely participating logically in the Established Church as the manifestation of Christ's temporal church in England at that moment. The "thousand-year sleep" of the church in England described in "Holy Sonnet" 18 (1. 5), where Donne asked which of the Roman, Anglican, and Calvinist churches was correct, refers us back significantly from the date of its writing to the seventh century A.D., roughly to 664, when the Council of Whitby according to the seventeenth-century Anglican position integrated the already existing independent English Church into the Roman organization. Even in his scurrilous anti-Jesuit tract, *Ignatius His Conclave*, Donne did not attack the validity of the Roman faith but only the details of its concepts of religious authority, communities, experience, and liturgy.[20] Whether such a reason for Donne's conversion psychologically and morally satisfied him is unanswerable.

Second, Donne's attitudes to speculation, being fundamentalist, were circumscribed by the prototypes of the Bible. The pursuit of metaphysical truth was bounded by the need of the human spirit to be guided by the Great Puritan warden of truth, Conscience. Conscience alone was sufficient to assure his understanding of the prototypes of God's revealed Word and their relevance to current history. The morality of the present was determined by the essential clarity of Biblical message rather than by the classical Graeco-Roman philosophical speculation identified, because of medieval tradition, with the Church of Rome. Donne's leading authority for his Biblical position in *Essays* was the excommunicated medieval Spanish Catholic monk Raymond de Sebund, who enjoyed considerable attention because of Montaigne's French translation of his work.[21] From his dependence on such an authority, there resulted his attitudes to history as a series of copies of Biblical prototypes. His understanding of history, not necessarily in conflict with the Counter Reformation world view, explains his conscious, intellectual engagement to the Established Church.

Donne's approach to sacred poetry conforms to Jesuit aesthetics when these involved no fictions obscuring the clarity of Biblical prototypes. It is therefore unnecessary to view Donne's practice of Jesuit or Protestant aesthetics, or both, as conflicting with either his residual Catholic sensibility or his later Anglican position. The "Second Anniversary" poem celebrates Elizabeth Drury in life as having been both the Jesuit temporal exemplar of the universal affection of joy and the Protestant historical copy of the prototypal Christ. In death, she was also become the yet other prototype, a "pattern," of both that affection and Christ for the reader living in the contemporary world after her (11. 497, 524).

In the body of Donne's poetry the "La Corona" and "Holy Sonnets," because of their qualities of distance from the world, appear as the poems written more strictly in Ignatian tradition. The prototypes of the Bible which they copy appear regularly at a distance from the reader and the poet as the gateway to experiences of universal emotion. In Donne's poems Protestant typology did not negate the baroque world view, but restricted its manifestations to Biblical types. In other poems like "The Crosse," "Good-friday 1613; Riding Westward" and "On the Authour's last Going into Germany," by contrast to "La Corona" and "Holy Sonnets," the Biblical types remain firmly in the foreground. There, they are prevailing points of comparison rather than of affectuous meditation.

In the light of the religious reaches of Donne's poetry, the meanings of some of his secular poems become clearer than they are in the light of uniquely non-religious explanations. A poem like the "Canonization" presented a pair a deceased lovers as a prototypal "pattern," like Elizabeth Drury of the "Anniversaries." However, they were examples of human rather than divine love in the contemporary world (1. 45). The "well wrought" burial "urn" of Donne's "sonnets" "canonized" his and his mistress' human affection for future lovers in the sense of making it officially written (11. 45, 33, 32). Saintly canonization was for Donne not the Roman declaration of the soul's abiding in heaven but the exemplification of the emotion of lovers in the lines of verse. Profane or secular love poetry imitated the exemplary role of sacred verse by serving as a prototype of human rather than divine love in the contemporary world. In that way, secular poetry conformed to Donne's fundamentalist prototypal view of sacred verse and to the Counter Reformation view of the presence of the affections in the universe and in verse.

Notes

[1]Rosemund Tuve, *Elizabethan and Metaphysical Imagery*, p. 27, and *passim*.

²Spingarn, *Literary Criticism,* pp. 11, 14; Lily B. Campbell, *Divine Poetry and Drama in Sixteenth Century England* (Cambridge, 1959), pp. 211-215; Bernard Weinberg, *History of Literary Criticism in the Italian Renaissance* (Chicago, 1957), I, pp. 32-33.

³*Poetics,* I, "Introduction," p. 5; John Milton, "Introduction," Book II, *The Reason of Church Government,* in *Complete Prose Works,* I, ed. D. M. Wolfe (New Haven, 1953), pp. 817-818; Sidney, *Defence of Poetry,* p. 25; Puttenham, *Arte of English Poesie,* p. 3; Ben Jonson, *Timber, Or Discoveries,* ed. Ralph Walker (Syracuse, 1953), p. 34.

⁴A. Dulles, "Mystery (In Theology)," *New Catholic Encyclopedia,* Vol. X (New York, 1967), p. 151.

⁵Scallon, *The Poetry of Robert Southwell,* pp. 80, 181; Story, "General Introduction," Alabaster, *Sonnets,* pp. xxii-xxiii; xxviii.

⁶Donatus (pp. 3-4) described the individual image of a poem as a "property." In scholastic philosophy the "properties" of a thing made up its essence. Aristotle described a "property" as "a predicate which belongs to the thing alone," in *Topica,* I, 5, 102a, trans. W. A. Picard-Cambridge, in *Works,* Vol. I (Oxford, 1955), ed. W. D. Ross.

⁷Spingarn, *Literary Criticism,* p. 21.

⁸Friedman, Revett, *Selected Poems,* p. xxi.

⁹Spingarn, *Literary Criticism,* p. 11.

¹⁰Ibid., pp. 29, 38.

¹¹Donne, *Ignatius His Conclave,* p. 67.

¹²Aristotle, *Poetics,* I, "Introduction," p. 5.

¹³Spingarn, *Literary Criticism,* p. 39.

¹⁴William Crashaw, *Iesuites Gospell,* pp. 3-5; Donne, *Ignatius His Conclave,* pp. 9, 67.

¹⁵Plato, *Sophist,* No. 265a, p. 1013; *Republic* XXXV (X, 595), p. 317.

¹⁶Bald, *Life,* pp. 39-40; Bossy, *English Catholic Community,* pp. 216-271; Henry Foley, s.j., *Records of the English Province of the Society of Jesus* (1875), vii, Part I; Janelle, *Southwell,* pp. 42, 44.

¹⁷Donne, *Devotions,* p. 3.

¹⁸Story, in the "General Introduction" to Alabaster's *Sonnets,* p. xxi, quotes John Chamberlain's comment: "Yesterday Alabaster the double or treble turncoat preached before the King at Whitehall, where there were many clergiemen that do not greatly applaud him, but say he made a curious fantasticall piece of worke"; Southwell's "Epistle" to his father, Richard, written from prison, arguing fiercely for his reconversion to Catholicism, circulated in numerous editions between 1596 and 1622: N. P. Brown, "Textual Introduction," *Short Rule of Good Life,* pp. xlvi-xlviii.

¹⁹Donne, *Pseudo Martyr* (London, 1610), pp. 83-84.

²⁰Donne, *Ignatius His Conclave,* pp. 11, 43, 61.

²¹Donne, *Essays in Divinity,* p. 7.

CHAPTER SIX

The Epigrammatic Style

1

The symbol of reading in English meditative verse was an image of words, writing, and type describing the reader's experience. With its literary depictions, moreover, the symbol was regularly used to discuss the epigrammatic qualities of the style that provoked meditative experience. While the symbol was a figure to which the reader could relate himself, it described the artistic activity going on in the poem. As it appears in Crashaw's "Sancta Maria Dolorem" and Southwell's "Saint Peters Complaint," for example, the symbol is important because it illustrates the changes that meditative verse wrought on current concepts of length, pungency, and structure of epigram.

Style appeared to meditative poets to have transformed epigram into a new genre of verse. And the symbol's elements of reading seemed to form the natural image to picture that transformation towards meditation.

The symbol of reading suggested a number of specific traits as well as broad characteristics about the epigrammatic style. First, the style encompassed the ends of the Jesuit imitation by words which was founded on principles of active, sentient human life. This imitation placed meditative poets stylistically in the Petrarchan tradition. However, second, because of the infusion of rhetorical values into meditative verse, conforming to the baroque world view, this Petrarchan imitation took a new turning. Its emotional basis came to be thought of as primarily tonal rather than only generally sensory as in the past. This alteration forced the redefinition of much poetic terminology. A single image that allowed the reader to explore the meaning of his experience also permitted him to pursue the meaning of poetry.

Finally, meditative poets concentrated their alterations to epigram by developing two sorts of paradoxes. If poetry appeared to have become epigram, and if epigram was the style of all poetry, poetry's figures were potentially paradoxical in the two ways that literary history appeared now to make possible. Paradox could be drawn both from its subject as in ancient forms of pungent verse and from its images as well, which the indefinite new lengthening of epigram seemed to invite. Of these changes, the symbol of reading summed up the reality imagistically in verse. Crahaw's "On the still surviving markes of our Saviours wounds" shows these changes at work:

> What ever story of their crueltie,
> Or Naile, or Thorne, or Speare have writ in Thee,
> Are in another sence
> Still legible;
> Sweet is the difference:
> Once I did spell
> Every red letter
> A wound of thine,
> Now, (what is better)
> Balsome for mine.

Of the historical influences converging in the epigrammatic style of the above passage, the symbol of reading served to bring the major trends of meditative tradition into relief illustratively. The symbol described the reader's experience of verse while also representing universal emotive forces. But, practically speaking, in terms of the nature of imagery, the symbol also described how the ancient enthymeme of classical rhetoric, Aristotle's metaphor of proportion, and paradox were the chief elements of epigram. The character of these trends is evident in the symbol's various elements about reading, writing, and books. The enthymeme was a foreshortened form of syllogism, the metaphor of proportion compared the relations between things rather than comparing the things themselves, and paradoxes in meditative verse, as the symbol of reading demonstrated, could be drawn from both meaning and image. Enthymeme, metaphor, and paradox, the latter two being discussed in the next chapter, were the meditative poet's practical tools for image-making. Other more theoretical questions like the tonal values of verse, the categories of metaphor, and the ends of verse imagery helped the meditative poet to refine his thoughts about his poems. However, they did not form the basis of the poet's practical attempts at the success of his lines, nor were they central to his concerns about the symbolism of his work.

Undoubtedly, the frequency of the symbol of reading in meditative verse in England from Southwell to Revett was due to several wide currents in the history of ideas. These included the popular Protestant "theology of the word," the authority of the last Books of Augustine's *Confessions* for the scroll-like character of creation, the rhetorical asumptions behind the astronomical terminology describing the baroque universe, and finally the current oratorical concepts of poetic imagery. To talk of poetry in images of language was the logical step for poets for whom verse was materially analogous to creation. There were book and scroll symbols in the works of other poets too. One thinks of Vaughan and Traherne. But the recurrence of the symbol of reading in meditative verse was also marked by the three characteristics of enthymeme, metaphor of proportion, and paradox specific to its meditative tradition.

2

The force of the enthymemic image, the first of the characteristics of meditative verse style, is most apparent in contrast with the syllogistic, traditional, and established form of epigram of the times. However epigrammatic, the enthymemic figure was not constructed on the three premises of the Aristotelian syllogism of classical epigram. Indeed, although Renaissance Jesuits were aware of the enthymemic figure's origin, they employed it conscious of and emphasizing its profound differences from syllogism. Accordingly, conforming to the classical tradition of enthymeme, in his imagery Crashaw presupposed the first of the three premises and the truth of the syllogism.

The enthymemic figure had been recommended by Aristotle in *Rhetoric* for the orator's use in convincing his hearer.[1] Aristotle had written that, contrary to the logician, the orator "presumed" rather than set out to prove "the truth" of his statements. With its sharp qualities of surprise, the figure made by using only the second and third premises rather than the whole syllogism was more suited to that end. With this rhetorical method the Ignatian tradition both in England and on the Continent fulfilled the sylistic ends of its emotive aspirations.

The aim of the classical oration to persuade passed into the imagery of meditative verse through the enthymeme by which persuasion had been supposed to take place. At the same time the immediacy of the emotion that Aristotle had attributed to the oration also passed into poetry. The Jesuit approach to verse identified the affections of poetry and oratory as of the same kind. It eliminated Aristotle's distinction between the emotion of the hearer for the realities described in the oration, and the emotion of the reader of verse for imitation as imitation. For Aristotle, a spectator might feel pity for a person in a tragedy whom he would have despised in real life, or disdain for a character in a comedy he would have otherwise loved on the street. No such distinction between a purely aesthetic emotion and a feeling for a real thing was possible for someone who composed or heard an oration. Aristotle said that the orator made his subject immediately "pitiable or terrible," whereas the poet only made it "appear" to be "as such."[2]

By relying on the enthymeme for the structure of imagery, the Jesuit approach to verse made impossible the separate affection in the experience of poetry. The traditional distinction between poetry and oratory on the grounds of imitation and emotion broke down. At first in *Ars Poetica* Donatus found it difficult to associate the purely aesthetic emotion that Aristotle attributed to poetic imitation as imitation with the new baroque poetry; consequently, he entertained rejecting his Greek Master's definitions of poetic tragedy and comedy springing from such purely mimetic emotion. Eventually, he accepted these definitions by eliminating their reference to plot on which Aristotle rested his case for the separate aesthetic emotion. Donatus replaced plot with the immediate emotive realities of the baroque world in the substance of verse (pp. 208, 311). In this way, the values of classical rhetoric came to alter the ideals of the *dolce stile nuovo* of Petrarchan tradition.

As the symbol of reading grew more popular for depicting the role of emotion in verse, the enthymeme seemed to explain the argumentative drift of a poet's imagery. To the continental Donatus, writing theoretically, enthymeme distinguished the contemporary meditative writer of epigrams from Scaliger, the great contemporary defender of pungent verse *(Ars Poetica,* pp. 309-310). It seemed to Donatus that Scaliger, like the later English epigrammatist Quarles in the seventeenth century, wrote his epigrams in completed syllogisms layered with images.

An epigram by Quarles on "The formall Christian" in *Divine Fancies* of 1636, a second "Bind fragrant *Rose-buds"* translated by Arwaker in his English version of the Jesuit Hugo's *Pia Desideria,* and another epigram by Quarles, "Lord, scourge my Asse" in *Emblemes* of 1634, dramatize the contrasting new road charted by the enthymeme in meditative verse. "The formall Christian" and "Lord, scourge my Asse" were developed on the three premises of the syllogism and were faithful to the structure of pungent epigram of classical Roman tradition. They also fulfilled the Protestant aim that Quarles described for epigram in "To the Reader" of his *Emblemes.* That aim had been for epigram to be "but a silent Parable" making up "Types" that "figured" an "allusion to our blessed Savior."[3] Interestingly, Arwaker's translation of Hugo's poem "Bind fragrant *Rose-buds"* did not fulfill this aim.

Quarles' original epigrams were didactic and exemplary and were characterized by their adaptation of Christian themes to Martial's kind of verse. Their themes elaborated upon the exemplary virtues of Christian life according to the standards of syllogistic logic. In the opening line of Quarles' first epigram, "the formall Christian's like a *Water-mill,"* one thing (the Christian) was classically predicated of another (the Water-mill) in the Aristotelian sense of predication as the act of attributing place to something among the ten metaphysical categories.[4] In the second line, representing the middle premise of a syllogism, "Until the *Flood-gate's* open, he lies still," yet a third thing ("the Flood-gate") was predicated of the second (the "still" wheel). In the third premise of the completed syllogism of the epigram, the first thing was finally predicated of the third ("his wheeles shall find the streame"). Such a syllogistic structure, appearing again in Quarles' "Lord, scourge," was absent in Arwaker's literal translation of Hugo's poem. There, in lines like "Bind fragrant *Rose-buds* to my temples first, / Then with *cool apples* quench my *fiery thirst*" (11. 21-22), written in imitation of Canticle 2.5, the enthymeme prevailed. Hugo's Jesuit technique was powerful enough to survive his Protestant editor's translation.

The same enthymemic technique as in Hugo was most evident in Crashaw's verse in England because of the converging influences of literary history. Unlike other English poets, Crashaw's literary career spanned from its beginning to end the crest of the meditative movement. The enthymemic technique prevailed consistently from his earliest epigrams like "And he answered them nothing" which appeared in an original Latin version in *Epigrammatum Sacrorum Liber* in his undergraduate Pembroke College days, to a very brief epigram like "Upon the Sepulchre of Our Lord" in *Steps to the Temple* of 1646 *(Poems,* pp. 25, 91, 86). The latter epigram, among Crashaw's shortest, reads *in toto,* "Here where our Lord laid his Head, / Now the grave lies buried." The epigram lacked the first premise of the syllogism that would have predicated the connection between Christ and his grave in the rock. The same premise was missing in the figures of the first slightly longer epigram in queston "And he answered them nothing," which deals with the mystery of creation. This epigram is constructed of three enthymemes each two lines long:

> O Mighty *Nothing!* unto thee,
> *Nothing,* we owe all things that bee.
> God spake once when hee all things made,
> Hee sav'd all when hee *Nothing* said.
> The world was made of *Nothing* then;
> 'Tis made by *Nothyng* now againe.

Each enthymeme states the same point pungently rather than proves it wittily. In the first couplet, the predication of the Christian God to a mystical omnipresent "Nothing" which would have formed the first premise of a syllogism is missing. Yet, on that absent predication rested the pungent attribution of "all things" to "Nothing" in the second line.

In Heywood's and Southwell's lines, which were written earlier than Crashaw's, the enthymeme was less pervasive for obvious historical reasons. Their literary movement had yet to mature. The enthymeme was also less apparent in Heywood's and Southwell's poems than in Alabaster's sonnets, which occupy a medial position in time in the history of meditative verse. However, in Heywood's later work the break into what may be largely understood as seventeenth-century enthymemic positions of imagery in meditative poetry was already accomplished. That break in his literary development appears in the short period of nine years which separates his early contributions like "Easter Day" in the first edition of *The Paradise of Dainty Devices*

(1576) from his later contributions such as "The Complaint of a sorrowfull Soule" and "Alluding his state to the prodigall child" in the third and last edition of *Paradise* (1585). Undoubtedly, Heywood's verse was constrained by the same miscellany traditions that inhibited Southwell and that checked the progress of the poetry of both into the forward reaches of Alabaster's writings. But in the last sixteenth-century edition of *Paradise,* appearing a brief four years after his spell as his order's mission leader in England, Heywood's verse showed the wider changes to epigram being born.

> O Sovereign salve of sinne, who does my soule behold,
> That seeks her selfe from tangling faultes, by striving to unfold,
> What plea shall I put in, when thou doest Summons send:
> To iudge the people of the earth to give the world an end,
> When every deede and worde, yea every secret thought,
> In open vewe of all the world, shall unto light be brought.
>
> (11. 1-6)

In such an early manifestation of English Ignatian verse as "Complaint," Heywood's three opening enthymemes left their first syllogistic premises unrevealed. Heywood never identified the "salve of sinne" of the opening line of his first stanza: "O Soveraigne salve of sinne, who doest my soule behold, / That seekes her selfe from tangling faultes, by striving to unfold" (11. 1-2). Nor did he reveal the "plea" that the soul should "put in" on doomsday in the third line, nor the "deed and worde" requiring his atonement in the fifth line. Each couplet of the opening six lines of his poem was conceived of as rhetorically expressive rather than as a philosophical explanation of human existence.

The development of the enthymemic tradition suggested by "Complaint" is brought into relief by the closing couplets of Heywood's earlier poem "Easter day." "Easter day" lacked the later poem's suggestive emotive level of meaning. Although it shared with "Complaint" the doggerel iambic meter of the Elizabethan miscellanies, it too introduced paradox early into its lines. But it ended, "Come thou my childe and dwell with me, / God Graunt us all, to see that glorious day," with the conceptual forthrightness of its opening, "All mortall men this day reioyce, / In Christ that you redeemed had" (11. 31-32, 1-2). By contrast, "Complaint" concluded with the reader still uninformed about the poem's logical issues like the poet's sin, plea, and salvation.

In the enthymemic fashion of such epigrammatic verse, the meditative poet adapted to his reader the aim of the classical orator to convince his hearer spontaneously. That he should support this aim conformed to the movement in his baroque world view away from the syllogistic presuppositions of scholastic logic. This did not mean that non-Catholic epigrammatists like Quarles and other Catholic epigrammatists who continued to follow the syllogistic tradition wrote mere uninspired imitations of their ancient classical models. Notably Donatus and yet another important Jesuit commentator, Matthew Rader (b. Innichen, 1561; d. Munich, 1634), who may be described as forward-looking for their time, were conscious that in matters of epigram they contradicted the strongly syllogistic views of contemporary conservative members of their order like Pontanus and Possevine.[5] But they did not describe the old epigram as aesthetically irrelevant, particularly Rader who was a leading Renaissance translator of Martial and who discussed epigram at length. In the work of those other epigrammatists for whom commentators like Pontanus and Possevine spoke, traditions of Renaissance discourse prevailed. Lewalski has discussed the role of discourse in other forms of rhetorical and yet meditative poetry, and they were not attacked as such by the baroque Jesuits who had taken another turning.[6] Except for the historical relevance of pointing out the difference here, these original uses of discourse belong to other studies like Webber's *The Eloquent "I"*.[7] The significant aspect of the enthymeme in Ignatian practices illuminating meditative poetry is that it was not discursive. Meditative verse made use of the expressive rather than of the explicative uses of rhetoric to which Renaissance discourse, because of its desire to show reason, was attached.

The differences between the explicative and expressive reaches of Renaissance rhetoric as manifested in the use of the enthymeme become obvious when we consider Donne's verse. Donne's religious sonnets, whether "La Corona" or "Holy Sonnets," his later sacred poems like "The Crosse," and such secular poems as "The Funerall" argued in vastly dissimilar ways. The differences demonstrated the tradition of rhetoric in the later Renaissance working in three separate fashions or ways. For example, in the religious sonnets discussed as Ignatian in Chapter V, that way was enthymeme, and it did not contradict the traditional epigrammatic quality of Donne's other poems. By contrast, in poems like "The Crosse" and "The Funerall," with due allowances for strong differences in the content of paradox, the epigram was pungent in the traditional ancient Roman sense of a poem suspending full meaning and aesthetic effect until its closing image. However, a secular poem like "The Funerall" respected the traditional epigram's free range of paradox while a religious poem like "The Crosse," influenced by fundamentalist typology, did not. The immediacy of Renaissance rhetoric bequeathed to Donne many forms of expression. In the differences between these forms the variety of his art as a poet, like his genius, found its expression.

In the history of English epigram, "The Funerall," typical of Donne's secular verse, was remarkable for preserving the paradox and pungent ending characteristic of ancient Roman epigram. The question of paradox related to the epigrammatic style belongs more aptly to the next chapter. For the moment, however, the conventional epigrammatic paradox, springing only from knowledgeable play on words, contrasts revealingly with the enthymemic character of Donne's religious sonnets. "The Funerall" fulfilled Gardner's judgment that Donne's art consisted in some measure in lengthening conventional epigram without losing its point.[8] Long in contrast to the original conception of epigram, the poem nevertheless concluded with the snap effect by which syllogism became witty verse. With its play first on the wreath of hair as the symbol of the "outward Soule," next as the product of a "better braine," and finally as the unexpected image of his funereal revenge, the secular poem was much more faithful to the free range of paradox of the traditional epigram.

Although "The Crosse" like "The Funerall" maintained the traditional single pungent closing of Roman epigram, the method of sustaining it was radically unconventional. "The Crosse" strongly bore signs of Donne's desire to pursue in the lines of poetry the discovery in nature of copies (the "Mast and yard," the "Globes frame," and others) of a Biblical type (the cross, ll. 19-23). A poem like "The Crosse" sought to keep the religious models of poetry clear in the fabric of verse as well as to imitate the traditional epigram. Fundamentalist typology in such verse constrained poetic antithesis. It confined the figures of Donne's central paradox to Biblical types and to their copies in the universe.

> Who can blot out the Crosse, which th' instrument
> Of God, dew'd on mee in the Sacrament?
> Who can deny mee power, and liberty
> To stretch mine armes, and mine owne Crosse to be?
> Swimme, and at every stroake, thou art thy Crosse;
> The Mast and yard make one, where seas do tosse;
> Looke downe, thou spiest out Crosses in small things;
> Looke up, thou seest birds rais'd on crossed wings;
> All the Globes frame, and spheares, is nothing else
> But the Meridians crossing Parallels.
> Materiall Crosses then, good physicke bee,
> But yet spirituall have chiefe dignity.
>
> *("The Crosse," ll. 15-26)*

In the first part of the central paradox of "The Crosse" Donne drew wit typical of ancient epigram from antithesis and at the same time he sought "material" crosses. Then, in the second part, he pursued "spiritual" crosses. Finally, the poem's pungent ending fused material and spiritual crosses unexpectedly into an exemplar of the religious life: "Then, doth the Crosse of Christ worke fruitfully / Within our hearts, when wee love harmlessely / That Crosses pictures" (ll. 25, 26, 61-63). The development of the extended paradox in "The Crosse" suggests the imposition of one typological layer of meaning upon another rather than the unbounded secular play of "The Funerall."

In Donne's religious sonnets, by contrast to his secular verse, the literalist representation of Biblical type was as equally striking as in his later sacred poetry. In this way, Biblical type demonstrated the consistency of the influence of theology on his sacred poems. In not one of his religious sonnets does a Biblical truth, character, or event appear decorated by symbol. However, the consistency of Donne's theology in his verse was not without its practical variants. The enthymemic character of the sonnets' imagery altered his respect for the historical representation of Biblical type quite strongly from that in "The Crosse." A style in which every image aspired to the qualities of enthymeme also aimed at a pungent effect in every one of those images. This pungent effect in every image made the one extended paradox of traditional epigram found in "The Crosse" impossible. Such a style prohibited the fusion of the typological layers of didactic Biblical verse in the extended paradox of traditional epigram. Without rejecting the literalist preservation of Biblical types, Donne's religious sonnets recreated type part by part in a variety of paradoxes. The sonnets thus fulfilled the stylistic standard of Jesuit meditative verse without forcing the poet to compromise his Anglican commitments.

> At the round earths imagin'd corners, blow
> Your trumpets, Angells, and arise, arise
> From death, you numberless infinities
> Of soules, and to your scattred bodies goe,
> All whom the flood did, and fire shall o'erthrow,
> All whom warre, dearth, age, agues, tyrannies,
> Despaire, law, chance, hath slaine, and you whose eyes,
> Shall behold God, and never tast deaths woe.
>
> *("Holy Sonnet"* VIII, ll. 1-8)

Geared to the meditative visions of *Exercises,* the enthymeme in Donne's religious sonnets depicted Biblical prototypes historically without the argumentation of the later sacred poetry. Without the need of fusing didactically Biblical type and copy in epigram as in "The Crosse," the imagery of the religious sonnets portrayed rather than explicated the nature of those types. This is particularly true of "La Corona" sonnets which, being meditations on Christian Mysteries, showed their Biblical types directly. It is less true of the "Holy Sonnets," which were meditations ostensibly on the self with less easily identified scriptural types.

However, the role of the enthymeme in "Holy Sonnets" did not alter from that in "La Corona." In both sets of poems every image and hence every enthymeme aspired after an antithetical effect proper to itself, different from that of the extended paradox of ancient epigram. "Holy Sonnet" 5 "I am a little world made cunningly," mixed images of the cleverness of divine creation and of darkness, and "Holy Sonnet" 6 "This is my playes last scene," confused images of drama, race, pilgrimages, and span. This mixture of images did not occur simply for the sake of some haphazard aesthetic profusion absent merely by chance from "The Crosse" and "A Hymne to Christ, at the Authors last going into Germany." Rather, Donne was attempting in the sonnets to create an enthymemic effect unnecessary to the other poems; he was organizing a series of compressed images into a provocative general picture of Christian truth emotionally significant to all men.

"Holy Sonnet" 5 suppressed the first premise of the syllogism underlying its opening four lines. This premise would state generally that the fall of creation sharpened Donne's consciousness of his own weak condition. The end of the poem's first quatrain reads that "blacke sinne hath betraid to endlesse night / My worlds both parts" (11. 3-4), and it leads us on little reflection to grasp the absence of that first premise. The poem's opening enthymeme fulfilled its end of provoking a picture of Donne's condition as racially common without his ever having stated its presuppositions.

In the meditative fashion of repeating epigramatic effects, the picture of Donne's condition served as the basis for the imagery of the poem's next couplet. Without its natural predilection for a very quick death, a predilection wholly unstated, the "cunningly" made personal "little world" of the first couplet would not tremble at the fateful prospect of death presaged in the second couplet. The feeling for the general fragility of the "little world" in which Donne imagined himself was to be an integral part of the reader's emotion without even being mentioned. Similarly, the profusion of time and space images in the octet of "Holy Sonnet" 6 depicted the terrifying proposition that the "last mile" of life is heaven-appointed. However, it masked the more pleasing prospect that human life was created at all only in order to end, and thence to enter into a better state. We act, we go on pilgrimages, we run, and we cross bridges to achieve the same vision, and all fourteen lines of the poem depict that vision rather than show us pilgrimages, running, and bridges.

3

The rhetorical values of persuasion that Donne's religious sonnets reveal were originally oral as the tradition of oratory understood them. That they should have easily become represented by the symbol of reading in meditative verse sprang from the fact that oratory, like reading, dealt with language. The emotive values of one discipline of language were simply fused into the symbolic values of another because of the ready association to be made between them. The use of typology as a philosophical instrument supported that fusion. The passage of the values of spoken rhetoric into the fabric of the silent meditative verse of Crashaw and of other English poets, through the figure of the enthymeme by which such values had been originally sustained in oratory, was natural. It followed easily on the already achieved presence of those values in baroque creation.

Thus, Crashaw's extended symbol of reading in "On the still surviving markes of our Saviours wounds" was also a typological analysis of the everyday seventeenth-century universe as he perceived it. The symbol of reading in the poem, with its emphasis on enthymeme, obeyed the existential prescriptions of the typological universe. The symbol imaged Christ's passion and was eternally emotive at one level of meaning and historically limited to Crashaw's figure at the other. Crashaw's theme was truly the sweetness to him of the similarity between the emotion pictured in a Biblical past and the feeling provoked by the present experiences of the seventeenth century. He was interested in the creative uses of typology for the expression of this sweetness which enthymeme made possible. Crashaw learned, he says, to "spell / Every red letter" in the New Testament account of Christ's passion as "A wound"; he intended to transmit the meaning of the Bible's typic "letters" into the emotive enthymemes of contemporary poetry. Accordingly, the concluding figure of the poem reads "Now, (what is better) / Balsome for mine," revealing the vitality of Biblical types for his verse experience.

The symbol of reading in "On the still surviving markes," fusing the values of a new world view with those of a number of ancient disciplines, was not poetic in our modern sense. Generally, we conceive of the poetic as something imaginatively figurative applied for vividness to the real, without the supporting force of universal myths. For us, the effect may or may not be pleasurable and it is most often deepening. The poetic is also to us practically speaking the arbitrary attribution of new meaning to old language. Such was not the case in "On the still surviving markes." There, the "poetic" was metaphoric according to the realities of the contemporary world. For Crashaw, the "poetic" was meant to be understood by experience. In the context of worldly experience, the symbol of reading was an instrument intended to analyze the poet's life. The written poem was a synthesis of experience described most vividly in its analytic symbol of reading.

Crashaw's reading symbol in "On the still surviving markes" recreated therefore the levels of experience of the baroque world by which such analyses and syntheses of life were achieved. The poem declared that "Or Naile, or Thorne, or Speare have writ" in Christ the degrading "story of their crueltie" at the Crucifixion (11. 1-2). However, their significance hardly rested on their allegorical record of past divine passion. With their revelation of the "still legible" meaning of the Biblical type "in another sence" in the contemporary world, the following two lines showed that going up the ladder to the next typological level of meaning in both verse and creation this passion continued to exist (11. 4, 3). In such a synthesis of the universe and experience in the first ten lines of "On the still surviving markes," Crashaw constructed an enthymeme. Through the use of enthymemes, the typological universe once recreated in verse, provoked meditation.

The enthymemes describing the experience of reading in Crashaw's epigram were repeatedly frustrated of their presuppositions. From the point of view of narrative continuity, the reader has the impression of beginning to read "On the still surviving markes" three times, once for each of its enthymemes. Our modern concept of the symbol as a figure standing cogently in the place of something else is also confounded. As the first premise of syllogism was dropped, we are never told what is the other "sence" in which the Biblical "story" of Christ's passion was repeated in the seventeenth century. Yet, as the classical orator's use of the enthymeme spread its roots in meditative verse, that unmentioned "sence" was the experience of meditation.

This meditative experience is present in the next four lines (5-8) of Crashaw's epigram as well. Characteristically, Crashaw developed a second enthymeme based on the symbol of reading in order to sustain the poem's original imagistic momentum. As these lines continued to truncate the epigram's logical flow to support emotive ends, the symbol of reading took a turning into questions of "spelling" and of "letters." The new enthymeme leaves unrevealed its underlying logical presuppositions about the relationship between the old Biblical type and its new contemporary copy, but its symbol nevertheless retains its rhetorical power of convincing. "Sweet is the difference" between the two "senses" of the written nails and thorns in Christ's passion and in present meditation, Crashaw wrote, after having only just told his readers in the first enthymeme that they were grandly similar.

In other poems like the trilogy to Saint Teresa, Crashaw extended the authoritative basis of his types to include contemporary religious writings. As a result of this, the ideas developed in his symbol of reading touched on concepts of history. Rather than the Bible alone as in "And he answered them nothing," current works like Teresa's autobiography *Vida* provided new types to judge seventeenth-century patterns of experience.[9] The trilogy's first poem "The Hymne," showing the symbol of reading fluctuating into many more variations than in Alabaster or Southwell, is an example. A new contemporary source of written types like Teresa's *Vida* extended automatically the basis of the moral authority of poetry. As the typological method appeared to become a primordial habit of mind, works of personal inspiration took on the validity of divinely revealed writings to justify the writing of religious verse.

Thus haue I back again to thy bright name
(Fair floud of holy fires!) transfus'd the flame
I took from reading thee, tis to thy wrong
I know, that in my weak & worthlesse song
Thou here art sett to shine where thy full day
Scarse dawnes. O pardon if I dare to say
Thine own dear bookes are guilty. For from thence
I learn't to know that loue is eloquence.
That hopefull maxime gaue me hart to try
If, what to other tongues is tun'd so high,
Thy praise might not speak English too; forbid
(By all thy mysteryes that here ly hidde)
Forbid it, mighty Loue! let no fond Hate
Of names & wordes, so farr praeiudicate.

("Apologie," ll. 1-14)

Crashaw's movement away from the exclusive authority of Biblical type in no way compromised his adherence to the baroque world view. The significance of the symbol of reading and of the enthymeme in Crashaw's verse based on that world view did not alter. Crashaw's theological conceptions of type and copy might differ from our Biblical idea of them which is essentially descended from the Reformers. We think of type and copy as strictly Biblical appurtenances, from which point of view we are probably closer to Donne than to Crashaw. But in the currents of Biblical and historical thought of the meditative tradition inspired by the Counter Reformation, type and copy were not so scripturally restricted.

As a fundamental intellectual discipline in an English poet like Crashaw, long before as well as after his conversion to Roman Catholicism, the typological method was wider in use than would be consonant simply with Biblical interests. This discipline, deriving its force from having subsumed the role of logic for the study of creation, had also become a creative tool for writing poetry. The symbol of reading reflected this new role of typology as a general discipline. Because of its natural affinity to creation, the reading symbol was used by meditative poets to describe verse as a mirror of the universe as well as of the Bible. Moreover, the frequency of the symbol's usage grew greater with time. Although the symbol did not appear in Heywood's verse, it rapidly became the dominant extended image in the English meditative verse that immediately followed. As such, the symbol represented the historical aspirations of this verse related to typology.

That eyes with errours may just measure keepe:
Most teares I wish that have most cause to weepe.

(ll. 31-42)

At about the same time that Southwell completed "Saint Peters Complaint" in the mid-fifteen-nineties, a brief nine years after Heywood's introduction of Ignatian meditation into English verse, the surfacing of the poet in the symbol of reading appeared already to have become a general practice. This method of the poet's appearance recurred in Alabaster's "New Jerusalem" Sonnet 43 "Thrice happy souls and spirits unbodied" roughly at the moment that "Saint Peters Complaint" was printed. Undoubtedly supported by the regular practice of the original ascetic exercise by all of its early practitioners, Heywood, Southwell, and Alabaster, the new habit of verse had quickly become a refined tradition. The poet like Alabaster in Sonnet 43 now disregarded the established rules of genre and grammar for those of symbol and aesthetics that supported the emergence of his figure in meditative topics.

The book imagery of the octet of Alabaster's sonnet developed three relative clauses. All of these were related to his role as a poet rather than to genre or grammar. The clauses qualified the simple subject of the unbodied "Thrice happy souls and spirits" of the first line, and they touched profoundly on the poet's life without ever becoming a grammatical sentence. The octet also concluded its description of the poet's role without developing the problematical statement characteristic of the first part of a sonnet. The rules of both grammar and sonnet genre were suffused into the aesthetic effect of the symbol of reading. More important than these rules was the meditation worked into the octet's relative clauses about books. The reference to the "three-leaved bible" and its "unfolded page" was followed by the picture of love being "read" as mystery. It was also followed by the second picture of the poet having "learned" love (ll. 3, 4, 6, 8). As variations on the same symbol, these images of reading and learning were the octet's sole element of unity. Symbol, rather than sense, became structure. The favorite image of the experience of reading appeared to the poet as a literal approximation of his baroque world and united that world's emotive meanings in his person. As the poem's octet cedes its place to the sestet, the symbol continues to play its unifying role and to supersede the rules of grammar:

Thrice happy souls and spirits unbodied,
Who in the school of heaven do always see
The three-leaved bible of one Trinity,
In whose unfolded page are to be read
The incomprehended secrets of the Godhead,

Who only read by love that mystery
And what you read is love's infinity,
Who learn by love, and love is what is learned.
O happy school whose master is the book,
Which book is only text, which text unwrit
Doth read itself, and they that on it look
Do read by being read, nor do they flit
From word to word: for all is but one letter,
Which still is learnt, but never learnt the better.

In Revett's "Lasarus *raised by our Saviour*" in the mid-seventeenth century, the symbol of reading played a less formative but not different role than in Alabaster's sonnet many years earlier. The emotional links between language, the world, and sensation had become less secure as the currents of the seventeenth century's literary preoccupations diluted the society's concept of the baroque universe. But some sixty years after the writing of Alabaster's sonnet No. 43, the symbol continued to allow the consideration of existential issues typologically. It had lost none of its power to serve the ends of long epigrammatic poems sustained by enthymemes.

That "Lasarus *raised*" should close with the reading symbol denoted the image's remaining force to describe the vestigial experiences of the baroque world. The occurrence of the reading symbol in Revett's poem continued the scattered reach for the baroque heights at which his verse as a whole no longer aimed. In the best tradition of that symbol, Revett's concluding image in "Lasarus *raised*" brought into its reaches the world, the poet, and verse. Because of its literary character, the metaphoric universe at the end of the poem appeared as the vanquisher of inferior death. Death was a mere imitation of a prototype in the eternal typological universe, and this prototype, as though fixed forever from the beginning of time, was the experience of poetry:

Death! alas where is thy *sting?*
Thy mortall once *invenoming?*
Thy *weakness see*
Puling Anatomy.
That o're this vanquisht corps didst rowl
And *breath'dst* upon
It thy *short fetcht corruption?*
Till thy dull weight squeez'd out the vexed soul?
Now that *turneth* thee *beneath,*
With a new *recruit* of *breath*
And *purges* out thy noysome *Aires*
By *smells* with which the soul from *Heaven* repairs;
Leaving the *Original* to see

For the English meditative poet, the new role of typology and hence of poetry came to be supported by the apparent new role of history. History had not ceased to produce types with the close of the Apostolic Age and with the last, Apocalyptic book of the New Testament. It continued to produce new ones like *Vida* conforming to the emotive spiritual certainties of the baroque world. The age of types, like the age of miracles, was not over. New experiences, such as those provoked by meditative verse, were always being born to copy new types generated by contemporary history.

In a time that supposed modern history to be everything that followed the Apostolic Age, the symbol of reading made cogent sense of typology, enthymeme, the world, and poetry all at once. In poems like the Teresan and Alexis trilogies, which are essentially unintelligible outside a typic approach to history, the symbol made whole periods of time manageable in imagery. With its variations on images of studying, letters of the alphabet, literary transcriptions, epistles, words and reading, the symbol enabled Crashaw to describe current events in poetry unrestricted by the defined limits of the Apostolic past.

Profoundly understood in rhetorical terms, historical items like religious writings came to be imaged by the symbol of reading. From its capacity to represent contemporary historical types, the symbol gained much of its strength. As Crashaw used it for example in "The Hymne," the symbol was not so much metaphoric as we understand metaphor. Instead, it possessed the connotative associations of simile that kept its historical basis clear. It bore a close likeness of being with the world rather than representing it in separate pictures. Because it tended to represent history directly to the seventeenth-century reader, the symbol of reading served to bring the new typic qualities of the contemporary world into relief. It appeared to enshrine the moral role of religious writings. Crashaw wrote in the "Hymne:"

> Those rare Workes where thou shalt leave writt,
> Love's noble history, with witt
> Taught thee by none but him, while here
> They feed our soules, shall cloth Thine there.
> Each heavnly word by whose hid flame
> Our hard Hearts shall strike fire, the same
> Shall flourish on thy browes. & be
> Both fire to us & flame to thee.
>
> (11. 155-162)

From this wide historical basis of the symbol of reading, the ancient Biblical type as well as history itself gained in poetic power. Liberated from the fixed character of the past by the new view of current history, Biblical type lost its inhibiting corrective appearance. It needed no longer to be only didactic. As the values of history were associated with

Scripture, a Biblical type like Christ's "Nailes" that "writ swords in" Mary's heart in Crashaw's "Sancta Maria Dolorem" (1. 7) became a living standard for poetic inspiration. This standard was not only a guide-line but also an experience that poetry was to create:

> O teach those wounds to bleed
> In me; me, so to read
> This book of loves, thus writ
> In lines of death, my life may coppy it
> With loyall cares
>
> (VI, 11. 51-55)

By supporting the aims of meditative poetry, the symbol of reading came to uphold Biblical as well as historical types for poetic composition.

4

The symbol of reading made periods of time figuratively manageable in the verse of other poets besides Crashaw too and was notable regularly for one thing. The symbol always served to situate these poets and hence the seventeenth-century readers in the general context of their themes. In the previous chapter we noted how the figure of the poet invariably surfaced in the English poetry that we are calling meditative verse. The symbol of reading described the nature of this surfacing consistently as one related to the themes of baroque typology. In "Saint Peters Complaint" Southwell identified his poem with its Biblical type, Jeremy's *Lamentations*. But its development beyond the limits of a mere unfelt picture of Jeremy's plaint led the poet to situate the nature of his present emotion in place and time: "My threnes an endlesse Alphabet do find, / Beyond the panges which Jeremy doth paint" (11. 39-40). In an epic invocation to the Muse of poetry in which the Muse became universal emotion earlier in the same poem, the symbol also appeared as an historical description of Southwell's literary work: "Be you O sharpest greeves, that ever wrung, / Texte to my thoughtes, Theame to my playning tung" (11. 35-36).

> Ambitious heades dreame you of fortunes pride:
> Fill volumes with your forged Goddesse praise.
> You fancies drudges, plungd in follies tide:
> Devote your fabling wits to lovers layes:
> Be you O sharpest greeves, that ever wrung,
> Texte to my thoughtes, Theame to my playning tung.

> Sad subject of my sinne hath stoard my mind
> With everlasting matter of complaint:
> My threnes an endlesse Alphabet do find,
> Beyond the panges which *Jeremy* doth paint.

The *coppie* it left with *Mortalitie,*
And with an *ante-dated* bliss comes on
To this *Preludious* resurrection.

In such a symbol Revett, finding the answers to life's mysteries, played the swan song of the literary sensibility of Ignatian tradition. In the "Transcrib'd" and "Victorious Sign" of the "Prime" section of Crashaw's "Office of the Holy Crosse" (11. 18, 20), this sensibility had received its firmest expression only a decade earlier. Revett also used the literary symbol in which the sensibility of Ignatian tradition had best expressed itself in English to sound the passing of that very sensibility.

5

Jesuit commentators in the meditative school conceived of the verse discussed in the symbol of reading as having become epigrammatic in a fortunate contemporary moment. That moment saw baroque poetry evolve to play its part in the cause of literary history. It appeared that the coming of the meditative experience of the Counter Reformation universe was a happy historical event to which the development of epigram had worked by Divine Providence for thousands of years. The epigram had supposedly originated in Antiquity as an inscription on the base of a statue; then supposedly it had developed into a slightly longer "inscription of an inscription" as lines were added to it to substitute for the statue from which it was eventually removed; and finally, as a short poem it appeared to have grown free of its ascriptive origins completely by becoming short independent verse of the Roman kind so admired by Martial's Jesuit editor, Raderus (pp. 9-10; Donatus, pp. 308-309).

As a short poem, liberated from even the revived statuary role that a sixteenth-century Scotsman like George Buchanan continued to ascribe to it, the epigram had reputedly started developing into a long poem somewhere mythically (though Jesuit commentators did not use that term) just before Martial's time.[10] Characterized initially by the three qualities of brevity *(brevitas)*, grace *(suavitas)*, and pungency *(argutia)*, epigram had, it appeared, in early stages, relinquished brevity (Raderus, pp. 10-12; Donatus, p. 310). Next, it gradually shed its quality of grace that, according to Hamilton and Hudson, strongly characterized one whole lyric branch of epigram, that of classical Greece, which was to be clearly distinguished from the Roman variety epitomized by Martial's work.[11] To the Jesuit commentators, ruggedness characteristic of Martial's verse appeared to have been the epigram's predestined historical development. They contended that gradually over the centuries, with the increase in the number of civilized men and with the spread of new forms of verse that this growth supposedly provoked, it was evident that grace was an inadequate term to describe epigram because it was applicable to all kinds of poems. Like brevity, the Jesuits argued, grace had been a valid formal rule for epigram only when once in a half-civilized world it had occupied the field of poetry unchallenged by the presence of other genres (Donatus, p. 312).

Finally, in that fortunate moment in the convergence of epigram and baroque world view covering the end of the sixteenth century and the first part of the seventeenth century, the genre had, it appeared, become noteworthy solely for the one quality of pungency. In the arguments of Raderus and Donatus, pungency was the epigram's only remaining characteristic. In his preface to his translation of Martial, Raderus wrote that in his day an "infinite number" of epigrams seemed to be composed "according to no fixed rule" except pungency (pp. 9, 12). Because of this aesthetic dominance of pungency, epigram came to describe the desired effect of all religious verse written in the emotive universe. The poet, Donatus said, made "a certain new construction in the style of things, actually appearing in the form of words," and in the context of his argument pungency came to speak for the rhetorical silence of language (p. 218).

Once separated from the other qualities of brevity and suavity, pungency characterized a genre of poetry called epigram that no longer had fixed shape. Pungency had always described an aesthetic effect and continued to do so. However, the Jesuit commentators concluded that the epigram, marked now solely by pungency, had become the genus of all verse, had ceased to be a mere genre, and no longer had to be written in the simple monostich of its original short, sharp form. It could, Raderus wrote, be written in "the lengthy distich, tetrastich, and even the decastich," for which Martial's long epigrams seemed to have been the forerunners. He added that the epigram could be written in elegies, two, four, or even ten times the length of its original genre such as, we might add, could be found in the Jesuit Remond's *Epigrammata et Elegiae*.[12] The epigram could also be written in the "phalaeic and iambic" genres and even in the "heroic" or epic (p. 10). Following the same line of argument, Donatus attributed pungency to more conventional genres and had trouble in conceding it to the lyric because of the traditional conception of lyric as smooth song. But eventually he did so, and finally he found pungency's great use even in the epic (p. 311). As the practice of Jesuit writers was invariably restricted to short forms of verse like the ode, panegyric, elegy, and lyric, the challenge and perhaps the impossibility of an epic poem in the epigrammatic style was never put to the test.

As the epigram got longer, its once terminal sharp effect became characteristic of the whole of long poems, elegies, lyrics, odes, and epics alike now also bearing that name. Pungency, which Raderus said gave the epigram "its sinew, strength, and sharpness," marked the whole of the new long poem. This inevitably led to the characterization of epigram as "a kind of song without rules" of genre *(ita genus carminis liberum est,* p. 11) covering all of poetry's kinds. In that pungency, Donatus found that "the imitation necessary for verse" was "served" (p. 312).

Pungency became the very foundation of the aesthetics of verse. In Donatus' argument, contemporary commentators like Scaliger and even other Jesuits like Pontanus and Possevine[13] were so desperately bound by ancient conception of the epigram as brief that they failed to see what its pungency was now doing as style (p. 310). Such an error in the arguments of two others of his fellow contemporary Italian critics Minturnus and Robortellus as well as in the writings of Scaliger, Raderus said, grew out of too much concentration "on the history" of the epigram. It spoke, he continued, for too little attention to epigram's higher and more important "poetic conception" as style which, he thought, he was now setting out to explain (p. 9).

Pungency became the quality of the whole of a long poem by growing characteristic of every one of its images from its first to its last. Whereas the old epigram had only one concluding pungent effect at its end, the new epigram had as many such effects as it had images. Justified, it seemed, by its appearance as the distinguishing feature of the long epigrammatic poems being written by Jesuit poets like Remond, Hugo, and Cabilliau in the literary background of English meditative writers, pungency at the end of a poem in the new style was not its logical conclusion. Rather, it merely "tested" its preceding paradoxes. Pungency at the close of a poem only reiterated a thought introduced earlier one final time (Donatus, p. 309). The epigrammatic style, Donatus continued, "carried out" the whole of a poem's pungency from beginning to end. The style produced "some pungency for the senses in individual sections of the poem and throughout the song as a whole," so that the last image of a poem "brought out" the pungency of its earlier parts (pp. 310-311). The reason for this, Raderus wrote, was that as the new epigrammatic poem ended, "a comparison was not so much rounded off" but rather the poem as a whole came "to a close through a similitude drawn in yet another direction" (p. 10). No longer associated with the logical conclusion of its thought, the close of the epigrammatic poem "was not led forth" logically from what preceded. Instead, it merely continued to express "the purpose of the preceding things" (Donatus, p. 309).

Having so replaced the logic of thought with the logic of sharp feeling, pungency left the pith of the poet's message mobile or amphibious within the poem. The thought of a poem was not conceived of as illogical but simply not as logically presented. Suggesting that a poem was a series of epigrams strung together, the style inspired Praz' description of Crashaw's "The Weeper" as *"non e infatti altro che un rosario de epigrammi o di madrigali malamente legati assieme."*[14] The style leads to the grouping of the writers under Ignatian influence with the German exclamatory school of Gryphius, Kuhlmann, and the Jesuit Frederich von Spee, whose verse according to Nelson described "in instantaneous terms the actual experience of eternity."[15] But even there the emphasis of the style on poetry as a string of epigrams isolated the Jesuit von Spee's sharp images of "night" and "light" recurring in various combinations in a poem like "The Spouse of Jesus Bewails her Passion," from the syllogistic narrative image patterns of a poem like Kuhlmann's "The Nativity of the Lord" or Gryphius' "On the birth of Jesus."[16]

Neither of these latter poems by Kuhlmann or Gryphius, nor even a strongly epigrammatic English poem like Herbert's "The Pulley," observed the rule of sustained pungency of the movement for which the non-traditional Jesuits spoke. The meaning of these poems was developed independently of aesthetic effect. They lacked that persistent union of meaning and pungency which the sustained epigrammatic quality of the new style supposed.

In "Nativity," Kuhlmann developed the conventional paradox of epigram with light praising darkness: "O Night! Whose moon the moon and sun did raise! / O Night! Where shines Whom moon and sun do praise!" (11. 10-11). In "On the birth of Jesus," Gryphius opened with a similar sort of paradox on the superiority of the clarity of darkness to light: "Night brighter than the sun where light is born: / Which God, who dwells in light, chose as his own!" (11. 2-3). And Herbert developed "The Pulley" on the proposition that God began to satiate man in order deliberately to leave him unsatiated: "He would adore my gifts in stead of me, / And rest in Nature, not the God of Nature."[17] But the narrative continuity of these poems, supported by the general logical development of their events, contradicted the closed effect of the images in the epigrammatic style. The reader can even come to an end of "The Pulley" and fully understand Herbert's basic meaning about God refusing to spoil man by bestowing on him all the gifts he had to offer, without ever grasping the nuances of the puns on "rest" and "restlesnesse" in the latter half of the poem pivotal to its traditional epigrammatic character (ll. 10, 14, 16, 17).

The division of meaning and pungent effect in the above poems was absent in the verse governed by the aspirations of the new style. Meaning was the expression of the universe's affections: no matter what they concerned, images had to reflect instantaneously that pungency by which these affections were experienced in verse. In von Spee's "The Spouse," a flame of love burns in the poet; epigrammatically, that is all the poem has to say as each of its images repeats its meaning: the "east and north winds freeze" this love rather than blow it out (11. 9-10), and, a little later at dawn, the sun begins "to court'sy with its light" in a reflexive action to describe that love (11. 21-24). As in Crashaw's "Bleeding Crucifix" and "The Weeper" or Southwell's "Upon the

Image" or Donne's "La Corona" sonnet "Ascention" or his "Holy Sonnet" 19, the substance, meaning, and imagery of verse rested on epigrammatically expressed emotive values. This was so in spite of the prominent influences of ancient genres converging in their lines.

For the sake of the new epigrammatic style, the conventions of all sorts of traditional poetic genres were creatively enlisted. As the style was in practice inclusive and not exclusive of inherited genres, their conventions supported its development. For example, Crashaw's "Bleeding Crucifix" displays many of the original traits of the Renaissance love lyric. By tradition, the lyric poem apostrophized the parts of the lady's person, comparing them to convergent streams (a practice that Herbert mildly satirized in "Jordan I," 1. 8). Yet, these well-worn lyric conventions failed to constrain the epigrammatic qualities of the nine stanzas of "Bleeding Crucifix" as Crashaw simply adapted the parts of the lady's person to Christ's body.

> Iesu, no more! It is full tide.
> From thy head & from thy feet,
> From thy hands & from thy side
> All the purple Riuers meet.
>
> What need thy fair head bear a part
> In showres, as if thine eyes had none?
> What need They help to drown thy heart,
> That striues in torrents of it's own?
>
> Thy restlesse feet now cannot goe
> For vs & our eternall good,
> As they were euer wont. What though?
> They swimme. Alas, in their own floud.
>
> Thy hands to giue, thou canst not lift;
> Yet will thy hand still giuing be.
> It giues but ô, it self's the gift.
> It giues though bound; though bound 'tis free.
>
> But ô thy side, thy deep-digg'd side!
> That hath a double Nilus going.
> Nor euer was the pharian tide
> Half so fruitfull, half so flowing.
>
> (ll. 1-20).

The first stanza of Crashaw's poem ironically displaced, as from the loved one to the lover, the tide of blood flowing at the Crucifixion from the person of the suffering Christ to the meditating poet. With equal pungency, the third stanza depicted Christ's nailed feet walking in a flood. Moreover, in Stanzas II through IV Crashaw apostrophized the parts of Christ's person as the meeting point of all the earth's rivers.

Stanza II apostrophized the head, Stanza III the feet, Stanza IV the hands, and Stanza V the side concluding with Stanza VI's apostrophe to the hair.

Similarly, "The Weeper" was a copy of a verse plaint. However, such a genre, once absorbed into the Counter Reformation literature of tears, was rife for the destitution of its traditional tone of lament that Crashaw imposed on it. The Magdalen's tears in the poem are successively imaged in epigrams of upward and downward motion and of liquid, dew, and balsam as they head happily with little plaint for their destination at Christ's feet thirty stanzas later.

Even in a poem like "Upon the Image of Death," the conventions of both the refrain and of incremental repetition of the ballad on which Southwell leaned heavily, ceded to the strength of the epigrammatic style. Rather than with this style, the conventions of the ballad appear to vie with the ascetic exercital structure of Ignatius' "election" which the poem also unwittingly contained *(Exercises,* pp. 62-63). With its preludial "composition of place" in the first stanza, with its five successive exercital points applied to the self in the second to sixth stanzas, with its two points applied to exemplary Biblical figures in the seventh and eighth stanzas, and finally with its recapitulation on the self in the closing sestet, Southwell's "Upon the Image of Death" deployed the exercital structure along the steps of ballad incremental repetition. But the poet left neither ballad genre nor exercital structure in its original shape. Ironically, the juxtaposition of the refrain of the ballad with a part of the exercital structure in every stanza created an isolated epigrammatic effect. This effect worked to the profound disintegration of the conventions of both the ballad and the ascetic exercise.

By contrast to Southwell's "Upon the Image of Death," neither Donne's "La Corona" sonnet on the "Ascension" nor his "Holy Sonnet" 19 on the "contraryes" meeting "in one (1. 1) displays structural parts of the ascetic exercise. But both sonnets were constructed of a series of pungent figures. Except that the two poems are each fourteen lines long and that each comes to a full stop after the eighth line, neither is a sonnet in the established sense of an octet elaborating on a problem in a relationship which the sestet resolves. Each sonnet shifts its address from the third person to the first in a semblance of argument, but pungency supersedes genre.

The octets of both Donne's sonnets are composed of two quatrains; the sestet of "Ascension" contains three couplets, and that of "Holy Sonnet" 19 two tercets. These subdivisions were conventional to the sonnet genre. However, instead of these traditional subdivisions supporting the genre's conventional arguments, they repeated concepts epigrammatically. The first quatrain of "Ascension" does not introduce a conventional sonnet resolution, but elaborates on the antithesis of the sun which, by its darkening at three o'clock on Good Friday, appeared nevertheless to have been hardily washed of its soiled dross in Christ's burning tears. This somber sun is also made quickly to prefigure the path of Christ's ascension in terms of the contrary emotion of joy:

> *Salute the last and everlasting day,*
> Joy at the uprising of this Sunne, and Sonne,
> Yee whose just teares, or tribulation
> Have purely washt, or burnt your drossie clay.

The same pungent figure of the path recurs in the second quatrain as Christ clears his own way through the clouds:

> Behold the Highest, parting hence away,
> Lightens the darke clouds, which hee treads upon,
> Nor doth hee by ascending, show alone,
> But first hee, and hee first enters the way.

Donne repeated the sharp image of the trodden path again in the first two lines of the sestet. There Christ paved it with blood: "O strong Ramme, which hast batter'd heaven for mee, / Mild lambe, which with thy blood, has mark'd the path." He invoked the idea of the path once more in the next two lines when Christ showed him the way to heaven by quenching his wrath in his own blood: "Bright Torch, which shin'st, that I the way may see, / Oh with thy owne blood quench thy owne just wrath." He called on it yet one final time in the closing couplet where Christ sent the Holy Spirit to show him the correct manner of writing verse: "And if thy holy Spirit, my Muse did raise, / *Deigne at my hands this crowne of prayer and praise.*"

The epigrammatic requirements of style in the above poems were supported in the arguments of the Jesuit commentators by corresponding claims for the development of wŏrld history. The history of Christianity, which was for these commentators the same thing as saying the history of the world, appeared to have conspired to cater to the needs of the pungency of epigram. Progressively, history seemed to have created more and more subjects suggesting perfect contraries and contrasts. Christ's incarnation seemed to have fused into the times and the spaces of creation the ideal antitheses of eternity and infinity for the maximum success of the pungency of epigram. The saints and other great Christians who had succeeded Christ through sixteen hundred years to the present day appeared to have proliferated, enriched, and variegated the contributions of contraries and contrasts of their divine master to the new style. Such opportunities had been denied by Divine Providence to the impoverished pagan ancestral epigrammatists of baroque Christian poets, like Martial, ungifted with Christian Revelation:

> Those poems [epigrams], produce the great motions and affections
> of the soul, of love, hate, envy, anger, disgust, hope, fear. Of all

these there are many more illustrations in our day than in Antiquity, more new monuments in the state than the profane and impious period of men at that time had. What did the founders of the human race, Adam and Eve, not give in abundance [as poetic subjects] when they fell into lamentable death and all hardships from the blessed and living state of glory, by faltering mortally? What did Samson, David, the Macchabees [not give us]? What, our Magdalen weeping a tear of love and sorrow everywhere? What did our martyrs of Herod, and heroes Lawrence, Ignatius, George, Catherine, Hagne, Agatha, and that other Lucy, by whose thousands of life's stories we overcome the superstitions of nations against us? And indeed the aptest and most arousing ideas [for epigrams] are suggested by the person of . . . Christ about whom much may be said in the form of contraries, in the covenant of whose life may be found mortality and eternity alike.

(Raderus, 11).

Notes

¹Aristotle, *Rhetoric,* I, 1, pp. 3-5; Cooper argues against the traditional appreciation of the enthymeme as a shortened form of the syllogism, "Introduction," *Rhetoric,* pp. xxv-xxix.

²Aristotle, *Poetics,* II, xxii, p. 37.

³Francis Quarles, *Divine Fancies* (London, 1636), p. 107; Hugo, *Pia Desideria,* trans. Arwaker, p. 182; Francis Quarles, *Emblemes,* first ed. 1634 (Cambridge, 2nd ed., 1643), p. 55. and Sig. A3.

⁴Aristotle, *Analytica Priora,* trans. by A. J. Jenkinson, in *Works,* I, general ed. W. D. Ross (Oxford, 1928), 246.

⁵*Jacobi Pontani de Societatis Iesu, Poeticarum Institutionum Libri III,* first ed., 1594 (Ingolstadt, 2nd ed., 1597), p. 168; *M. Valerii Martialis Epigrammaton libros omnes,* Ingolstadt, 1599. The copy used here is the third revised edition of 1627. Donne attacked Raderus in an epigram, *Works,* p. 78, and in *Conclave,* p. 67.

⁶Barbara K. Lewalski, "Donne's *Devotions,"* *Renaissance Quarterly* (Summer, 1977), XXX: 2, p. 263.

⁷Joan Webber, *The Eloquent "I"* (Madison, Wisc., 1968), pp. 11-12.

⁸Helen Gardner, "Introduction," John Donne, *The Elegies and the Songs and Sonnets* (Oxford, 1965), p. xxvi.

⁹Teresa of Avila, *Los Libros de la Madre Teresa De Jesu . . .Un tratado de su Vida* (with frontispiece), Salamanca, 1587, translated into English as *The Lyf of the Mother Teresa of Iesus, Foundresse of the Monasteries of the Descalced or Bare-footed Carmelite Nunnes and Fryers . . . By W. M. of the Society of Iesus,* Antwerp, 1611.

142 THE EMOTIVE IMAGE

[10]H. H. Hudson, *The Epigram in the English Renaissance* (Princeton, 1947), p. 106.

[11]G. H. Hamilton, *English Verse Epigrams* (London, 1965), p. 6; Hudson, *The Epigram in the English Renaissance*, p. 6.

[12]*Francisci Remondi Societatis Iesu Epigrammata et Elegiae.* Antwerp, 1606.

[13]For example, Scaliger's epigram, "S. Benedictus," in *Iulii Caesaris Scaligeri Viri Clarissimi Poemata Sacra* (Coloniae, 1600), p. 57.

[14]Praz, *Secentismo e Marinismo*, p. 231.

[15]Lowry Nelson, *Baroque Lyric Poetry* (New Haven, 1961), p. 27.

[16]Frederich von Spee, "The Spouse of Jesus Bewails Her Passion;" Quirinus Kuhlmann, "The Nativity of the Lord"; and Andreas Gryphius, "On the Birth of Jesus," in *European Metaphysical Poetry*, ed. Frank J. Warnke (New Haven, 1961), pp. 163, 209, 185.

[17]George Herbert, "The Pulley," (11. 13-14), *Works*, ed. with commentary by F. E. Hutchinson (Oxford, 1941), p. 160.

CHAPTER SEVEN

Metaphor and Paradox

1

For the enthymeme and for the symbol of reading in meditative verse, Aristotle's metaphor of "proportion" or of "analogy" as he called it was indeed a powerful ally. Marked by the qualities of surprise that meditative poets expected of the epigrammatic style, the metaphor of proportion appeared to be their natural poetic figure. The metaphor made the pungent effect of the enthymeme poetic and, without the metaphor, the enthymeme would have seemed merely oratorical. In *Poetics* and *Rhetoric*, Aristotle had spoken of the metaphor in terms of paradox; meditative art consisted in expanding the limits of this paradox to the dimension of new Christian absolutes.

The metaphor of proportion was the last of Aristotle's four kinds of metaphor, and it now became the fashionable way of stating enthymeme in verse.[1] Its lively qualities, which appeared to have once been the reserve of the venerable syllogistic epigram of antiquity and of the conservative-minded epigrammatists of the seventeenth century, now seemed to make possible epigram as meditation. Rather than the closing pungency of the old short epigram, the metaphor of proportion now recreated that pungency in the new long epigram. Comparing the relationships between things rather than the things themselves, it provoked that inner world of personal experience characterized by the sensation and universal emotion necessary for meditation. The metaphor became the manner of stating in language those emotions, now human, now universal, now temporal, now eternal, that the enthymeme sought to awaken in the readers of a meditative poem. Epigrammatic effect seemed to have come to speak for the rhetorical silence of the words of a poem, and the metaphor of proportion kept that oral effect of rhetoric alive.

The two main characteristics of the metaphor of proportion appeared to realize simultaneously the aims of epigram and of Christianity. These characteristics were called "antithesis" and "actuality" by Aristotle and they came to make possible the visionary and emotive dimensions of both epigram and the baroque Christian world.[2] The metaphor's "antithesis," which Aristotle said put things "side by side," sparking a "surprise effect," now came to cover the Counter-Reformation absolutes of matter and spirit. Its "actuality," which Aristotle said "invested" its "contraries" with "life" and an "effect of activity," now infused these Christian absolutes with an appearance of daily relevance.[3] The result of this, wrote Donatus, was that the metaphor of proportion "delighted the senses" and "activated the highest motions of the soul" simultaneously. In this way, Donatus continued, the metaphor made "concession to the senses and to action in the spirit" which the Ignatian meditation sought (pp. 223, 224, 218).

The metaphor of proportion achieved its far-reaching meditative aims not in the context of Aristotle's original intentions but in the framework of the baroque world view. The world view determined the emotional dimensions of the metaphor as universal rather than as purely human as Aristotle had intended them. The "contraries" related to the metaphor's characteristic of "antithesis" were no longer time-bound, human, and earthly. They became infinite as the meditative thinkers of the late sixteenth and early seventeenth centuries understood such abstract terms — "Aeternity," as Crashaw wrote, was "shutt in a span" ("Nativity," 1. 80). Accordingly, the images expressing such antitheses were marked by the absolute contrasts of space and infinity, time and eternity, and sensation and spiritual "affection" of Christian mythology.

> Wellcome, all WONDERS in one sight!
> AEternity shutt in a span.
> Sommer in Winter. Day in Night.
> Heauen in earth, & God in MAN
> Great little one! whose all-embracing birth
> Lifts earth to heauen, stoopes heau'n to earth.
>
> Yet when young April's husband showrs
> Shall blesse the fruitfull Maja's bed
> We'l bring the First-born of her flowrs
> To kisse thy FEET & crown thy HEAD.
> To thee, dread lamb! whose loue must keep
> The shepheards, more then they the sheep.
> To THEE, meek Majesty! soft King
> Of simple GRACES & sweet LOVES.
> Each of vs his lamb will bring
> Each his pair of sylver Doues;
> Till burnt at last in fire of Thy fair eyes.
> Our selues become our own best SACRIFICE.
> ("Nativity," ll. 79-84, 97-108).

Similarly, Aristotle had described the metaphor's other characteristic of "actuality" as a quality that put "things before the eyes." Actuality made the hearer "see the thing occurring now." This characteristic was

submitted to the same visionary conditioning as "antithesis."[4]
"Actuality" came to give life in poetry to a meditation that, as Ignatius
had described it, made man see his contemplated Christian Mystery
"with the eyes of the imagination" as if he were present at its first
occurrence long ago (*Exercises*, p. 37; *Overthrow*, p. 44; *Meditations*, I,
p. 41). In this way the "actuality" of the metaphor made it possible to
express in verse the values of Augustinian memory on which the
vividness of the original ascetic meditation was founded. "Actuality"
permitted in poetic imagery Augustine's reconstruction of memories
"into future actions, events and hopes . . . as if they were present."[5]
The metaphor of proportion's "actuality," supported by its first quality
of "antithesis," came therefore to conjoin all the strands of thought
converging in the original meditation into the yet further dimension of
poetic imagery.

   If it is true that the enthymeme released the poet from having to
conceive of the epigram as a short poem, it is equally correct to say that
the metaphor of proportion fused verse meditation into a cogent unit. As
recommended by Aristotle, the metaphor could be drawn in a long
version with an "as" and "so" construction, and in a foreshortened
version without that construction. Both versions spoke for the coherence
of verse. Though intelligible principally according to the values of
oratory, the metaphor of proportion united the arguments of a poem's
enthymemes into a conceptually consistent ikonic image. The structure
of the metaphor alone permitted this.

   That is, as *Poetics* speaks of it, the metaphor of proportion compared
the relationship between things "A" and "B" to the relationship between
things "C" and "D." As Aristotle said, the more things "A" and "B"
differed from things "C" and "'D" the more "actuality" and "antithesis"
the metaphor possessed. With Donatus imitating him some milleniums
later, Aristotle used the example of the relationships between the Greek
mythical god Dionysius and his orgiastic wine-drinking cup, and the god
of war Mars and his shield (Donatus, p. 220). As Dionysius was to his
cup, wrote Aristotle, so was Mars to his shield.[6]

   Founded on such relations, the metaphor of proportion was not based
on the metaphysical categories of Aristotle's other three kinds of
metaphor. These kinds transferred one thing from, or substituted it into,
another genus, species, or category completely (Donatus, pp. 219-220).
The first kind of metaphor transferred a thing in the category of genus
into the category of species (like a ship "at anchor" into a man
"standing"). The second kind transferred a species into the category of
its genus (like "ten thousand" replacing "a large number" in a
description of Ulysses' good deeds). The third kind transferred a thing in
one species into another species (like a bronze sword "drawing" instead
of "severing" the life of its victim). These three sorts of metaphor
compared and contrasted things in the very categories at the basis of the

ancient scholastic approach to matter and form. They also presupposed the assent of the poet to the world view inspired by that approach. However, the metaphor of proportion, not based on these categories, did not presuppose that assent. For this reason, even though the metaphor of proportion undoubtedly erupted into several manifestations with the general revival of classical learning in the Renaissance, its prominence over other forms of imagery in meditative verse bespoke the current disillusionment of the Counter Reformation with the former world view.

Donatus spoke of the metaphor of proportion with surprise as though after the two milleniums since Aristotle described it he was uncovering the metaphor for men for the first time. He wrote that it alone of all kinds of image possessed wholly the Renaissance criteria of proportion and similitude. However, both the long and short varieties of the metaphor, conforming to the long and short versions of the Metaphysical conceit pointed out by Williamson, must have been as well known to the Renaissance as the other parts of *Rhetoric* and *Poetics.*[7] Donatus' surprise before the metaphor therefore rested not so much on its existence as on its support of baroque love of contraries (p. 220).

The wide occurrence of the metaphor of proportion in Donne shows the breadth of its Renaissance influence. The Jesuits also drew from this influence, and it is hardly conceivable that all instances of the metaphor of proportion in Donne's poetry, where it prominently performed other functions besides the meditative, sprang from Jesuit practices. For example, the long version of the metaphor occurred in secular poems by Donne like "A Valediction: forbidding mourning": "As virtuous men passe mildly away . . . / So let us melt, and make no noise" (11. 1, 5); in "The Extasie": "As our blood labours to beget . . . / So must pure lovers soules descend" (11. 61, 65); and in "The Funerall": "As 'twas humility . . . / So, 'tis some bravery" (11. 21, 23). The short version is found in yet more examples like "The Sunne is spent, and now his flasks / Send forth light squibs, no constant rays" in "A nocturnall upon S. Lucies day" (11. 3-4), and "But neere worne out by loves securitie, / Shee, to my losse, doth by her death repaire" (11. 12-13) in "The Dissolution," and "Call her one, mee another flye, / We'are Tapers too, and at our owne cost die" in "The Canonization" (11. 21-22).

Because the metaphor of proportion was not solely in the province of the meditative tradition, as the above poems show, it contributed to the singularity of that tradition more by its tendency to become its exclusive source of imagery than by its presence. And, though the metaphor of proportion certainly testified to the disaffection of the Counter Reformation mind with syllogistic logic in matters of poetry, its ability to afford a retreat from such logic was not enough. The metaphor had also to be able to open the way to practical avenues for poetry. These avenues respected the concepts of ascetic meditative experience and the new world view's typological values, and they distinguished the appearance of the metaphor here from its other contemporary manifestations.

By its emphasis on the comparison of the relationships between objects, the metaphor of proportion released the poet to conceive of metaphor as a typological reflection of his baroque universe. If the meaning of this universe was always emotional as the Counter Reformation understood the affections, the relationship between objects came to speak for that emotional typological level in creation. The objects themselves came to speak for the world of time and space, that is, the domain of sensory experience. If a poem was about eternal love, then the relationships of all its metaphors of proportion or of "analogy" demonstrated that love, and all of its related and unrelated objects in which its enthymemes were arranged made that love felt. The task of the poet was to develop his compared relationships into as many antitheses as he thought necessary to fit his idea of a worthy experience of the emotive sublime.

The condensed metaphor of proportion favoured the meditative poet more than the long variety. That it should have done so was the result of the charged character of its paradox. The short variety of the metapher dropped the second object in the first of its two relations, and the first object in its second relation, just as Aristotle and later Donatus had described the figure.[8] Where the long version of the metaphor had read that "A" is to "B" as "C" is to "D," the short version now read compressedly, and even more antithetically, that "A" is "D," as, for example, "We are Tapers too" in "The Canonization" (1. 21), or the "Sun dyall in a grave" in "The Will" (1. 51).

> Then all your beauties will bee no more worth
> Then gold in Mines, where none doth draw it forth;
>   And all your graces no more use fhall have
>   Then a Sun dyall in a grave.
>   Thou Love taughtst mee, by making mee
> Love her, who doth neglect both mee and thee,
> To 'invent, and practise this one way, to 'annihilate all three.
>   (ll. 48-54).

The Jesuit meditative tradition adjusted this version of the metaphor appearing in Donne's secular verse both to its standard of absolute antitheses of time and eternity and to its emotive enthymemes. In this way, the metaphor ceased to be merely secular and became meditative. The metaphor also bespoke grammatical constructions approaching those of enthymeme, facilitating its passage into Jesuit aesthetics. Both being originally rhetorically devised by Aristotle, the metaphor of proportion and enthymeme rested on like rhetorical and grammatical values as opposed to norms of logic. It was by these values that standards of baroque universality were achieved. In its condensed version, particularly in the case where its original propositions supposed long clauses, the metaphor differed from the enthymeme no more than in matters of definition. In practice in meditative verse, the metaphor was an imaged version of the enthymeme rather than its distracting pictorial counterstatement. Through imagery, the unadorned enthymeme of classical tradition assumed the pungent qualities of ancient epigram. In this fashion, the Counter Reformation fused the two ancient arts of oratory and epigram into a new one.

2

In this convergence of enthymeme, metaphor of proportion, and paradox, the meditative poem was a way of being, of existing, of fulfilling one's self rather than an isolated religious act. Its tone was not the medieval *contemptus mundi* but what might be called the late Renaissance *via mundi Deo*. Such a reflection of the self and the world in verse was naturally intense. Positing emotion as the substance of poetry, its intensity seemed intelligible only in terms of two imitations.

The meditative poem came to be spoken of as a combination of two imitative processes in order that it might be discussed at all. Each of its imitations answered respectively to one of the two major typological levels of meaning in creation, eternal emotion and time-bound matter, for which Jesuit poetry was developed. As the art of poetry in practice worked exactly to the opposite result of the division implied by the two imitations, this separation of image and meaning was theoretical. However, such a separation made possible the discussion of the aesthetic effect of imagery as distinct from its imitated objects.

With his argument for the separation of reasoning from matter in the oration in *Institutio Oratoria,* Quintilian, on whose authority much Jesuit aesthetics relied, appeared to support that trend in poetry to which his declarations on rehetoric were applied. Eloquence, he had written, was divided into "that which is expressed and that which expresses." Moreover, earlier than Quintilian, Aristotle drew refined connections between image and meaning in his first three kinds of metaphor, but he implied the necessary separation of image and meaning in the fourth kind. This metaphor, he said, was constituted of the attachment of the "concepts" of some things to others.[9]

The separation of matter and meaning which had run through the arguments of the masters of classical rhetoric now came to serve the idea that poetry contained no conventional argument or logical narrative. This conception supported a view that verse was invariably about an eternal emotion that was beyond narration and discussion. The classical separation of image and meaning that had furthered arguments about rhetorical language now upheld the view of a meditative poem as a series of emotive effects picturing matter. As the meditative poem contained no argument, its emotive meaning was discussed in terms of its aesthetic effect. To discuss style meant also to discuss meaning. The things of the world that had once made up part of the oratorical argument now made up parts of figurative language conveying nothing but feeling.

> O gracious spheres, where love the Center is,
> A native place for our selfe-loaden soules:
> The compasse, love, a cope that none can mis:
> The motion, love that round about us rowles.
> O Spheres of love, whose Center, cope and motion,
> Is love of us, love that invites devotion.
>
> O little worldes, the summes of all the best,
> Where glory, heaven, God, sunne: all vertues, starres:
> Where fire, a love that next to heaven doth rest,
> Ayre, light of life, that no distemper marres:
> The water, grace, whose seas, whose springs, whose showers,
> Cloth natures earth, with everlasting flowers.
>
> What mixtures these sweet elements do yeeld,
> Let happy wordlings of those worlds expound,
> But simples are by compounds farre exceld,
> Both sute a place, where all best things abound.
> And if a banishd wretch gesse not amisse:
> All but one compound framde of perfect blisse.
>
> I outcast from these worlds exiled rome,
> Poore saint, from heaven, from fire, cold Salamander:
> Lost fish, from those sweet waters kindly home,
> From lande of life, strayed pilgrim still I wander:
> I know the cause: these worldes had never a hell
> In which my faults have best deservde to dwell.
>
> O Bethelem cisternes, *Davids* most desire,
> From which my sinnes like fierce Philistims keepe,
> To fetch your drops what champion should I hire,
> That I therein my withered heart may steepe.
> I would not shed them like that holy king,
> His were but tipes, these are the figured thing.
>
> (*"Saint Peters Complaint,"* ll. 403-432).

The separation of image and meaning which in a number of guises runs through Jesuit writing answered to yet another hypothetical distinction. It conformed to the theoretical separation of meaning and matter in the typological world which Jesuit commentators made. As was the world, so was meditative verse. While the imitation of things corresponded to the exigencies of the time-bound world, the imitation by words relating to aesthetic effect stood for the significant eternal emotive exigencies of that world.

Donatus was the most definite and the clearest of all the commentators in making the separation of image and meaning and arguing for two imitations. To claim that a poem had two imitations and not one as most contemporary theorists argued, required courage in an age that held itself bound by the authority of the ancients. Quintilian and Aristotle might have supported the separation of matter and meaning, but never suggested two imitations. With neither past nor present authority to quote, Donatus proceeded with circumspection. However, his committal to the two imitations was complete. It enabled him to clarify points of style that an argument about verse solely on the grounds of imitation of the world would have kept obscure. To respect the authority of the ancients who had discussed poetry in terms of only one imitation, Donatus was not only bound to find out what the ancients meant, but to do what they said.

This need to justify himself in terms of the authority of the past led Donatus to break from it to explain the nature of the present. Donatus' argument deferentially began with a conventional statement that poetic imitation was related to song (p. 7). But his belief in the two imitations was soon apparent and he no longer approached mimetic art conventionally (p. 71). Joining in a single poem the two traditions of Aristotelian and Petrarchan imitations that his own age quarrelled over regularly as though they were hopelessly irreconcilable, Donatus called them *imitatio rerum* and *imitatio verborum*. [10]

Donatus' argument for the separation of image and meaning had similar consequences of divisive effect when it arose in the works of other Jesuit commentators. Unlike Donatus, other commentators did not necessarily bring the theory of two imitations to the forefront of their arguments; however, their general approach to imitation had essentially the same divisive purpose. The authority of the past was resolutely abandoned in the face of the rhetorical exigencies of the new universe.

Handling the same emotive dimensions of verse as Donatus, the French Jesuit Charles Pajot (b. Paris, 1609; d. Flèche, 1686), for example, had pertinent comments, though late. He referred to these dimensions of verse in varied conceptions of sound much as Raderus touched on them in terms of pungency. Pajot's writings came late in the history of baroque aesthetics and he is certainly a minor figure, but his *Ars Poetica* is nevertheless interesting. In an *imitatio verborum,* figurative language appeared to assume tonal values unattributable to *imitatio rerum.* "Verse," wrote Pajot in his lexicon of poetic terms, "seems to progress" not by configurations or pictorial patterns of imagery but "by certain feet or steps of sound" like "men walking." This suggested more the movement of music's "tonal patterns" as an "analogue of emotive life" described by Langer in our own century than conventional verse.[11] Pajot also added that a poem was "a certain apt composition of syllables" containing pitches and volumes, and Crashaw at the beginning of "Adoro te" laid great stress on the sense of the "ear" as the way of experience in his poem (1. 10). But such sound was all unheard as it advanced through the measures of verse by the pungency that gave living form to its rhetorical silence.

By the "imitation by words," whether or not Donatus, Pajot, and Raderus invariably called it by that name, the Jesuit writers tended to develop their views on imagery. Their argument about stylistic imitation as *verborum*, or as "feet of sound," or as pungency described a poem's imitated eternal affections in the terminology of figurative language. For example, for Pajot the *dictio* became any indirect way of saying something, and in his discussion of stylistic imitation it came to cover many traditional categories of trope (pp. 16-17). For Donatus, by a similar approach to stylistic imitation, the meaning of metaphor grew even more inclusive. It came to signify the kinds of figurative language that other commentators of the age generally classed beneath scheme (pp. 219-220). The three kinds of substitutions of imagery covering seventy-five percent of the territory that Aristotle had meant by metaphor now signified almost nothing that the philosopher had understood by the term.

By extending the range of metaphor indefinitely, for example, Donatus made it synonymous with *figura*. Such a conception of metaphor as *figura* gave it value as a form "higher" than mere trope. This elevation of metaphor had also occurred in literary history before the seventeenth-century manifestations of Jesuit poetry.[12] However, in the currents of the Counter Reformation, this approach to metaphor as *figura*, in addition to serving literary theory, responded to the practical needs imposed on verse by typology. The needs generated by the typological character of the world exerted the same sort of formative pressure on the Jesuit idea of metaphor which Aristotle's concept of matter and form had applied to his idea of the metaphor too.

3

Of such baroque metaphor, paradox was the living form. The metaphor of proportion's two kinds of paradox conjoined a poem's typological levels into a single aesthetic effect. There is nothing unusual about the presence of paradox either in any given image or in the full length of a poem. Its singularity in the epigrammatic style was not its presence but the original manner of its appearance and the yet more unusual method of its continuity. Paradox did not grow out of the rearrangement of the roles of things, which is our usual way of creating it, whether or not we group things according to Aristotle's categories. Rather, paradox in the style was made to emerge more intricately both out of the forced contrasts between things and out of the likeness of their relations.

Paradoxes were drawn equally from the meaning and from the objects of a metaphor. In such an approach to figurative language, meaning and image were in practice identified as one. The poet did not have to worry about a paradox which rested on image keeping the meaning of the image clear. The objects in the relationships in the Jesuit tradition's favorite metaphor of proportion were regularly pictured in their original shapes. The objects in one relationship of a metaphor might be Christian and those in the other relationship might be originally classical. There is the goddess Maja in Crashaw's "Nativity" hymn (1. 98) as well as the Virgin Mary. But as none of these classical and other Christian subjects ever came to represent one another by the "transference" that both we and Aristotle usually think of as metaphor, paradoxes could be drawn from either a metaphor's relationships or its objects. No symbol or other form of "transference" interfered with drawing paradox from either. As long as the poet sustained the effect of the opening paradox of his poem, he was free to create as many new metaphors as the objects of their relationships suggested. The objects forming the basis of the comparison in one metaphor became the basis for the relationships and the likeness of yet another metaphor.

The making of paradox might appear to us as a useless complication of the art of imagery. However, in a world conceived of as typological such paradox was a much more logical way to make poetry than is our or Aristotle's concept of metaphor as transference or substitution. As the universe was already thought of as metaphoric, it was much more pertinent to suggest that poetry was the art of intensifying the experience of the already existing symbolic world all around oneself, rather than setting out to create symbols from nothing. The poetry of Heywood who introduced Jesuit verse onto English soil demonstrated such a role for paradox.

> The wandring youth, whose race so rashlie runne,
> Hath left behinde, to his eternall shame:
> The thriftlesse title of the Prodigall sonne,
> To quench, remembrance of his other name.
> Mate now devide, the burthen of his blame,
> With me, whom wretchlesse thoughtes entised still:
> To tread the trackt of his unruly will.
>
> ("*Alluding his state,*" ll. 1-7)

The central paradox of poems like Heywood's "Easter day" ("By death, with death sing we with voyce," 1. 3) and his "Alluding his state to the prodigall child" ("The wandring youth, whose race so rashlie runne, / Hath left behinde . . . / The thriftlesse title," 11. 1-3) augured the general drift of meditative verse yet to come. Particularly as his father was John Heywood the epigrammatist, Heywood need not be imagined as deliberately appropriating paradox and metaphor of proportion. Nor need he be pictured as consciously instituting as by manifesto a practice of meditative verse in England. Heywood's poetry heralds the coming of that verse by his response to certain literary and philosophical exigencies of the times into which other Englishmen also drifted by conviction. Heywood did not introduce Martial into the living culture of Renaissance England, as his father had already accomplished for his country that revival of an ancient poet's art that was spreading throughout the Continent. But under the pressure of the gestating baroque Catholic world, Heywood's verse was, nevertheless, the first to betray signs of the influence on English epigram of the love of stylistic antithesis and meditative temper. Because of the cultural forces it represented, the love of this style was also soon to spread among many of his compatriots.

The truth of this appears in Alabaster's and Southwell's literary performances a mere decade later. In the work of these writers it was already impossible to confuse the favorite antithesis of meditative paradox with the witty sharpness of some of Sir Philip Sidney's poems written at about the same time. A paradoxical metaphor like the "points of sin" of a soldier's armour "against the skies" in Alabaster's Sonnet 26 ("Another of the same," 1. 5), or a metaphor of a similar nature about the "wrastling winds with raging blasts / Still" holding Southwell "in a cruell chace" in "The prodigall childs soule wracke," stress antithesis rather than Sidney's witty comparisons. Such a comparison appears in Sidney's image of himself as both "a horseman to my horse" and "a horse to love" in his relationship to the lady "Stella" of his sonnet.[13]

The difference between the two kinds of sharpness, Alabaster's and Southwell's on the one hand and Sidney's on the other, was not only the result of tonal disparity. It could be argued that such disparity arises out of the distance that always separates sharp verbal play touching on religious matters from a similar play on secular issues. But more than the realms of Renaissance "decorousness" applied to either religious or profane imagery was at stake.[14] The world views being different, paradox in meditative poetry sought consistently to reflect absolute Christian antitheses as a basic constituent element of verse. By contrast, Sidney's sharpness of figure was "decorous" in the Renaissance rhetorical sense for ornament as adjunct layered onto meaning, such as Puttenham described.[15]

For much the same reasons the traits of paradox present in Alabaster's and Southwell's verse reappeared in Donne's "La Corona" and "Holy Sonnets." They distinguished Donne's work from the "decorous" sharp imagery in Sidney's verse too. Both Donne's religious sonnets and the sonnets of Sidney's sequence to Stella are fourteen lines long, but that is about their only conventional similarity. Already, in Donne's sonnets the art of paradox had taken the additional new turning into the taut series of antitheses characteristic of the flowering of English meditative verse in Crashaw. Donne's art of antithesis also bespoke a more developed practice of meditative poetry, as verse came more and more to reflect a world constituted of forever pressing absolute contraries of matter and emotion.

> 3. *Immensitie cloystered in thy deare wombe,*
> Now leaves his welbelov'd imprisonment,
> There he hath made himselfe to his intent
> Weake enough, now into our world to come;
> But Oh, for thee, for him, hath th'Inne no roome?
> Yet lay him in this stall, and from the Orient,
> Starres, and wisemen will travell to prevent
> Th' effect of *Herods* jealous generall doome.
> Seest thou, my Soule, with thy faiths eyes, how he
> Which fils all place, yet none holds him, doth lye?
> Was not his pity towards thee wondrous high,
> That would have need to be pittied by thee?
> Kisse him, and with him into Egypt goe,
> *With his kinde mother, who partakes thy woe.*
>
> *("Nativity,"* La Corona 3)

"Holy Sonnet" I about the impossible death of an immortal soul is an example of the transformation of a genre by paradox. The poem succeeds one paradox ("Thou hast made me, And shall thy worke decay?") with another ("Repaire me now, for now mine end doth haste,") and with yet another ("I runne to death, and death meets me as fast," 11. 1-3). To interpret these lines as representing the development of the conventional problem of a sonnet octet is to fail to grasp their central point which was that all three of their propositions were theologically impossible to Donne as well as to his first readers. An immortal soul could not die, man and not God was responsible for human salvation, and death was fixed not by man or by death itself but by Divine Providence. From such theological impossibilities there sprang all the force of Donne's paradoxes reflecting the exigencies of the Christian mythological universe for which his theology spoke.

That Crashaw's world a few years later was less dark than the sombre universe of Donne's first "Holy Sonnet" did not indicate that the meditative art of paradox had changed. The greater brightness of his world suggested rather that paradox and verse meditation had flowered, and that the older tradition of the sonnet with its explorations of the darker emotions originally related to the self had faded into history. As in Revett's "Christmas day," the favorite meditations now tended to be more regularly on the happier events of Christian history. These reflected directly the great positive eternal emotions like love and joy in the poet's world of time. Crashaw's "Nativity" and "Epiphanie" hymns and Revett's "Lazarus raysed by our Saviour" and "Ascension day" were among their best poems and this suggests consequently the maturity of their meditative movement as it gradually receded from the past's preferences of theme and genre. "Nativity" and "Epiphanie" fulfilled the meditative tradition of paradox in two of Christianity's happiest historical and most miraculous events even though the poet is hampered in achieving his effect by the superficial choral, phonal, and antiphonal sections with soloists like the Magi and shepherds.

"Nativity" and "Epiphanie" were strings of paradoxes as were "The Weeper" and "The Teare," a fact that their underlying historical, theological, and narrative traditions tend to obscure. The two poems were above all meditative forms of communication with the forces of a baroque world. Only secondly were they stories of the birth of Jesus and the Coming of the Magi. "Nativity's" first paradox compared the relations on the one hand between Christ and the visitation of the shepherds, and on the other hand between the sun and the physical sight of the shepherds: "Come we shepherds whose blest Sight / Hath mett love's Noon in Nature's night" (11. 1-2). Though springing from the contrast of "love's Noon" and "Nature's night" (1. 2), paradox rested on the double meaning of the word "Sight." In the first line "Sight" meant physical vision and insight. The relations between noon, night, and the meanings of sight controlled the poem's imagery, as the remainder of its lines elaborated on them into more paradoxes. Outside of these relations, Crashaw's images in "Nativity" lacked purpose.

Similarly, the continuity of "Epiphanie" rested on Crashaw's paradoxes. The role of his imagery was to expand the possibility of paradox, and the emotive character of one image led to the emotive context of the next. The central paradox of the poem was founded on the relations between Christ and the brightness of the sun, and on the relation between the coming of the Magi and the sunrise on January 6 (the Twelfth Day of Christmas, the former feast of the Epiphany in the Roman liturgy). The poem repeatedly compared the Magi as worshippers and the sun as a representation of Christ. The paradox of this central comparison emerged in the poem's very first metaphor: the morning on the January 6 in question incurred a "sweet mistake" for believing that it could literally cast light on the world once Christ was born to illuminate it spiritually (1. 2). The paradox recurred immediately in the description of the Magi as the "East." The Magi come to seek light in the yet blind eyes of the new-born Christ-child

(1. 14), but they also search for it in the figure of Christ likewise
described as "the world's great universal east" some lines later (1. 24).

Bright BABE! Whose awfull beautyes make
The morn incurr a sweet mistake;
(2.) For whom the' officious heauns deuise
To disinheritt the sun's rise,
(3.) Delicately to displace
The Day, & plant it fairer in thy face;
   [1.] O thou King of loues,
    [2.] Of lights,
    [3.] Of ioyes!
(*Cho.*) Look up, sweet Babe, look vp & see
   For loue of Thee
   Thus farr from home
   The EAST is come
To seek her self in thy sweet Eyes
(1.) We, who strangely went astray,
   Lost in a bright
   Meridian night,
(2.) A Darkenes made of too much day,
(3.) Becken'd from farr
   By thy fair starr,
Lo at last haue found our way.
(Cho.) To Thee, thou Day of night!
   Thou east of west!
Lo we at last have found the way.
To thee, the world's great vniuersal east.
The Generall & indifferent Day.

(ll. 1-25)

Continuity in this verse was not a matter of pictorial coherence but of
verbal self-propulsion. One emotive image led to the next. Now, though
the shared vision of the baroque world has long passed, the modern
reader still remembers the previous image in the relations of the next
paradox.

Under the impetus of such paradox, the phonal and antiphonal
sections of both "Nativity" and "Epiphanie" were inessential to their
structure. They suggest the disposition of certain images rather than the
basis of structure. A seventeenth-century church musician would have
found impossible the task of setting either of Crashaw's poems to music
according to the plainsong and the Gregorian chant which his age
understood as hymnal. Perhaps modern atonal music with its deliberate
suppression of sound patterns called melody might serve their
adaptation to music better. As the epigrammatic style's antithesis took

precedence over genre, "Nativity" and "Epiphanie" were united by paradox rather than by their superficial hymnal structures. Neither poem has anything to say in the sense of the general argumentative responsories of hymns. Each speaks through a number of suggestive antithetical ideas uniting the vague, once conventional parts of traditional church music.

For example, the solo and choral sections of "Nativity" alternately redefine the paradox about Christ and the shepherds by altering repeatedly their different religious and natural implications. Christ is paradoxical, then the shepherds are paradoxical, next the sun above them, then the star that guided the shepherds. Similarly, the solo parts of the Wise Men and the phonal and antiphonal sections of "Epiphanie" do not provide the logic of its movement. Nor does the fact that these divisions are shorter and less clearly defined in "Epiphanie" than in "Nativity" obscure the shared paradoxical basis of their continuity.

In "Nativity" and "Ephiphanie" paradox rather than hymnal structure supplied Crashaw with relations for his succeeding metaphors of proportion. The schematic arrangement of paradox counted rather than the elaborate patterns of ideas, images, and symbols that went into numerous expressions of genre in the Renaissance. Such schematic arrangement makes the traditional categories of genre and figure to which theorists like Puttenham and Sidney in *The Arte of English Poesie* and *A Defence of Poetry* held so deeply seem unimportant.[16] The success of the meditative poem was the degree of its paradoxical intensity. It was not the capacity of poetry's genres and figurative language to conform to the rich categories of Renaissance literary terminology.

As were the categories of figurative language and genre, the creatures, personalities, and objects depicted in poems like Crashaw's two so-called hymns were reduced to the stylistic reaches of paradox. The repetition of paradox failed to give coherent pictorial value to Crashaw's lines. An image like that of the sun in "Epiphanie" recurs many times without developing more into a coherent visual picture than it does in a short poem like "New Year's Day" where it is repeated only a few times. As the image served exclusively the repetition of the poem's central paradox, it possessed no cumulative pictorial dimensions. Likewise, devoid in "Nativity" of their independent metaphoric life in original pastoral tradition, the lushly classical sheep-tending figures of Tityrus and Thyrsis appeared primarily for their epigrammatic effect. They no longer served to people a wistful, literary, allegorical dream-world which they had not created.

At the height of the meditative tradition in England, therefore, Crashaw's images possessed a quality of the phoenix. They persistently appeared only to be consistently destroyed. As the figure of the sun in the short "New Year's Day" suggests, the role of metaphor was determined by the "proportional" needs of a poem. Once the need for new relationships between objects passed, the role of the metaphor had for the moment ended. The beginning of "New Year's Day" identified the sunrise as the harbinger of day (11. 1-2). As the closing lines of the poem shifted the meaning of the sunrise from earthly time to Christ, the metaphor of proportion concluded: "The morn shall come to meet thee here / And leave her own neglected Sun" (11. 31-32). The poem's coherent level of meaning was not pictorial but made up of numerous yet rapidly disappearing antitheses along which the poem's central paradox was repeated. In such a central paradox, the relationships between objects in the metaphors of "New Year's Day" were forever changing.

4

In the face of such constant change, Crashaw's poems did not invariably lack subordinate narrative structures. Poems such as "Nativity," "Epiphanie," "The Teare," and "The Weeper" lacked cogent narrative action. But others like "Sancta Maria Dolorem," the verse letter "To the Countess of Denbigh," and the first verse letter to Mrs. "M.R." display certain subordinate structures. These serve to bring their verse fabric into relief. This is particularly true of the two verse letters that follow almost part for part the steps of the classical oration. Their use of the classical oratorical structure in no way obscures their equally informative meditative experiences described in "Sancta Maria Dolorem," where the narrative, though not oratorical, is also interesting.

"Sancta Maria Dolorem" is narrative in that it describes the meditative experience in several symbols of reading. The juxtaposition of certain paradoxes is made to say something about the experience. The poem's main paradox was that Mary at the foot of the Cross resembled a text and was the object of Crashaw's meditation; yet, she compelled him to identify with her in her contemplation upon Christ. Crashaw repeated this paradox of identity in such a way that he could be expected to conclude by meditating on Christ. Mary, we are told, comprehended Christ's death by questioning her own pain, and Crashaw likewise comes to do this in the tenth stanza. He concludes by asking the Virgin Mary for help and suffers Christ's sorrow that she herself experienced at the foot of the Cross (11. 98-100).

The poem's later paradoxes make explicit the details of the meditative experience depicted in the first stanza. The metaphor of the sixth stanza which compares a book and a man copying it with Christ and Mary, is pertinent (11. 51-60). Though such lines tell us nothing about the metaphor's objects that the poem's opening paradox has not already suggested, they depict a whole new aspect of the poet's meditation. The meditation now concentrates on the poet rather than on Mary in spite of the fact that the poem was originally a "ritualistic" hymn to Christ's mother.[17]

O teach those wounds to bleed
In me; me, so to read
This book of loues, thus writ
In lines of death, my life may coppy it
With loyall cares.
O let me, here, claim shares;
Yeild somthing in thy sad praerogatiue
(Great Queen of greifes) & giue
Me too my teares; who, though all stone,
Think much that thou shouldst mourn alone.
(VI)

In the verse letters "To the Countess of Denbigh" and to Mrs. "M.R.,"
the structure of the classical oration, like the description of the
meditative experience in "Sancta Maria Dolorem," served the
epigrammatic style. Moreover, in both poems the structure of the oration
runs parallel with parts of Ignatius' exercital structure. These structures
appear as paradoxes, and they support the recurring central antitheses of
the poems. They function in both verse letters much as did the ancient
ballad and Renaissance lyric conventions in Southwell's "Upon the
Image of Death" and Crashaw's "Bleeding Crucifix."

The structure of the oration contained a number of parts conforming
loosely to the structure of the exercise. Conjoined in the paradoxes of the
verse letters, the parts of both structures provided Crashaw with the
material for his imagery. They also supported the emotive ends of the
epigrammatic style. How they could do so rested on their original
disposition in their respective disciplines. Briefly, the structure of the
oration in *Rhetoric* was made up of a proem or a prologue, sometimes a
"connecting link" that followed, next the statement of facts, then the
proof (the latter two being the pivotal sections) and finally the epilogue.
Another part, a "prejudice," might appear between the proem and the
statement of facts for the orator to clear away his hearer's prejudice
against his subject. In Quintilian's *Institutio* III. ix. 1, the proem and
epilogue were called the exordium and the peroration respectively, and a
"refutation" sometimes appeared between the proof and the peroration.[18]
Crashaw worked these parts of the oration into his paradoxes with the
parts of the exercise, namely the prelude, the colloquies (usually three),
sometimes an analysis, and finally the application of the senses, with
which in the lines of verse they could be made roughly parallel because of
their shared argumentative qualities.

In Crashaw's poetry the structure of the oration, like that of *Exercises,*
was present with the attraction it possessed for him. The dialectic of the
oration was altered to paradox and its argument was replaced by style.
The oration's structure did not appear in its ancient rhetorical role with
its original vocation to persuade. Rather, it emerged conditioned by the

images of the central paradoxes of Crashaw's verse letters. The repetition of certain images related to rhetorical structure according to the norms of the epigrammatic style became the instrument for Crashaw to transfer such structure into verse. The three lines in the first verse letter to Mrs. "M.R." (11. 8-10), which are roughly equivalent to Aristotle's "connecting link" between the proem and the statement of facts, reiterate the images of the poem's opening. They introduce a new paradox and also sustain the momentum of the poem. For Aristotle the connecting link enabled the hearer to identify himself with the orator's topic, and Crashaw described the volume for Mrs. "M.R." as mounting to a very beautiful and rewarding level of experience in the nature of verse: " . . . confidently look," he wrote, "To find the rest / Of a rich binding in your Brest" (11. 8-10). The technique of repeating paradoxes in Crashaw's verse letters was not restricted to an unimportant sub-part of the oratorical structure. It was symptomatic rather of the breadth of his art in both poems. This technique recurs throughout both poems, fusing the whole older rhetorical structure with the much younger but ever-present exercital structure.

In the beginning of the verse letter to Mrs. "M.R.," the paradox of "So here a little volume, but great book! / A nest of new-born loves" forms the classical "proem" or "exordium." But it also serves as a poetic way of making the Ignatian Prelude. Aristotle had described the "proem" as the equivalent to "the prologue in poetry" or the "prelude in music," paving the way for what follows by putting the hearer in the right emotional frame of mind for the rest of the speech.[19] Aristotle's prelude now came also to recreate figuratively the vividness of the Ignatian Prelude's "composition" of place, persons, and incidents. The vividness of Crashaw's lines contradicted the asceticism of his thought. However, this was not an issue in a poetic art that served as the meeting ground of the already dissimilar arts of oratory and ascetic meditation.

At the beginning of the verse letter "To the Countess of Denbigh" the same two dissimilar arts of oratory and exercise were fused. They are presented to the reader in a more intense series of paradoxes than in the opening lines of the poem to Mrs. "M.R." Yet, the new art remained inalterably that of epigram as emotive force. Crashaw's address to the Countess betrayed the fundamental sensibility of that conception of epigram as it transformed the rhetorical proem and the exercital prelude into one of extended paradox. The Countess was described in lines that converted her personal state into a meditative object. In a quick succession of antitheses, she is first a "heav'n besieged Heart" standing irresolute "at the Gate of Blisse." Next, she suffers from a spiritual condition, "whose Definition is, A Doubt / Twixt Life and Death, twixt In and Out" (11. 1-2, 5-6). Paradox served to demonstrate the unacceptable character of the Countess' religious indecision as, having become the topic of Crashaw's meditation, she suffered his attempts to persuade her to settle her convictions.

If the paradoxical fusion of the first stages of oratorical and exercital structures in Crashaw's verse letters was intense, the welding of "statement of facts" and three Ignatian colloquies that followed in both poems was characterized by antitheses of yet greater complexity. With this complexity, Crashaw rose to the challenge of the greater length of the structural parts involved. Being elastic in its application, the epigrammatic style met the demands of the detailed similarities of the "statement of facts" and of the "colloquies" on verse, with a modulated complexity of antithesis. The effect of the colloquies was similar in both verse letters. In three rapid affirmative declarations about his gift of a book to Mrs. "M.R.," and in three probing questions to the Countess, paradox was adapted to the orator's enumeration in his "statement of facts." By such "a persuasive exhibition of his subject," the classical orator had prepared to launch into his proof; now, paradox in the written word became the new instrument of rhetorical conviction.[20] Crashaw's lines to the gentlewoman illustrate the role of paradox in its new rhetorical and exercital context:

> It is, in one choise handfull, heavenn; & all
> Heavn's Royall host; incamp't thus small
> To prove that true, schooles use to tell,
> Ten thousand Angels in one point can dwell.
> It is love's great artillery
> Which here contracts it self, & comes to ly
> Close couch't in your white bosom: & from thence
> As from a snowy fortresse of defence,
> Against your ghostly foes to take your part,
> And fortify the hold of your chast heart.
> It is an armory of light
> Let constant use but keep it bright.
> (11. 11-22).

The paradoxes about the "handfull" of "heavenn," the "great "artillery," and the "armory of light" in the letter to Mrs. "M.R." (11. 11, 15, 21), and the antitheses about the "Magick-Bolts," the "fantastick Bands," and the "Birth" of the "brave Soul" in the letter to the Countess of Denbigh (11. 11, 13, 15), repeat the same idea successively. The reiteration then of certain images, one of the chief habits of the epigrammatic stylists, became for Crashaw an instrument for transferring oratorical structures into verse. By repeating such antitheses, Crashaw narrated the facts of his rhetorical case with the emotive savouring of the once ascetic colloquies that Heywood had introduced, though without oratorical structure, into English verse long ago.

As the verse letters developed into their "proof" sections, their paradoxes became progressively more epic or panoramic. Their antitheses also widened. The graduated intensity of both poems represented Crashaw's attempt to convince his reader by increasingly wide paradoxes. These paradoxes ranged the full distance from matter to infinite emotion. The Countess' spiritual condition was at first described in fairly detailed paradoxes connected with the forces of nature: "Both Winds and Waters urge their way, / And murmure if they meet a stay" (11. 39-40). However, as the description of her condition unfolded, its paradoxes became more profuse. Crashaw showed a spiritual rather than a material force lying behind the workings of nature and hence her condition too. The sources of imagery also increased as the poet intensified the end of his proof with the antithetical figure of a magnet originating in emblem literature. The Countess was drawn by love prefigured in the magnet as much as was nature in the earlier paradoxes: "So lumpish Steel, untaught to move, / Learn'd first his Lightnesse by his Love" which spiritually governed the universe (11. 51-52).

The intensification in the proof section of the verse letter to Mrs. "M.R." proceeded at a slower pace than in the poem to the Countess. Crashaw was developing a point by point Ignatian application of the five senses. From this application he drew his images, relaxing paradox and broadening antithesis. But the poem's central paradox about emotion and reading grew nevertheless progressively sharper as the value of the woman's experience became clearer with every sense's epigrammatic application.

The first antithesis of the proof section of the letter to Mrs. "M.R." described the application of the ear to sound. Its paradox centered on the tonal stillness of a massive spiritual force. Above this supposedly absolute stillness was heard the series of whispers communicating truth to the hearer's soul, demonstrating that the spiritual force of the preceding paradox was there at work (11. 65-67). With the application of the last sense, taste, after sight, smell, and touch (11. 70, 77, 82), the description of the spiritual experience of the Countess, with her final understanding of Christ, drew rapidly to a close (11. 90-94).

The intensification of paradox noticeable in both verse letters led to the "epilogue" or "peroration" of the oratorical structure. In the epilogue of the poem to the gentlewoman, the final broadening of paradox took the shape of antitheses between a number of absolutely sensory things like spices, sweets, and treasures (11. 110-116, 119), and the infinite spiritual moral qualities in the person of Christ (11. 118, 119, 124). By contrast, in the poem to the Countess, the antitheses of the epilogue were between intangible objects, victory, courage, and life on the one hand and defeat, cowardice, and death on the other. These antitheses were less broad too than in the poem to "M.R." (11. 79-90). However, their effect as they repeated paradoxically the woman's indecision was likewise to bring out one final time the sharpness of the preceding figures of the poem. Antitheses characterized the presence of the rhetorical structure in both verse letters and distinguished the structure's influence from its formative role elsewhere in Renaissance works. The oratorical structure also appeared in Sidney's *Defence of Poetry* and in the speeches of the devils in Book II of *Paradise Lost*. But there its influence was other than the aesthetics of Ignatian tradition.[21]

To understand the force of the Ignatian poetic in England such as in Crashaw's verse letters, a full survey of all continental poetry is unnecessary. Out of the development of the Counter Reformation, which was international, there were nevertheless distinguishing marks in England. Although Italian writers appeared to produce the more prominent poetic theorists and the French often seemed the best philosophical interpreters of the general movement of Jesuit thought, the English may have been the best and most consistent practitioners of verse meditation. Many factors existed to make the poetic in England strong and distinct. The symbol of reading and the help it gave to contemporary poets from Heywood to Revett to discuss poetry are only a single example.

English meditative poetry answered to a vision of the world, whether that vision was always immediately, directly inspired by Ignatian poetics or not. Ironically, that Jesuit-inspired poetry might be more clearly delimited on British soil than elsewhere may be due to the unfavourable political position of the Church there between 1580 and 1650. We say ironically because, as we recede in time from that troubled period, the Counter Reformation and the Reformation appear to be more and more the forces of similar movements of thought and art, inspired by a single disaffection with the former thousand-year-old world view, having little to do with the political strains that they then appeared exclusively to support.

Notes

[1]Aristotle, *Rhetoric*, III, 10-11, pp. 208-211; *Poetics*, II, xxv, p. 41.
[2]Aristotle, *Rhetoric*, III, 9, pp. 204-205.
[3]Aristotle, *Rhetoric*, III, 10, 9, 11, pp. 209, 204-205, 211.
[4]*Rhetoric*, III, 11, 10, pp. 211, 207-208.
[5]Augustine, *Confessions* X, viii, 14, p. 209.
[6]*Poetics*, II, xxv, p. 41; *Rhetoric*, III, 11, pp. 211-212.
[7]George Williamson, *The Donne Tradition* (New York, 1958), p. 87; *Rhetoric*, III, 11, pp. 213-215.
[8]*Rhetoric*, III, 11, p. 215.
[9]Quintilian, *Institutio Oratoria*, III, V, 1, 4 Vols., ed. H. E. Butler (Cambridge, Mass., 1953), Vol. I, p. 397; *Rhetoric*, III, 11, pp. 211-212.
[10]A. J. Smith, "Theory and Practice in Renaissance Poetry: Two Kinds

of Imitation," *Bulletin of the John Rylands Library,* XLVII (1964), pp. 213, 217.

[11]Charles Pajot, *Ars Poetica complectens; 1. Varia Versuum et odarum genera; 2. Methodum facilem et brevem componendi versus; Universam Quantitatem seu quae regulis Joannis Despauterij continentur,* Paris, 1645. The copy used here is of the fifth edition, Paris, 1666, p.7; Suzanne K. Langer, *A Theory of Art* (New York, 1951), p.238.

[12]Erich Auerbach, "Figura," *Scenes From the Drama of European Literature* (New York, 1959), pp. 25-26.

[13]Sir Philip Sidney, "Sonnet 49," 11. 1-4, *The Poems,* ed. William A. Ringler Jr. (Oxford, 1962), p. 189.

[14]Tuve, *Elizabethan and Metaphysical Imagery,* pp. 104, 109.

[15]Puttenham, *The Arte of English Poesie,* pp. 137-138.

[16]Puttenham, *The Arte of English Poesie,* pp. 42-59; Sidney, *A Defence of Poetry,* p. 27.

[17]Martin, "Commentary," *Poems,* p. 448.

[18]Aristotle, *Rhetoric,* III, 13, p. 220; Quintilian, *Institutio,* III, ix, 1, Vol. 1, p. 515.

[19]Aristotle, *Rhetoric,* III, 14, p. 221.

[20]Quintilian, *Institutio,* IV, ii, 31; i, 7, Vol. II, p. 67.

[21]K. O. Myrick, *Sir Philip Sidney as Literary Craftsman* in *Harvard Studies in English,* Vol. XIV (Cambridge, Mass., 1935), pp. 52-53; John Milton, *Paradise Lost,* IX, 1, 549, in *Paradise Lost and Selected Prose,* intro. by Northrop Frye (New York, 1971), p. 212.

Index

Act of Supremacy, pp. 88, 112.
Agony in the Garden, p. 16.
Alabaster, William, pp. IX, X, 1, 2, 4, 5, 8n.8, 23, 26, 50, 52, 54, 61, 63–66, 69, 71, 73–74, 76, 78–79, 84, 90–91, 112, 121, 153; *Apparatus in Revelationem*, pp. 5, 9n.14, 26, 40; *Ecce Sponus Venit*, p. 36n. 29; "Incarnation Sonnets," p. 88; Sonnets 1, "The night, the starless night of passion," pp. 5, 91–92; 3 to 6, "The Portrait of Christ's death," p. 88; 10, "Though all forsake thee, lord," pp. 64; 13, "My soul within the bed of heaven doth grow," p. 90; 15, "My soul a world is by contraction," pp. 17, 40, 49, 64, 76; 19, "A Divine Sonnet," pp. 72, 73; 21, "Upon Christ's Saying to Mary," p. 88; 26, "Another of the same," p. 153; 30, "Upon the Crucifix," p. 88; 31, "Upon St-Paul to the Corinthians," p. 40; 32, "Upon the Crucifix," p. 88; 34, "Upon the Crucifix," p. 88; 38, "The Eternity," p. 72; 43, "New Jerusalem," pp. 132–33; 47, "Lord, I have left all," p. 40; 48, "My friends, whose kindness," p. 40; 50, "To his Sad Friend," p. 76; 53, "A preface to the Incarnation," pp. 40, 69, 72; 58, "Christus Recapitulatio Omnium," p. 106; 62, "Omnia Propter Christum Facta," p. 69; 68, "A Morning Meditation," p. 106; 70, "A Morning Meditation," pp. 95–96; 75, "A New Year's Gift to my Savior," pp. 65, 88.
Allison, A. F., and D. M. Rogers, *A Catalogue of English Books*, p. 80n.6.

Ambrose, Isaac, p. 52.
Antwerp, Jesuit College, p. 3.
Aphrodite, p. 13.
Apollo, p. 13.
Apostolic Age, p. 130.
Aquinas, Thomas, pp. 15, 22, 41, 50, 58n.17, n.18, 76–77; *In Perihermenias*, p. 56n.5; *Summa Theologica*, pp. 34n.5, 35n.17; *Treatise on Man*, pp. 56n.1, n.2, n.4, 57n.6, 58n.12, 80n.12.
Aristotle, pp. 4, 15, 29, 31, 37–38, 41, 83, 85, 118, 119; *Analytica Priora*, p. 141n.4; *Of the Categories*, pp. 23, 31, 56n.5, 120, 152; *On Interpretation*, p. 57n.5; *De Partibus Animalium*, p. 36n.33; *Poetics*, pp. 9n.13, 84–85, 103–104, 115n.3, n.12, 119, 141n.2, 143, 145–146, 151–152, 163n.1, n.6; *Rhetoric*, pp. 15, 34n.4, 73, 119, 141n.1, 143–148, 151–152, 159–160, 163n.1, n.2, n.3, n.4, n.6, n.7, n.8, n.9, 164n.18, n.19, 80n.9; *On Soul*, p. 56n.5; *Topica*, p. 115n.6.
Arwaker, Edmund, trans. *Pia Desideria*, by Herman Hugo, pp. 52–53; 59n.25, 120–121, 141n.3.
Auerbach, Erich, *Scenes From the Drama of European Literature*, p. 164n.12.
Augustine, of Hippo, pp. 41, 76, 78; *Confessions*, pp. 56n.1, n.2, 80n.14, n.15, 118, 145, 163n.5; *Trinity*, pp. 57n.10, 80n.13.

Bacon, Francis, pp. 33, 57n.8, 105.
Bagshaw, Christopher, *A True Relation*

165

of the Faction, p. 9n.11.

Bald, R. C., *John Donne, A Life*, pp. 2, 7n.4, 115n.16, 58n.20.

Balsamo, Ignatius, *Instruction How to Pray and Meditate Well*, trans. Thomas Everard, p. 15.

Banister, John, *The Historie of Man*, pp. 29–30, 36n.35.

Barnes, Barnaby, *A Divine Century of Spirituall sonnets*, pp. 61, 79n.1, 101.

Bauhusius, Bernard, p. 8n.5.

Bayley, Lewis, p. 52.

Beaumont, Joseph, pp. 15, 57n.8, 61, 79n.1.

Bellarmine, Robert, pp. 18–20, 27; *Explanatio in Psalmos*, pp. 21, 35n.18; *Of the Eternall Felicity of the Saints*, trans. Thomas Everard, pp. 18–20, 34n.10, n.11.

Bennet, Joan, *Five Metaphysical Poets*, pp. 79, 81n.17.

Berry, Boyd M., *Process of Speech*, pp. 54, 59n.28.

Bertonasco, Marc, *Crashaw and the Baroque*, p. 8n.5.

Bettinus, Marius, p. 8n.5.

Bible, pp. 13, 26, 53–54, 87–89, 110–111, 113–114, 124–125, 129–131; "Apocalypse," p. 130; "Canticles," p. 121; "Corinthians," p. 26; "Daniel, Book of," p. 26; "Genesis," p. 22; "Jeremy," p. 131; New Testament, pp. 24, 53–54, 88, 111; Old Testament, pp. 24, 53–54, 111.

Biderman, Jacob, *Deliciae Sacrae*, pp. 8n.5, 31, 36n.42, 54.

Blundeville, Thomas, *His Exercises . . . Cosmographie*, pp. 19, 35n.15.

Boccacio, p. 101.

Borgia, Francis, pp. 65, 74, 80n.10.

Bossy, John, *English Catholic Community*, pp. 8n.9, n.10, 9n.11, 115n.16.

Boyle, Robert, p. 52.

Brahe, Tycho, p. 33.

Brerely, John, *Virginalia*, pp. 61, 79n.1, 101.

Bright, Timothy, *Treatise of Melancholy*, pp. 28, 30, 36n.31.

Brinkley, Stephen, trans. *Exercise of a*

Christian Life, by Gaspard Loarte, p. 59n.26.

Britt, Matthew, trans., *The Hymns of the Breviary and Missal*, p. 58n.18.

Brodrick, James, *Saint Ignatius Loyola, The Pilgrim Years*, p. 58n.14.

Brown, Nancy Pollard, p. 2; ed., Robert Southwell, *The Poems*, p. IX; "The Structure of Southwell's 'Saint Peters Complaint'," *MLR*, p. 7n.4, n.5; ed., *Two Letters and Short Rule of Good Life*, by Robert Southwell, pp. 34n.8, 115n.18.

Bruno, Vincenzo, *An Abridgement of Meditation*, trans. Richard Gibbons, pp. 37, 55n.1.

Buchanan, George, p. 134.

Bunney, Edmund, trans. *A Book of Christian Exercise*, by Gaspard Loarte, pp. 53, 59n.26.

Burton, Robert, p. 19; *The Anatomy of Melancholy*, pp. 19, 35n.14, n.16.

Bush, Douglas, *English Literature in the Earlier Seventeenth Century*, p. 8n.5.

Cabilliau, Baldinus, p. 136.

Campbell, Lily B., *Divine Poetry and Drama in Sixteenth Century England*, p. 115n.2.

Campion, Edmund, s.j., pp. IX, 111.

Camus, Albert, *The Plague*, p. 34n.2.

Cavalier poetry, p. 109.

Chamberlain, John, p. 115n.18.

Church Fathers, p. 21.

Coleridge, Samuel Taylor, *Biographia Literaria*, p. 57n.7.

Constable, Henry, pp. 8n.10, 9n.11, 101.

Cooper, Lane, ed., Aristotle, *Rhetoric*, p. 141n. 1.

Copernicus, pp. 19, 33.

Cornford, F. M., trans., Plato, *Republic*, p. 9n.13.

Coronary prayers, pp. 65, 96.

Cowley, Abraham, p. 64.

Crane, William G., "Introduction," *The Garden of Eloquence*, by Henry Peacham, p. 80n.9.

Crashaw, Richard, pp. IX, X, 1–7, 15, 24, 50, 53–55, 63–64, 69, 76, 84, 92–

93, 119, 127–129, 154; "Adoro te," pp.
4, 5, 16, 50, 53, 69–70, 78, 86, 98;
"Alexias" elegies, pp. 2, 8n.6, 107,
130: "The First Elegie," p. 108; "The
Seconde Elegie," pp. 14, 108; "The
Third Elegie," p. 108; "And he an-
sewered them nothing," pp. 121, 128;
"Description of a Religious House," p.
76; "Dies Irae," pp. 50, 69; "Dives asking a drop," p. 8n.6; "Easter day," p.
88; *Epigrammatum, Sacrorum Liber*,
pp. 44, 58n.11, 121; "Epiphanie"
hymn, pp. 87–88, 93–94, 155–158;
"Glorious Assumption," p. 14; "Holy
Nativity," pp. 5, 87–88, 93–95, 96,
144, 152, 155–158; "Lauda Sion," pp.
4, 5, 24, 50, 53; "Musick's Duell," pp.
2, 8n.6; "New Year's Day," pp. 157–
158; "Office of the Holy Crosse," p.
134; "On hope," pp. 64–65; "On the
still surviving markes of our Saviours
wounds," pp. 118, 127–128; "Our Lord
in his Circumcision," p. 88; "Sancta
Maria Dolorem," pp. 50, 88, 93–94,
117, 131, 158–159; "Sospetto d'Herode," pp. 5, 14, 17, 19; *Steps to the
Temple*, p. 121; "The Teare," pp. 2,
8n.6, 155, 158; "To Lessius His Rule of
Health," pp. 2, 44; "To our Lord upon
the Cross," p. 88; "To the Countess of
Denbigh," pp. 2, 16, 71, 98, 109–110,
159–163; "To the Name," pp. 4, 5, 40,
51, 53–54, 65, 69–70, 107; Trilogy to
Saint Teresa, pp. 107, 128, 130:
"Hymne to . . . Sainte Teresa," pp.
5–6, 107, 128, 130; "Apologie for the
Fore-going Hymne," pp. 4, 107, 129;
"The Flaming Heart," pp. 107–108;
"Upon the Bleeding Crucifix," pp. 16,
138–139, 159; "Upon the Sepulchre of
Our Lord," p. 121; Verse letters to
"Mrs. M. R.," p. 102: "Ode Praefixed
. . . to a little Prayer-book given to a
young Gentlewoman," pp. 2, 4, 98,
100, 159–163; "To the same Party,
Councel concerning her Choise," p.
159; "Vexilla Regis," pp. 50, 69–70,
88, 110; "The Weeper," pp. 2, 8n.6, 76,
136, 139, 155, 158; "Water made

Wine," p. 88.
Crashaw, William, pp. 21, 53, 79n.4,
111–112; "Dialogue, Betwixt The
Soul and the Body of a damned Man,"
p. 111; *The Jesuites Gospell*, pp. 8n.6,
110, 115n.14.
Crooke, Helkiah, *A Description of the
Body of Man*, pp. 28–30, 36n.31, n.35.

Daniells, Roy, "Baroque Form in En-
glish Literature," *University of
Toronto Quarterly*, pp. 31, 36n.40.
Dante Alighieri, pp. 20, 22, 35n.21.
Dayrell, John, *A Treatise of the Church*,
pp. 21, 35n.19.
Dionysius, p. 145.
Dobell, Bertram, p. 8n.8.
Donatus, Alexander, pp. 15, 102, 123;
Ars Poetica, pp. 15, 34n.6, 43, 44,
57n.8, 83, 95, 103–104, 108, 115n.6,
119–120, 134–136, 144–147,
150–151.
Donne, Henry, p. 112.
Donne, John, pp. IX, 1, 2, 3, 23, 32, 50,
54, 55, 61, 62, 63–66, 71–74, 79, 84,
90, 111–114, 124–125, 129; "Anniver-
sarie poems," pp. 3, 7n.4, 102, 114:
"The First Anniversary," pp. 2, 110;
"The Second Anniversary," pp. 24, 25,
114; "The Canonization," pp. 90, 114,
146, 147; "The Crosse," pp. 111, 114,
123–126; *Devotions Upon Emergent
Occasions*, pp. 7n.4, 26, 29–30, 32
36n.34, 115n.17; "The Dissolution," p.
146; *Essays in Divinity*, pp. 25,
36n.28, 53, 113, 115n.21; "The Extasie," p. 146; "The Funerall," pp. 29,
123–124, 146; "Goodfriday 1613.
Riding Westward," pp. 49, 114; "Holy
Sonnets," pp. X, 4, 26, 63, 64–66, 74,
80n.5, 114, 123, 125–126, 153–154:
1: "Thou hast made me," pp. 13, 17,
64, 154; 5: "I am a little world," pp.
73–74, 126; 6: "This is my playes last
scene," p. 126; 7: "At the round earths
imagin'd corners," p. 125; 10: "Death
be not proud," pp. 16, 87; 12: Why are
wee by all creatures," pp. 46, 106–
107; 13: "What if this present," p. 91;

14: "batter my heart," p. 63; 16: "Father, part of his double interest," pp. 64–65; 17: "Since she whom I lov'd," pp. 65, 112; 18: "Show me deare Christ," pp. 63, 113; 19: "Oh, to vex me," pp. 17, 138–139; "A Hymn to Christ, at the Author's last going into Germany," pp. 111, 114, 126; *Ignatius His Conclave*, pp. 26, 36n.29, 103, 110, 113, 115n.11, n.14, n.20, 141n.5; "La Corona" sonnets, pp. X, 4, 65–66, 74–75, 80n.5, 96, 114, 123, 125, 153–154: 1: "Deigne at my hands," pp. 92, 96, 102; 2: "Annunciation," p. 88; 3: "Nativitie," pp. 88, 154; 4: "Temple," p. 88; 5: "Crucifying," pp. 74–75, 88; 6: "Resurrection," pp. 88, 89; 7: "Ascension," pp. 89–90, 138–140; "A nocturnall upon S. Lucies day," pp. 25, 146; *Poems* (1633), p. 65; *Pseudo-Martyr*, pp. 30, 36n.36, 113, 115n.19; "Raderus," p. 141n.5; "A Valediction Forbidding mourning," pp. 73, 146; "The Will," p. 147.

Douai, Jesuit College at, pp. 3, 42.

"The Dream of the Rood," p. 16.

Drury, Elizabeth, pp. 25, 26, 114.

Dulles, A., *New Catholic Encyclopedia*, p. 115n.4.

Edmonds, See Weston, William.

Elias, the prophet, p. 47.

Elyot, Thomas, p. 46; *Castle of Helth*, pp. 30, 36n.37.

Enoch, the prophet, p. 47.

Everard, Thomas, pp. 15–16, 20, 33, 37; trans. *Instruction How to Pray and Meditate Well*, by Ignatius Balsamo, pp. 34n.7, 38, 40–42, 45; trans. *Of the Eternal Felicity of the Saints*, by Robert Bellarmine, p. 20; trans. *The Practise of Christian Perfection*, by Francis Borgia, pp. 74, 80n.10.

Ferrar, Nicholas, *The Story Books of Little Gidding*, pp. 52, 58n.19, 59n.21.

Fletcher, Iain, "Introduction," *Partheneia Sacra*, pp. 8n.10, 9n.12.

Floyd, John, pp. 21, 37–38; *The Overthrow of the Protestant Pulpit-babels*,

pp. 8n.6, 21, 38–42, 44–45, 67, 145.

Foley, Henry, *Records of the English Province of the Society of Jesus*, p. 115n.16.

Francis of Sales, p. 47.

Freeman, Rosemary, *English Emblem Books*, p. 9n.12.

Friedman, Donald, ed., Eldred Revett, *Selected Poems*, pp. IX, 100, 115n.8.

Frye, Northrop, intro., *Paradise Lost and Selected Prose*, p. 164n.21.

Fulke, William, *A Most pleasant Prospect Into the Garden of Naturall Contemplation*, pp. 19, 34–35n.12, 35n.14.

Galileo, p. 33.

Gardner, Helen, pp. 2, 124; "Introduction," Donne, *Divine Poems*, pp. 80n, n.5, n.11; "Introduction," John Donne, *The Elegies and the Songs and Sonnets*, p. 141n.8; "The Poetry of Meditation by Louis Martz" (review), *Review of English Studies*, p. 7n.4; ed., William Alabaster, *Sonnets*, pp. IX, 8n.8.

Garnet, Henry, p. 9n.11.

Gerard, John, p. 2.

Gibbons, Richard, trans. *An Abridgement of Meditation*, by Vincenzo Bruno, pp. 37–42, 44–45, 48, 55–56n.1, 57n.8, 67, 71, 103–104; trans. *Meditations Upon the Mysteries of our Holy Faith*, by Luis de la Puente, pp. 37, 40, 42, 55–56n.1, 57n.8, 145.

Granada, Luis de, pp. 21, 27–29; *Devotions*, trans. Francis Meres, pp. 27–28, 30, 35n.18, 36n.30, n.32; *The Sinners Guyde*, p. 34n.9.

Grierson, H. J. C., ed. John Donne, *The Poetical Works*, pp. IX, 80n.5.

Grosart, A. B., ed. *The Complete Poems of Joseph Beaumont*, p. 79n.1.

Grundy, Joan M., ed. *The Poems of Henry Constable*, pp. 2, 7n.2, 9n.10, n.11.

Gryphius, Andreas, pp. 137, 142n.16.

Halewood, William, *The Poetry of Grace*, pp. 2, 7n.4, 53, 59n.27, 79n.4.

Hall, Joseph, "The Art of Divine Medita-

tion," *Works*, pp. 52, 59n.23, n.24.
Hamilton, G. H., *English Verse Epigrams*, pp. 134, 142n.11.
Harvey, Christopher, trans., *The Scoole of the Heart*, by Benedict van Haeftan, pp. 24, 35–36n.26.
Harvey, William, p. 33.
Hawkins, Henry, pp. 33, 49; trans. *The Devout Hart*, by Stephen Luzvik, pp. 54, 59n.29; trans., *Fuga Saeculi. Or the Holy Hatred of the World*, by Johannes Maffei, p. 58n.15; *Partheneia Sacra*, pp. 2, 8n.5, n.6, n.10, 9n. 12, 30, 44, 54.
Herbert, George, pp. 15, 61, 94; "The Pulley," p. 137; "Jordan I," p. 138, 142n.17.
Heywood, Elias, pp. 3, 112.
Heywood, Jasper, pp. IX, X, 1, 2, 3, 4, 5, 6, 23, 54, 61, 63, 66, 70, 76, 78–79, 84, 85, 93, 97, 112, 121, 129, 152–153, 161, 163; "Alluding his State to the Prodigall Child," pp. 13, 14, 16, 62, 85–86, 99–100, 122, 152–153; "Beyng troubled in mynde, he writeth as followeth," pp. 16, 61, 71, 85; "Complaint of a sorrowful Soule," pp. 4, 76, 86, 98, 122; "Easter day," pp. 88, 93, 121–122, 152–153; "Look oe'r you leap," p. 86; *The Paradise of Dainty Devices*, pp. IX, X, 2, 121–122; "A witty and pleasant conceit," p. 86.
Heywood, John, p. 153.
Hooker, Richard, p. 105.
Hopkins, Richard, p. 21.
Howell, Wilbur S., *Logic and Rhetoric in England*, pp. 35n.22, n.24; *Poetics, Rhetoric and Logic*, p. 35n.23.
Hudson, H. H., *The Epigram in the English Renaissance*, pp. 134, 142n.10, n.11.
Hugo, Herman, *Pia Desideria*, pp. 8n.5, 31, 36n.41, 53, 54, 59n.25, 120–121, 136, 141n.3.

Ignatius Loyola, pp. IX, 33, 66, 77–78; *Spiritual Exercises*, pp. IX, X, 1–2, 15, 17, 30, 32–34, 37–41, 43–50, 52, 54, 55, 56n.3, 58n.14, n.18, 62, 66–67, 70, 72, 86, 89, 95, 97–101, 125, 139, 145, 159–161.

James I, p. 112.
James, Thomas, *The Jesuites Downfall*, p. 9n.11.
Janelle, Pierre, *Robert Southwell The Writer, A Study in Religious Inspiration*, pp. 2, 7n.2, 8n.10, 9n.11, 115n.16.
Jessop, Augustus, *One Generation of a Norfolk House*, p. 8n.9.
John of the Cross, p. 47.
Jonson, Ben, p. 85; *Timber, Or Discoveries*, p. 115n.3.
Julian of Norwich, p. 47.

Keane, Henry, ed., Ignatius Loyola, *The Spiritual Exercises*, pp. IX, 56n.3.
Koestler, Arthur, *Darkness at noon*, p. 34n.3.
Kuhlmann, Quirinius, pp. 137, 142n.16.

Langer, Suzanne, K., *A Theory of Art*, pp. 151, 164n.11.
Lany, Benjamin, Master, Pembroke College, p. 58n.11.
Lessius, Leonard, *Hygiasticon*, pp. 2, 8n.7, 44, 80n.13.
Lever, J. W., *The Elizabethan Love Sonnet*, p. 80n.8.
Lewalski, Barbara K., pp. 2, 123; *Donne's Anniversaries and the Poetry of Praise*, p. 7n.4; "Donne's Devotions," ed. A. Raspa, *Renaissance Quarterly*, pp. 7n.4, 59n.22, 141n.6; *Protestant Poetics and the Seventeenth-Century Religious Lyric*, pp. IX, 59n.22, 80n.4.
Lewis, C. S., *English Literature in the Sixteenth Century*, p. 79n.4.
Leys, M. D. R., *Catholics in England*, p. 8n.10.
Little Gidding, pp. 52, 58n.20.
Loarte, Gaspard, *The Exercise of a Christian Life*, pp. 53, 59n.26.
Lok, Henry, *Ecclesiastes . . . English Poesie*, pp. 61, 79n.1.
Loretto, pp. 70, 79n.1.
Lovejoy, A. O., *The Great Chain of Being*, p. 36n.39.

Lucifer, p. 14.
Luzvic, Stephen, *Cor Devotum*, trans. Carolus Musart, p. 59n.30; *The Devout Hart*, trans. Henry Hawkins, pp. 54, 59n.29, n.30.

Machiavelli, p. 46.
Maffei, Johannes, *Fuga Saeculi*, trans. by Henry Hawkins, pp. 49, 58n.15.
Maja, p. 152.
Manresa, p. 48.
Marino, Giambattista, "Sospetto d'Herode," pp. 5, 9n.15.
Mars, p. 145.
Martial, pp. 120, 123, 134–135, 140, 153.
Martin, L. C., ed. Richard Crashaw, *Poems, English, Latin and Greek*, pp. IX, 7n.5, 8n.5, n.6, 57n.7, 58n.17, n.20, 79n.4, 164n.17.
Martz, Louis Lohr, pp. 2, 7n.3, n.4, 72, 97; *The Paradise Within*, p. 58n.18; *The Poetry of Meditation*, pp. 2, 7n.3, n.5, 36n.29, 56n.1, 80n.5, n.6, n.11.
Marvell, Andrew, p. 94.
McDonald, J. H., ed., Robert Southwell, *The Poems*, p. IX.
Meres, Francis, trans., *Devotions*, by Luis de Granada, pp. 21, 27–28, 34n.9, 35n.18.
Metaphysical poetry, pp. 4, 90, 109.
Michael, Archangel, p. 14.
Milton, John, p. 85; *Paradise Lost*, p. 163; *The Reason of Church Government Urged Against Prelaty*, p. 115n.3.
Minturnus, p. 136.
Mitchell, W. F., *English Pulpit Oratory*, pp. 2, 7n.4.
Molina, Antonio, *A Treatise of Mental Prayer*, trans. John Sweetnam, pp. 75, 79n.3.
Montagu, Walter, p. 33; *Miscellania Spiritualia*, pp. 30–31, 36n.38.
Montaigne, Michel de, p. 113.
More, Anne, pp. 65, 112.
More, Thomas, pp. 3, 46, 112.
Moses, p. 22.
Mount Olivet, p. 88.

Moxon, T. M., ed., Aristotle, *Poetics*, p. 9n. 13.
Mueller, Janelle M., "The Exegesis of Experience, Dean Donne's *Devotions*," *JEGP*, pp. 2, 7n.4.
Musart, Carolus, trans. *Cor Deo Devotum*, by Stephen Luzvic, p. 59n.30.
Muzio, pp. 102–104.
Myrick, K. O., *Sir Philip Sidney as Literary Craftsman*, p. 164n.21.
Mystery, Christian, pp. 65, 86–92, 96, 125.

Nelson, Lowry, *Baroque Lyric Poetry*, p. 142n.15.
Neo-Platonism, pp. 43, 67, 79.

Pajot, Charles, *Ars Poetica*. pp. 150–151, 164n.11.
The Paradise of Dainty Devices, pp. IX, X, 2, 121–122.
Parsons, See Persons.
Peacham, Henry, *The Garden of Eloquence*, pp. 73, 80n.9.
"The Pearl," p. 16.
Pembroke College, Cambridge, p. 58n.11.
Persons, Robert, p. 9n.11; trans. *The first Booke of Christian exercise*, by Gaspard Loarte, p. 59n.26; *A True Report of the death and martyrdome of M. Edmund Campion*, p. IX.
Petrarch, Francis, pp. 5, 117, 120, 150.
Plato, pp. 79, 95, 103, 110; *The Republic*, pp. 9n.13, 84, 115n.15; *The Sophist*, pp. 57n.8, 115n.15.
Pona, Francesco, p. 8n.5.
Pontanus, Jacobus, pp. 123, 136, 141n.5.
Possevine, Anthony, pp. 21, 123, 136; *Apparatum Sacrum*, p. 21.
Praz, Mario, *Secentismo e Marinismo in Inghilterra*, pp. 8n.5, 136, 142n.14.
Primum Mobile, p. 19.
Ptolemy, pp. 19, 50.
Puente, de la, Luis, *Meditations Upon the Mysteries of our Holy Faith*, trans., Richard Gibbons, pp. 37, 55–56n.1, 57n.8.
Puristic verse, pp. 67, 103.

Puttenham, George, *The Arte of Englishe Poesie*, pp. 73, 80n.9, 85,
115n.3, 153, 157, 164n.15, n.16.
Quarles, Francis, pp. 120, 123, 141n.3.
Quintilian, *Institutio Oratoria*, pp. 148–
150, 159–161, 163n.9, 164n.18, n.20.
Raderus, Matthew, *M. Valerii Martialis
Epigrammaton*, pp. 123, 134–136,
140–141, 141n.5, 151.
Ramsay, Mary Paton, *Les Doctrines Mé-
diévales chez Donne*, pp. 2, 7n.4,
57n.8.
Ramus, Peter, *The Logicke*, pp. 23,
35n.24, n.25.
Raspa, Anthony, ed., John Donne, *Devo-
tions Upon Emergent Occasions*, pp.
7n.4, 36n.34.
Rastell, John, *Book of Purgatory*, pp. 19,
35n.15.
Recorde, Robert, *The Castle of Knowledge*, pp. 19, 35n.13, n.16.
*Records of the English Province of the
Society of Jesus*, See, Foley, Henry.
Remond, Francis, *Epigrammata et Elegiae*, pp. 8n.5, n.6, 135–136, 142n.12.
Renold, P., *The Wisbech Stirs*, p. 9n.11.
Restoration, The, p. 3.
Revett, Eldred, pp. IX, X, 3, 6, 54, 55,
61, 63, 76, 78–79, 84, 92, 97, 118, 163;
"Ascension day," p. 155; "Astraea recall'd," p. 109; "Christ nailed and
wounded on the Cross," p. 88; "Christmas Day," pp. 87–88, 94, 155; "Innocents Day," pp. 13, 14; "Jacobs Vision
at Bethnel," pp. 40, 77; "Jesus Wept,"
p. 6; "The Jewes attempting to stone
our saviour," p. 14; "Lasarus *raised by*
our Saviour," pp. 133–134, 155;
"Lazarus and Dives," p. 88; "Meditation," p. 71; "The Nymph," p. 109;
"Our Saviour circumcis'd," p. 88; "Our
Saviour cradled in the Manger," p. 6;
Poems (1657), pp. IX, X, 3; "The
Sepulchure," p. 6; "The Taper," pp.
100–101; "The Teare," p. 6; "The Water Made Wine," pp. 6, 88.
Rheims, Jesuit College, p. 3.
Ribadeneira, Pedro, p. 24; *Catalogus*

Scriptorum Religionis societatis Jesu,
pp. 24–25, 36n.27.
Richeome, Louis, *Holy Pictures of the
mysticall Figures*, trans. of *Tableaux
Sacréz*, pp. 21–22, 35n.20.
Roberts, John, "The Influence of the
Spiritual Exercises of St. Ignatius on
the Nativity Poems of Robert South-
well," *JEGP*, pp. 2, 7n.4.
Robinson, Eloise, ed. *The Minor Poems
of Joseph Beaumont*, pp. 57n.8, 79n.1.
Robortellus, Franciscus, pp. 102–104,
136.
Rogers, D. M., See A. F. Allison.
Rogers, Richard, p. 52.
Rolle, Richard, p. 47.
Roman College, pp. 3, 15.
Ross, Malcolm M., *Poetry and Dogma*,
p. 79n.1.

St-Omer, Jesuit College, p. 3.
Sancer, John, See Stephen Brinkley.
Satan, pp. 13–14, 64.
Scaliger, Julius Caesar, pp. 136,
142n.13.
Scallon, Joseph D., *The Poetry of Robert
Southwell*, pp. 2, 7n.2, 115n.5.
Schaar, Claes, "Commentary," *Sospetto
d'Herode*, p. 9n. 15.
Scribanus, Charles, *Amphitheatrum
Honoris Jesuitici*, pp. 2, 8n.6.
Sebund, Raymond de, p. 113.
Seminarist priests, pp. 3, 9n.11.
Shakespeare, William, pp. 47, 49; *Ham-
let*, p. 58n.13; *Richard II*, p. 58n.16;
Troilus and Cressida, p. 58n.16.
Sharland, E. Cruwys, ed. *The Story
Books of Little Gidding*, by Nicholas
Ferrar, p. 58n.19.
Sibbes, Richard, p. 52.
Sidney, Sir Philip, pp. 63, 67, 85,
153–154, 164n.21; *A Defence of Po-
etry*, pp. 79n.2, 115n.3, 157, 163; *The
Poems*, p. 164n.13.
Smith, A. J., "Theory and Practice in
Renaissance Poetry: Two Kinds of Im-
itation," *Bulletin of the John Rylands
Library*, pp. 163–164n.10.
Sommervogel, Carlos, *Bibliothèque de la*

Compagnie de Jésus, p. 34n.6.
Southern, A. C., *Elizabethan Recusant Prose*, p. 80n.6.
Southwell, Richard, pp. 112, 115n.18.
Southwell, Robert, pp. IX, X, 1, 2, 3, 4, 5, 23–24, 50, 54, 55, 63, 66, 70, 71, 76, 78, 79, 84, 87–88, 93, 118, 153; "At home in Heaven," p. 65; "The Author to his loving Cosen," pp. 67–68, 102; "Burning Babe," p. 93; "Davids Peccavi," pp. 14, 68; "Decease Release," pp. 84, 86; "Epistle Unto His Father," pp. 34n.8, 115n.18; "A Holy Hymne," pp. 40, 50, 87; "Josephs Amazement," pp. 77, 88; "Life is but Losse," p. 16; "Lifes death loves life," p. 13; "Looke Home," p. 63; "Loves Garden grief," p. 13; "Man's Civill War," p. 68; "Man to the Wound in Christ's side," pp. 88, 100; "Mary Magdalen's Blush," p. 88; "Of the Blessed Sacrament of the Aulter," pp. 23–24, 39, 50, 98–99; "A Phansie turned to a sinners complaint," pp. 77, 86; "The Prodigall childs soule wracke," pp. 13, 85, 100, 153; "Saint Peters Complaint," pp. 2, 3, 4, 16, 43, 49, 85, 88, 105, 117, 131–132, 149; "The Sequence on the Virgin Mary and Christ," pp. 14, 88; *Short Rule of Good Life*, pp. 15–16, 18, 34n.8, 44, "Sinners Complaint," p. 65; "Sinnes heavie load," p. 87; "To the Reader," pp. 67, 103; "Upon the Image of Death," pp. 137–139, 159; "A Vale of Teares," pp. 43, 99–100, 105–106; "The Virgin Mary to Christ on the Cross," p. 88.
Spenser, Edmund, "A Hymn of Heavenly Love," p. 81n.16; "Letter to Raleigh," pp. 43, 57n.9.
Spingarn, J. E., p. 67; *History of Literary Criticism in the Renaissance*, pp. 9n.13, 80n.7, 115n.2, n.7, n.9, n.10, n.13.
Story, G. M., ed., William Alabaster, *Sonnets*, pp. IX, 8n.8, 80n.8, 115n.5, n.18.
Strada, Famianus, pp. 43, 57n.7; *Prolusiones Academicae*, pp. 43, 44, 57n.7,

102–104, 108.
Sweetnam, John, trans. *A Treatise of Mental Prayer*, by Antonio Molina, pp. 52, 64, 70–71, 75, 79n.3.
Synan, Edward, p. 56n.5.
Teresa of Avila, pp. 47, 128, 130, 141n.9.
Thesaurus Hymnologicus, p. 7n.5.
Tillyard, E. M., *The Elizabethan World Picture*, p. 36n.43.
Traherne, Thomas, pp. 78–79, 118.
Tuve, Rosemund, *Elizabethan and Metaphysical Imagery*, pp. 35n.25, 114n.1, 164n.14.
Ulysses, p. 145.
Van Dorsten, J. A., ed. *A Defence of Poetry*, by Sir Philip Sidney, p. 79n.2.
Van Haeftan, Benedict, pp. 24, 33; *Schola Cordis*, pp. 24, 35–36n.26.
Van Laan, "John Donne's *Devotions* and the Jesuit *Spiritual Exercises*," *SP*, pp. 2, 7n.4.
Vaughan, Henry, pp. 78–79, 118.
Viegas, Blasius, *Commentarii Exegetici*, pp. 21, 35n.18.
Von Spee, Frederich, pp. 137, 142n.16.
Walker, Alice, See G. D. Willcock.
Walker, Ralph, ed. Ben Jonson, *Timber*, p. 115n.3.
Wallace, K. R., *Francis Bacon on Communication and Rhetoric*, p. 57n.8.
Wallerstein, Ruth, *Richard Crashaw, A Study in Style and Poetic Development*, p. 8n.6; *Studies in Seventeenth Century Poetic*, p. 35n.25.
Walley, See Garnet, Henry.
Walpole, Henry, pp. IX–X, 111.
Warnke, Frank, pp. 1–2, 11; *European Metaphysical Poetry*, p. 142n.16; *Versions of the Baroque*, pp. 7n.1, 34n.1.
Warren, Austin, *Richard Crashaw: A Study in Baroque Sensibility*, p. 8n.5.
Webber, Joan M., p. 2; *Contrary Music*, p. 7n.4; *The Eloquent "I"*, pp. 123, 141n.7.
Weinberg, Bernard, *History of Literary Criticism in the Italian Renaissance*, p. 115n.2.

Weston, William, p. 9n.11.
Whitby, Council of, p. 113.
White, Helen, *English Devotional Literature*, p. 80n.6.
Willcock, G. D., and Alice Walker, eds, *The Arte of English Poesie*, by George Puttenham, p. 80n.9.
Williamson, George, *The Donne Tradi-*

tion, pp. 146, 163n.7.
Wisbech, p. 8n.11.
Wolfe, Don M., ed. Milton, *Reason of Church Government*, p. 115n.3.

Yahweh, pp. 5, 53–54, 111.

Zeus, p. 13.